OECD ECONOMIC SURVEYS

2000-2001

Turkey

OECD

ORGANISATION FOR ECONOMIC CO-OPERATION AND DEVELOPMENT

ORGANISATION FOR ECONOMIC CO-OPERATION AND DEVELOPMENT

Pursuant to Article 1 of the Convention signed in Paris on 14th December 1960, and which came into force on 30th September 1961, the Organisation for Economic Co-operation and Development (OECD) shall promote policies designed:

- to achieve the highest sustainable economic growth and employment and a rising standard of living in Member countries, while maintaining financial stability, and thus to contribute to the development of the world economy;
- to contribute to sound economic expansion in Member as well as non-member countries in the process of economic development; and
- to contribute to the expansion of world trade on a multilateral, non-discriminatory basis in accordance with international obligations.

The original Member countries of the OECD are Austria, Belgium, Canada, Denmark, France, Germany, Greece, Iceland, Ireland, Italy, Luxembourg, the Netherlands, Norway, Portugal, Spain, Sweden, Switzerland, Turkey, the United Kingdom and the United States. The following countries became Members subsequently through accession at the dates indicated hereafter: Japan (28th April 1964), Finland (28th January 1969), Australia (7th June 1971), New Zealand (29th May 1973), Mexico (18th May 1994), the Czech Republic (21st December 1995), Hungary (7th May 1996), Poland (22nd November 1996), Korea (12th December 1996) and the Slovak Republic (14th December 2000). The Commission of the European Communities takes part in the work of the OECD (Article 13 of the OECD Convention).

Publié également en français.

Table of contents

●●●●●

Boxes

Tables

BASIC STATISTICS OF TURKEY

THE LAND

Area (thousand sq. km)	779	Major cities, 1990 (thousand inhabitants):	
Agricultural area (thousand sq. km), 1995	275	Istanbul	7 309
Forests (thousand sq. km)	202	Ankara	3 237
		Izmir	2 695

THE PEOPLE

Population, 1999 (million)	65.8	Civilian labour force, 1999 (million)	23.2
Per sq. km, 1999	84	Civilian employment	21.5
Annual rate of change of population,		Agriculture, forestry, fishing	9.7
1989-1999	1.8	Industry	3.3
		Construction	1.2
		Services	7.3

PRODUCTION

Gross domestic product, 1999 (TL billion)	77 374 802	Origin of GDP, 1999 (per cent):	
Per head, 1999 (US$)	2 807	Agriculture, forestry, fishing	15.0
Gross fixed investment, 1999 (TL billion)	16 863 754	Industry	28.8
Per cent of GDP	21.8	Services	56.2
Per head (US$)	612		

THE GOVERNMENT

Public consumption, 1999 (per cent of GDP)	15.2	Public debt, end-1999 (per cent of GDP)	47.8
Central government current revenue, 1999		Domestic	29.3
(per cent of GDP)	23.5	Foreign	18.5

FOREIGN TRADE

Commodity exports, 1998, f.o.b.		Commodity imports, 1998, c.i.f.	
(per cent of GDP)	13.6	(per cent of GDP)	23.2
Main exports (per cent of total exports):		Main imports (per cent of total imports):	
Machinery and transport equipment	15.1	Machinery and transport equipment	39.7
Other manufactures	59.4	Other manufactures	24.2
Food and live animals	14.0	Chemicals and related products	14.3

THE CURRENCY

Monetary unit: Turkish lira	Currency unit per US$, average of daily figures:	
	1995	45 738
	1996	81 281
	1997	151 595
	1998	260 473
	1999	418 984

This Survey is based on the Secretariat's study prepared for the annual review of Turkey by the Economic and Development Review Committee on 2 November 2000.

•

After revisions in the light of discussions during the review, this Survey was submitted to the Committee for approval on 16 November 2000.

•

The previous Survey of Turkey was issued in July 1999.

•

The text of the original Survey is preceded by a policy reassessment in light of the financial crisis which erupted in Turkey on 22 November 2000. It takes account of the policy responses agreed between the authorities and the IMF on 21 December 2000 and is published under the authority of the Secretary-General.

Policy reassessment in light of the end-2000 financial crisis

Summary

At the end of 1999, Turkey embarked upon an ambitious stabilisation programme, aimed at achieving single digit inflation by 2002. Central to the programme have been firm monetary and exchange rate policies, set so as to provide a nominal anchor for reducing inflation expectations, sounder public finance aimed at eliminating the principal source of inflation pressures, and wide-ranging structural reforms designed to liberalise and modernise the economy. Significant progress was made during 2000. But a severe banking crisis blew up in late November, accompanied by a massive capital outflow. The crisis revealed a number of important stress points in the programme, located in the vulnerability of the banking sector and the sensitivity of foreign confidence to a widening current account deficit against the background of delays to the structural reform programme. An IMF-led emergency package has succeeded in normalising the situation and policies have become stronger in the light of the crisis, due to the renewed momentum that has been given to the structural reform programme. The crisis has resulted in much higher real interest rates, which put a burden on the budget and banking system and will undermine economic performance if long sustained. However, in the short term they contribute to stability in that they help (via slower growth) to contain the current account deficit and also provide support to the exchange rate anchor, which is crucial for guiding inflation expectations. Most importantly, they underscore the commitment to meet the original end-2001 inflation target, and as markets become convinced that the target can be met, capital inflows should resume and interest-rate risk premia should fall. Strengthening the banking system and following through on privatisation commitments are key elements in re-establishing policy credibility. For the longer term, the challenge is to recapture growth momentum and translate it into sustained economic convergence, as a basis for prospective entry into the European Union. Boosting per capita income requires a major reorientation of government functions from interventionism to guaranteeing the framework conditions for a strong market economy. The structural component of the programme recognises this and contains the necessary ingredients for successful change in this direction, provided it is fully implemented. It contains initiatives in areas as diverse as budget control, liberalisation and privatisation of utilities, banking, social security, and agriculture. In parallel, the 1999 earthquakes have concentrated attention on the need to improve the management and planning of urban and regional development, which should help to bring overdue changes to the structure of economic governance, including fiscal federal relations. Successful completion of all aspects of the stabilisation programme and related governance reforms would ensure that Turkey enters the 21st century with a more modern, market-oriented and efficient economy, able to meet its economic and social goals.

How did the crisis develop?

The trigger for the crisis was the emergence of financial problems in some, typically mid-sized, banks which had positioned themselves aggressively for continuing declines in interest rates via longer term investments which were highly leveraged by short-term funds. The underlying tensions appear to have been the widening current account deficit and delays to the privatisation programme which were causing interest rates to rise from September, and more markedly from around mid-November. The above-mentioned banks were forced to sell their government bond holdings at a loss to maintain liquidity in the face of the increasing cost of funds. Consistent with its monetary policy goals, the central bank was at first constrained from stepping in to ease these liquidity problems. Around 20 November, as rumours about the illiquid banks spread, first-tier banks cut their lines of credit to the interbank market and international participants exited the overnight market, unwilling to accept Turkish bank risk. This exacerbated market pressures and hence portfolio losses of the exposed banks.

These events resulted in an increasingly severe liquidity squeeze, pressure on overnight interest rates and government bond yields, widening Eurobond spreads, and growing bank distress. The squeeze had its counterpart in an excess dollar demand and pressure on central bank foreign exchange reserves. To protect the banking system and to limit the rise in interest rates, the central bank suspended its net domestic asset target and provided massive liquidity to the system during the week of 22-30 November. But despite this injection of liquidity, overnight rates climbed to triple digits around 28 November as capital outflow accelerated due to growing fears that the programme was no longer sustainable. To stem the reserves outflow, the central bank announced a return to its net domestic asset upper limit, which was to be reset as of 1 December at its 30 November value. However, overnight rates continued to rise up to 2000 per cent, as liquidity being supplied to the market again became short.

The capital outflow was only halted, and devaluation fears allayed by the announcement on 6 December of a large IMF package amounting to over $10 billion, including $7.5 billion from the Supplemental Reserve Facility (SRF),[1] in addition to $5 billion from the World Bank,[2] aimed at supporting the government's pledge to address the recent turmoil by strengthening the financial sector and accelerating privatisations. On the same day, the markets were reassured by the decision of the independent Banking and Supervision Agency to take over the nation's sixth largest private bank (Demirbank), which had been a main source of the liquidity problems, under the deposit insurance fund. International and domestic confidence was also bolstered by an announcement by the Treasury that it would provide a full guarantee of the deposits and credits of Turkish banks. The following week, the Treasury secured a $1 billion syndicated loan from international banks meeting in London, to signal their support for the programme.

As of the end of December, overnight interest rates had fallen to under 100 per cent, and Eurobond spreads had narrowed, while the benchmark government bond yields remained in the neighbourhood of 80 per cent, still double pre-crisis levels (Figure A). The net domestic assets of the

Figure A. **Interest rate developments**
2000

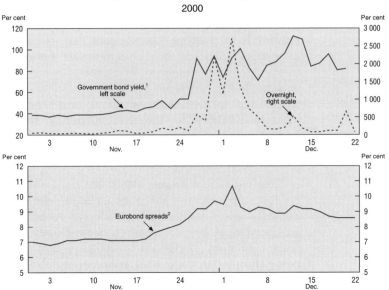

1. Secondary market, composite of original maturity.
2. OECD calculation based on yield spread between Turkish and Euro-$ government bond with 10-year maturity.
Source: Central Bank of Turkey, Bloomberg.

Figure B. **Central bank net domestic assets and gross reserves**
US$ billion, end-week data, 2000

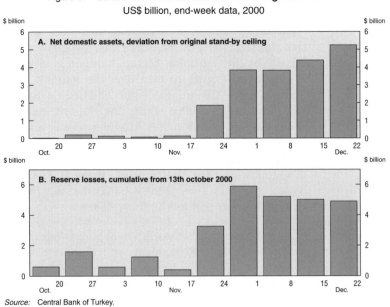

Source: Central Bank of Turkey.

central bank remained some $5 billion above their original stand-by target level of $1.75 billion (Figure B). The reserves outflow had been arrested and partially reversed; in all more than $6 billion in central bank reserves (around one-quarter of the total) flowed out during the crisis. These reserve losses will be gradually replenished by the SRF inflows over the course of the coming year.

Why is the banking system weak?

The *Survey* describes at some length the fragility of the Turkish banking system which made it susceptible to such a crisis. It also describes the substantial steps taken to strengthen supervision, especially through the establishment of an independent bank supervision agency and the intro-duction of internationally accepted prudential and account-ing rules. The loss of investor confidence which led up to the crisis had its roots in the vulnerability of the banking system during the process of adjustment to a low inflation regime. This included the unmasking, due to greater competition, of bad management practices in particular among smaller banks. More generally, there was a heightened exposure to interest and default risks as banks turned to consumer lending and other operations that incurred growing maturity mismatch to replace former high-yielding uncovered bond arbitrage, but often without having developed the expertise to deal with these risks. Exposure to exchange risk also grew sharply: banks' net open positions nearly doubled during the first nine months of 2000 as they continued to make use of very short-term foreign funding to lock in longer-term domes-tic nominal yields (*i.e.*, before falling as expected in parallel with inflation).[3] The new bank supervisory authority was a catalyst in revealing how deep-rooted the problems have been and how slowly they have been addressed. But, having become operational only a little more than two months prior to the crisis, it had not been able to forestall the develop-ment of these problems.

An action plan to rehabilitate eight banks under the administration of the deposit insurance fund since end-1999 was announced by the new Banking Board on 16 November. This contained the following main points: *i*) a timetable run-ning to end-April 2001 was specified for the sale of the banks to eligible bidders; *ii*) the banks would be run jointly by a board of six independent experts until they were sold; and *iii*) the Board would receive $6.1 billion from the Treasury in the form of bond issues in order to recapitalise the banks under administration.[4] Unease about the banking system grew despite, or perhaps in reaction to these major initiatives. The failure to close or resolve more rapidly the balance-sheet problems of the bad banks meant that they had to offer high deposit interest rates in order to keep operating, while benefiting from public protection, fostering moral hazard and "unfair" competition in the sector at large. In this respect, the action plan of the new Banking Board was perceived as too slow, while remaining silent on the possible need for more bank takeovers. In particular, the $6.1 billion bond issue for bank bailouts was seen as raising government debt and adding pressure to credit markets. Ongoing criminal investigations, since late October, into some of the banks in receivership greatly added to market nervousness, given the potential for repercussions in the remainder of the sector.

What were the macroeconomic tensions?

The *Survey* also describes two sources of macroeconomic tension which could provide an explanation for the increase in interest rates even prior to the crisis, namely the growing current account deficit and the overshooting of the inflation target in 2000. Even so, the assessment given in the *Survey* is that neither of these tensions would have been sufficient in themselves to derail the stabilisation programme, provided the 2001 inflation target was adhered to, fiscal policy was tightened to reduce excess demand and the structural reform programme progressed as planned.

The growing external imbalance was evidence of an unsustainable boom in demand, exacerbated by the impacts of higher world oil prices and the weakening of the euro. The 2000 deficit was projected by the OECD at 4.6 per cent of GDP, but more recently by the authorities at 5 per cent. Inflation was clearly above target, indicating problems in reducing expectations to levels consistent with wage moderation and the preservation of Turkish competitiveness. Moreover, monthly inflation rates continued to rise since mid-year, as the demand boom fed into consumer prices.[5] The latest figures show a year-end inflation overshoot of 14 per cent, compared with 10 per cent estimated by the OECD in the *Survey*. The implied likely real appreciation of the exchange rate over the 2000-01 period would now be somewhat higher than the 20 per cent that was estimated in the *Survey*.

In mid-November, in advance of the crisis, new fiscal measures were taken to address the widening current account deficit and the slow convergence of inflation. The primary surplus target (IMF definition) was raised from 3 per cent of GDP in 2000 to 5 per cent in 2001. OECD calculations, based on the *Economic Outlook* 68 (*December* 2000) projections for Turkish growth, suggest that this represented a tightening in the structural budget stance between the two years of some 5 per cent of GDP. However, the growing political difficulties in implementing the structural reform programme may have had a negative impact on sentiment. The inability to sell a block share of Turk Telekom accounted for about half of the $4 billion shortfall in 2000 privatisation receipts while complications in the contracting process for energy privatisations delayed the inflow of direct investments into that sector. The failure to pass state banking privatisation legislation, in turn, delayed the approval of a $780 million World Bank loan. These delays obviously affected both fiscal policy and the capital inflows necessary to finance the growing current account deficit. Legislation was finally passed on 15 November to deal with the state banks. These banks are to be privatised by 2003 (with an extension of 1½ years if necessary). In preparation, they will pass from state enterprise to corporate status and the estimated $21 billion in their outstanding duty losses will be taken over by the Treasury.

What are the implications for the stabilisation programme?

Despite the crisis, the government has confirmed that it would maintain the integrity of the disinflation programme. The details of the government's revised programme for 2001 were made known with the release of a new Letter of Intent on 21 December. The overriding priority has been signalled as reaching the original inflation target of 12 per cent by the end of 2001 and limiting the current account deficit to within 3½ per cent of GNP. The exchange rate regime is unchanged as is the incomes policy. Fiscal policy has been adjusted to cope with an implicitly weaker growth picture, with unchanged targets for the primary surplus, implying an even more severe degree of fiscal tightening in cyclically-adjusted terms. Tax measures have been announced as the principal means, and the intention is to further increase taxes if inflation and current account slippage persist. The intention of the original (1999) letter was to put more of the adjustment on the side of spending, but this has been abandoned, as expenditure reductions still amount to only ½ per cent of GDP. The tax measures remain largely *ad hoc* extensions of temporary measures.

The monetary framework has undergone some adjustment. The end-quarter target for net domestic assets of the central bank will be gradually lowered over the first six months of the year to eliminate about 50 per cent of the excess net domestic assets (NDA) created during the crisis, while remaining within a narrow corridor around this downward path within quarters. In the event of higher-than-expected capital inflows, NDA limits will be lowered in order to avoid an excess increase in the money supply, in turn limiting the potential downward movement in interest rates. In this sense, the "no-sterilisation" rule has been relaxed in favour of an element of monetary policy autonomy. After July, with the gradual move to a more flexible monetary regime during the period of widening exchange rate bands, NDA targeting will become even more flexible. The central bank would at the same time shift toward inflation targeting, an important step in the direction of clarifying the medium term framework.

Structural policies are being implemented more rigorously. As part of the measures taken to restore confidence, tenders for 33.5 per cent of Turk Telekom (plus rights on the executive committee) and 51 per cent of Turkish Airlines (with the state continuing to hold a privileged share) were announced on 14 December, and the electricity law (to liberalise and privatise the sector) was submitted to Parliament. A timetable has been set for receipt of bids and completion of the sales (structural benchmarks) and for enactment of the electricity law (a structural performance criterion). Total privatisation receipts of $6-7 billion are now targeted for 2001. Other structural benchmarks or performance criteria have been set for: the balances of the state enterprises in the electricity sector (benefiting from upward adjustments in energy prices), the sale of the eight banks (the strategy for the other three banks taken over by the deposit insurance fund more recently will be announced early in the year), the introduction of new banking regulations on internal risk management (to be adopted soon and implemented as of 2002), the incorporation of extra-budgetary funds into the budget (the government intends to keep six extra-budgetary funds, in contrast to its November statement that all such funds would be eliminated), and the support prices for wheat (which will follow inflation targets).

What are the chances of success?

The crisis has forced a major re-adjustment of the macroeconomic parameters of the programme which should ease the tensions noted earlier. Higher real interest rates should lead to a significant weakening of domestic demand and growth, and in this sense help both in bringing the current account back under control and in moving toward achieving the inflation targets. The decision to pass through crude oil price increases into consumer prices could have a one-off effect on headline inflation, but is necessary in order to arrest the large deficits which have emerged in the state energy sector enterprises. However, the faith of the public in the inflation targets may have been shaken by the crisis, potentially complicating the task of incomes policy in breaking the inertia of inflationary expectations. A notable gap in the programme has been that there is no effective institutional framework in place that would allow for forward-looking wage agreements to be struck in the private and state enterprise sectors and to assure an equitable distribution of the costs of disinflationary adjustment. Thus far, civil servants, minimum wage earners, and farmers have borne the brunt of the adjustment, as their incomes are subject to state influence and control. Other sectors, notably unionised and white-collar workers and bond holders, have reaped large real windfalls from the decline in inflation, as they have continued to benefit from nominal wage growth or interest rates incorporating previous higher levels of inflation. Moreover, under new legislation to strengthen the banking system, commercial banks will contribute little to the large structural tax effort this year, as generous tax deductions are the main instrument for voluntary mergers and consolidation of the banking system. Therefore, it would appear to be even more important to follow the *Survey's* advice to achieve a social consensus and to bring state enterprise workers' wages into line with inflation targets, which will help to balance the social burden of tighter fiscal and incomes policies.

At the same time, fiscal goals have become more difficult because higher real interest rates are likely to persist for a while. This faces the banks and government with higher funding costs, adding to bank fragility and, *ceteris paribus*, raising the fiscal deficit and debt. Accelerated bank takeovers and recapitalisation of public sector banks will imply a one-time, perhaps large increase in the public debt, which even though cost-effective (in the sense that delayed action would have implied greater costs later on), may further impact negatively on the government's debt service. The Treasury has now taken on the domestic and foreign liabilities of the entire banking sector as a contingent liability. Thus, new tensions have arisen on the fiscal side, and have been partly reflected in the introduction of further new tax measures. It will be important that the primary surplus be raised sufficiently to prevent fiscal balances from worsening and feeding into inflation expectations (for which there is ample precedent in the past), if necessary by reducing expenditure. The challenge for banking reform is likewise now greater than prior to the crisis, in particular as unlimited Turkish lira-deposit insurance – introduced after the 1994 crisis, just recently reformed and now, in effect, reintroduced – was a major source of banking system moral hazard in the past.

What about monetary policy?   The credibility of the disinflation effort, and adherence to the monetary framework, in particular the "no-sterilisation" (quasi-currency board) rule whereby capital inflows and outflows are to be the sole source of money supply changes, has been made more difficult to maintain because of slowness in addressing the problems of bank fragility and the impediments (evident in delays in the privatisation process) which inhibit the inflow of foreign capital. Looking forward, the challenge is to return to a framework conducive to capital inflows, especially direct investment. The episode shows that abandonment of the monetary rule, and *a fortiori*, the aim of price stabilisation, would make this goal more difficult. Turkey's experience has shown that the extra liquidity created simply flows out through the capital account and drains reserves given the necessity to stick to the pre-committed exchange rate depreciation path in line with inflation targets. If the exchange rate path were to be abandoned, there would be an inevitable return to the previous unsustainable configuration of high and volatile inflation and real interest rates. Timely and transparent action to pre-empt bank problems from developing into insolvency or systemic proportions seems to be an important corollary of these lessons. In hindsight, an earlier take-over of the banks with evident liquidity problems (or even earlier prompt corrective actions to forestall liquidity problems from arising in the first place), might have defused the incipient crisis. The commitment to implement by 2002 the legislation on internal bank risk management (including risk-adjusted capital adequacy ratios) is an encouraging step in this direction and fulfils a *Survey* recommendation, although coming later than hoped for.

Overall implications of the crisis

While the crisis has had the effect of exposing major tensions in the programme, it has forced a stronger focus on reform, and has had a salutary effect in underscoring the importance both of transparency and of staying on track on structural reforms in order to sustain capital inflows. In this respect it has also reinforced the main message of the *Survey*, namely that the stabilisation programme has to be seen as a whole. Within the programme, the impressive progress that is being made on economic "fundamentals" – particularly in the domain of fiscal and monetary policy – is dependent on the rigorous implementation of comprehensive structural reforms. The acknowledgement of this reality has evoked a clear commitment to the programme, supported by rapid and effective action from the international community. The authorities are demonstrating by their actions a resolve to preserve the progress achieved thus far. Rigorous implementation offers the prospect for a gradual normalisation in interest rates which will further relieve tensions. In sum, the renewed urgency in introducing reforms to and/or restructuring the budget, the private banking sector, the public sector banks and the utilities scheduled for privatisation have re-established the integrity of the stabilisation programme. The nature of these reforms are discussed in the *Survey*.

Notes

1. The SRF is a short-term loan facility for countries in balance of payments crisis but demonstrating sound policies. It carries a relatively high interest rate and will be released in seven payments until 15 November 2001. The first tranche of $2.25 billion was made available on 22 December, along with $550 million for the 4th/5th tranches of the regular stand-by (with $2.35 billion remaining).

2. On 22 December 2000 the World Bank approved the new Country Assistance Strategy for Turkey which aims at support of up to $5 billion for a three-year period. As a first step in implementing the strategy the Bank also approved two operations for Turkey: a $778 million Financial Sector Adjustment Loan (FSAL) to support the government's efforts to reform the financial sector and a $250 million Privatisation Social Support Project (PSSP) to mitigate the negative impact of privatisation of the state-owned enterprises. The first tranche of the FSAL ($385 million) was disbursed on 22 December 2000.

3. The exposure to exchange risk may be larger than is apparent, moreover, because some of the forward cover taken in order to satisfy bank supervision regulations is of dubious quality.

4. In accounting terms, these bonds are a liability of the deposit insurance fund, to be exchanged for the bad loans from the balance sheets of banks under its administration. Revenues from the sale of the banks and the recovery of bad assets, as well as the con-tributions of the banking system to the deposit insurance fund, will be used to repay the Treasury. The bonds are tradeable, though they are considered as non-cash debt since they are not auctioned in the primary market.

5. The rise of world energy prices, on the other hand, did not feed through into final con-sumer prices during this period as they were absorbed in the form of rising deficits of the state economic enterprises in the energy sector.

Pre-crisis assessment and recommendations

A recovery is under way, supported by a disinflation programme which offers an opportunity for sustained growth

Following a severe recession, the economy is now in the process of recovery, with growth of around 7 per cent expected this year. The global financial fragility and political uncertainty which blighted economic developments in late 1998 and 1999 have now dissipated, to be replaced by the beneficial influences of a favourable external environment, a more settled political climate and post-earthquake reconstruction. Most importantly, the negotiation of a tough, and, so far, highly credible, stabilisation programme with the International Monetary Fund has led to a marked fall in interest rates. It should be recalled, however, that the recovery is taking place from a base of an overall unsatisfactory economic performance. Real GDP per person has only managed to grow at 1½ per cent over the 1990s, below the OECD average and well below rates achieved by the most successful emerging economies. The challenge now is to translate the current upswing into a sustained increase in living standards. In this respect, the current stabilisation programme offers the best chance, perhaps for some considerable time to come, to attain a path of balanced, non-inflationary growth while achieving a degree of convergence with the EU, for which Turkey is now a candidate. The strategy rests on three central pillars: a combination of monetary, exchange rate and incomes policies designed to bring down inflation expectations; a fundamental fiscal adjustment; and wide-ranging structural reforms to improve governance and create a more-market-oriented economy.

Exchange-rate targeting and monetary restraint are central to the new programme

The core of the new monetary and exchange rate strategy is to shift from a policy of accommodation, focused on maintaining the real exchange rate and stabilising liquidity conditions, to one based on a pre-announced rate of currency depreciation and limited money creation. Under this approach, which restricts the depreciation of the lira against a currency basket to the *target* rate of increase in the wholesale price index (20 per cent in 2000), the exchange rate becomes a nominal anchor. Operationally, capital inflows/outflows are not sterilised, so that interest rates are fully market-determined. Monetary autonomy is further constrained by indicative ceilings on net domestic assets, with an accompanying floor on international reserves. This is to prevent monetary conditions from becoming too expansionary as a result of the possible liquidity needs of the public sector. The fact that monetary expansion will depend wholly on foreign inflows means that the programme has some of the central elements of a currency board. This forward-looking and pro-active attitude to inflation control represents a vital shift from the previous more accommodating approach and has been backed by a prices and incomes policy whereby increases in civil servants' salaries and the minimum wage, together with agricultural support prices and rents, will be based on projected rather than past inflation.

Interest rates have fallen and implementation of the monetary programme is on track...

Interest rates began to fall in the latter half of 1999 prior to the agreement on the IMF programme, both because of financial-market anticipation of its adoption and of a growing awareness of the central bank's less accommodating role *vis-à-vis* inflation. The programme's announcement triggered a decline in rates from 90 to under 40 per cent. Inflation has been falling back since March and, in spite of some unfavourable external developments, particularly the sharp rise in international oil prices, it has declined to the lowest level since 1986. A key contribution to this fall has come from the rigorous implementation of the monetary and exchange rate framework, the criteria for net domestic assets and net international reserves having been fully observed so far. The "no-sterilisation" rule and supporting performance criteria act as safeguards against possible monetary indiscipline – one of the potential weaknesses of an exchange-rate based stabilisation approach being that open-market operations can compensate for shifts in foreign capital inflows – adding to the credibility of the disinflation programme. Moreover, the identification, from the outset, of the "exit strategy", whereby after June 2001 there will be a gradually widening symmetrical band around a central parity prior to floating, should help to prevent any loss of policy credibility associated with the eventual shift to a more flexible exchange-rate regime. An early decision on the monetary framework to be adopted for the medium term, preferably based on inflation targeting, would reinforce this credibility and further reduce uncertainty, with associated benefits in terms of lower interest rates.

... but there has been some inflation slippage...

Such a clarification is all the more important because, despite substantially lower inflation, the inflation target of 25 per cent by the end of 2000 will not be realised. OECD projections, which take account of actual price movements in the first ten months, suggest an overshoot of around 10 per cent in 2000 due to contracted increases in some wage and price sectors (most importantly rents), as well as the overhang from high inflation in the early months of the year. The achievement of the 25 per cent threshold will be deferred to early 2001. Confidence in the programme should be maintained even if inflation overshoots moderately, as long as the pace of structural reform proceeds as planned. However, this slippage should not be allowed to undermine the rapid achievement of price stability. Effective management of monetary and fiscal policies as defined in the programme, together with the effective implementation of the full structural reform agenda are the keys to achieving this. But confidence in the programme would be weakened, and the achievement of its objectives rendered more difficult, if intermediate inflation targets are persistently overshot. For this reason, the government needs to make utmost efforts to meet its inflation target for 2001, set at 12 per cent. The continued credibility of this target is vital to underpin forward-looking wage outcomes and preserve external competitiveness.

... and private wage behaviour needs to adapt

A notable gap in the programme is that there is not at present an effective institutional framework in place that would allow forward-looking wage agreements to be struck in the private and state-enterprise sectors and assure an equitable distribution of the costs of disinflationary adjustment. If the private sector unions concerned succeed in winning wage increases considerably above the inflation target, as they are demanding, this could have a negative impact on inflation. The government's intention is that the recently-reconvened Economic and Social Council should be effective in achieving an agreement among the social partners on a formal joint declaration in support of the government's disinflation targets, as well as on price and wage guidelines for 2000 and 2001. Such a forum has proved useful to the attainment of disinflation programmes in other OECD economies and as argued in the previous *Survey* is a potentially valuable instrument for building a consensus for change based on non-inflationary growth, the fair distribution of any real wage adjustments and adherence to the fiscal adjustment process.

... and the current account deficit constitutes a future risk

Concerns also attach to the increase in the current account deficit. By September 2000, the level of the current account deficit ($6.8 billion) was already more than four times higher than the full-year deficit for 1999. The rise in international oil prices and stronger domestic demand – in response to lower interest rates and real exchange rate appreciation – have led to a surge in imports, while exports of goods and services have recovered more sluggishly, apart from the tourism sector which appears set to produce results at least as strong as 1998. The disinflation programme involves some real appreciation of the Turkish lira which, though it should be supportable because the programme is reducing enterprise financing costs, will negatively impact on export performance. OECD projections, based on a deceleration in GDP growth from its current 7 per cent rate to 4 to 5 per cent over the next two years, suggest that the current account deficit could widen to over 4 per cent of GDP this year before moderating to between 3 and 4 per cent over the next two years. This should be financeable provided the programme is implemented as planned, as the government has been increasingly successful in financing more of its deficit abroad. Nevertheless, excessive wage settlements could exacerbate the already disadvantageous trend in relative unit labour costs and accelerate the deterioration in the trade balance. This would be especially dangerous if the demand for imports began to reflect perceptions by private agents that they should bring forward consumption because of scepticism about future inflation and future higher interest rates. The measures introduced to cool the expansion of domestic consumption include a rise in consumer credit fees, an increase in the tax on luxury automobiles and the continuation of "temporary" tax measures. Normally, short-term interventionism of this sort should be ruled out, but the stakes are high and, if the credibility of the programme is at risk, such measures should prove useful. Indeed, the authorities should and do stand ready to take further fiscal action to control the external deficit if needed.

Stability of the public debt is attainable in 2000, after a period of unsustainable government borrowing

Chronic fiscal deficits have been the principal factor contributing to inflationary inertia in Turkey, and the main source of economic disequilibrium and fragile investor confidence. Financing the budget deficit through domestic borrowing has put pressure on the central bank to supply liquidity while also pre-empting the bulk of domestic credit resources. Lending to the government (which has been highly profitable) has diverted banking-sector activity away from commercial-loan operations, depriving the enterprise sector of capital. The large amount of debt redemption required by the country's very short-term maturity structure has tended to trigger periodic unsustainable upward spirals in auction interest rates and debt service commitments whenever foreign capital has dried up. The situation became especially critical in 1999, when the combination of unprecedentedly high real interest rates and recession caused the debt dynamics to become so adverse that the ratio of net public sector debt to GDP rose from just under 45 per cent to 62 per cent of GDP. The first priority of the fiscal adjustment has been to stabilise the ratio. The necessary steps have now been taken, via tax and primary expenditure measures, to generate a primary surplus which should, in conjunction with privatisation revenues, stabilise the debt ratio in 2000 and allow it to decline thereafter.

*The budget is on
track but primary
spending
pressures need
to be contained...*

So far the fiscal programme is on track. For 2000, the primary surplus of the consolidated public sector will be 3 per cent, slightly exceeding target, while the 2001 programme aims at a surplus of 5 per cent, which is higher than programmed earlier. However, ensuring that the fiscal adjustment is sustainable over the medium run will be a complex task, involving action to ensure that the tax system is more efficiently run and the tax base widened, and that deficiencies in expenditure control are corrected, especially with regard to off-budget entities. Correcting structural deficiencies in the budget process is crucial because much of the "up-front" fiscal rebalancing is currently stemming from the decline in interest payments, from short-term increases in tax rates which will need to be phased out and from the cyclical buoyancy of revenues. While central government primary spending is under control, it is still 3½ per cent of GNP higher than in 1998 and the primary deficit of the rest of the public sector is expected to exceed target, largely because of the deteriorating finances of the state-owned enterprises. These spending overruns need to be resisted, while at the same time ensuring that a greater share of public-sector resources go to welfare-enhancing areas such as education and health.

*... and the new
comprehensive
approach
to budgeting
needs to be
implemented
for medium-term
fiscal
consolidation
to be achieved*

The probability of the current disinflation strategy being successful, and confidence being maintained, has been greatly enhanced by the breadth and comprehensiveness of the fiscal measures being undertaken. The evidence from past stabilisation attempts is that if they are not accompanied by structural reforms, they are ineffectual. The stabilisation programme thus aims to tackle deficiencies in the budget system along a wide front, improving the efficiency of tax administration and codifying budget practice in a single "fiscal law"; regularising and ultimately eliminating the use of extra-budgetary funds; suppressing the quasi-fiscal activities of the state banks and tackling the deficits of the state-owned enterprises. Whereas the central government consolidated budget deficit amounted to 11.6 per cent in 1999, the public sector as whole, defined to include the above entities and their unpaid "duty losses" (see below), ran a deficit of 23.3 per cent of GNP. The process of bringing off-budget entities – often created to avoid proper scrutiny – back on budget has begun. By mid year 27 of the 74 extra-budgetary funds had been eliminated. The correction of the fiscal balance of the overall public sector, rather than the central government narrowly defined is probably the most radical and overdue elements in the rather long history of stabilisation packages, distinguishing the current adjustment programme from previous efforts and providing a vital underpinning to its potential success.

The problem of the state banks is being dealt with, but requires privatisation

Under the disinflation programme, control over the quasi-fiscal activities of the state banks also plays a crucial role in enhancing budget transparency and accountability. The incremental "duty losses" of these banks, incurred as a result of subsidised lending operations performed on behalf of the government, reached 8.2 per cent of GNP in 1999 and were one of the main contributing factors to the deterioration in the consolidated public deficit. With the decline in interest rates, the (revised) formula for subsidised lending has implied its virtual elimination as of March 2000, at least on a flow basis. Settling the government's outstanding obligations with respect to duty losses, which amounted to an estimated 11.4 per cent of GDP at the end of 2000 ($21 billion), will be more difficult, but for the first time appropriations were included in the 2000 budget for direct cash payments to state banks in order to compensate for the losses incurred in the early months of 2000. Settling this issue is essential for the next phase of privatisation. Two banks (Emlak and Halkbank) are to be privatised relatively quickly. Ziraat, which has almost $12 billion in uncollected assets *vis-à-vis* Treasury, will take longer due to its size and complexity. To maintain momentum, it is important that the pre-privatisation financial, operational, and capital recovery plans be published and implemented as expeditiously as possible.

The banking reform seeks to prepare banks for operating in the new non-inflationary environment

The *banking reform* seeks to strengthen the banking system as it adapts to a low inflation environment. Banks have become used to easy profits, via unhedged foreign borrowing to finance the purchase of high-yielding government paper, as well as domestic trading in that paper. These activities led to a significant build-up of off-budget positions in the form of open positions and "repos", which respectively carried high exchange and interest rate risks, as well as a steady crowding out of traditional loans by government securities in the asset portfolio. The disinflation programme implies a major structural shift in the banks income possibilities, to more commercially-oriented sources. There is a danger (with ample precedent) that a post-stabilisation credit boom, with the banks scrambling to diversify their activities, could lead to an increase in non-performing loans, banking problems and further monetary accommodation if the proper credit risk assessment procedures are not applied. Inflation control requires a healthy banking system, unmotivated by moral hazard. The banking legislation introduced in late 1999 is critical in these respects. It has created an independent bank supervisory agency and brought prudential standards into line with international norms, notably the requirement to present bank accounts on a consolidated basis and strengthen loan classification rules. The new agency has yet to deal with the eight banks that have been in the Deposit Insurance Fund since end-1999, to set a precedent for bank resolution, while prudential standards may need to be further toughened, for example to include risk-rated capital ratios. It is important that the new agency use its powers effectively and with full independence from political influence.

The inefficiencies of the state economic enterprises still pose a challenge

One of the severest tests of the programme comes from the continued inefficiency and deficit-proneness of the state economic enterprises (SEEs). The emphasis on transparency and accountability should, in principle, result in greater operational and financial efficiency of the SEEs. But, as noted, some will run higher deficits in 2000 than allowed for. Widening financial losses are due as much to a lack of operational and organisational efficiency as to short-term factors. Without restructuring and privatisation (or corporatisation), pressure from the public sector wage bill will remain the most important potential source of budgetary and inflation weakness. The success of the disinflation programme depends on implementing structural reform measures which inject more market-based incentives into hitherto state-sponsored economic activities, which will inevitably involve some redeployment of labour from over-manned companies to faster-growing liberalised sectors.

After delays,
the privatisation
programme
is now picking up
speed, but
there are some
problems

An important impetus to the *privatisation programme* has been given by the recent clarification of its legal framework, including the right to international arbitration where domestic and multinational interest conflict. In addition, the government has cultivated a new image of transparency, with a reinvigorated and well-managed Privatisation Administration in charge of all privatisations apart from telecoms and energy. This has boosted public confidence in the process. In the utilities sectors, where most of the key policy issues arise, the authorities are taking steps toward a market model as dominant positions are being privatised, splitting up vertically-integrated networks and setting up independent sectoral regulators. OECD experience shows that ensuring adequate competition at the outset is critical, as it is often too late to inject competition once privatised positions are entrenched. In this context, the following concerns stand out:

– In *electricity*, the shortcomings of the BOT (build-operate-transfer) method of obtaining more efficient generating capacity are becoming increasingly apparent. Under the BOT contracts, the public electricity generator is locked into paying companies prices for certain quantities of power which it would not be able to recover were consumers able to purchase power from a more competitive generating sector. Such price guarantees create large contingent liabilities for the government and greatly retard the shift to a market model as the average remaining length of contracts is 20 years. Turkey cannot wait 20 years to create competition in this sector. Ways should be found to reconcile these existing contracts with the creation of competition among more efficient generators entering under the new market-based system. This would reduce losses in the public electricity-generating company and bring lower prices to consumers, while expanding badly-needed capacity in the sector.

– In the *telecommunications* sector, only one of two auctioned mobile phone licences has been sold, which limits future competition, despite Turk Telekom being awarded a fourth licence. The incumbent retains its monopoly over fixed line services until the full shift to the market model after 2003, and even then current regulations require majority Turkish ownership of value-added services. The momentum of the privatisation of Turk Telekom has stalled recently as the government was not able to attract bids for a 20 per cent block sale, partly due to concerns about insufficient management rights attached to the share but also to changing market conditions. The problem of minority private investors having sufficient scope to improve efficiency in companies where the government is the majority shareholder owner is an important one with perhaps wider applicability, and will have to be resolved.

In both sectors, the effectiveness of the new regulators would be compromised if significant informational asymmetries *vis-à-vis* companies were to arise. Thus, to sustain competition it is important that the transmission owners do not also own generation capacity, that generation capacity is divided among a sufficient number of independently-owned generating companies, and that the various distribution networks are under separate ownership. The regulators and the competition authority must make sure that the conditions required for effective competition are fulfilled as network industries are privatised, even if this is at the expense of privatisation revenues.

Agricultural reform offers possibilities for greater efficiency and equity

Concerning the system of *agricultural support*, it is larger, in relation to GDP, than in the OECD as a whole by a wide margin – 8¾ as against 1½ per cent. This reflects mainly the far higher share of agriculture in national output in Turkey, as subsidy rates are similar. However, at its present income level and production structure Turkey cannot afford such a generous scheme. Most of it takes the form of price supports, which push up inflation and hurt the urban poor for whom food is a major expenditure. The politicised decision on year to year price supports distorts and destabilises agricultural activity, while direct budget subsidies for inputs encourage their inefficient use. Moreover, richer farmers are most able to benefit from the scheme's largesse. Consistent with previous OECD recommendations, the government has embarked on a radical overhaul which seeks to consolidate all forms of agricultural support into a targeted lump sum transfer by the end of the stabilisation programme. The planned speed and reduction in the overall level of support, to under 1 per cent of GDP, represents a severe adjustment which the government will need to cushion with appropriate training, support, and extension services for farmers. As with the other components of structural reform, it will be more important to secure a viable system of support than to achieve abrupt reductions in financial dis-savings. But if compensatory payments are needed they should be fully transparent and strictly temporary.

Social security reform has reduced financing pressures, but further measures are needed to achieve balance

Soon after the 1999 earthquakes, the government passed a landmark *social security reform* bill which addressed glaring problems in the public pension system, such as lack of a minimum retirement age, short contribution periods relative to generous payouts, poor enforcement of collections and tolerance of a variety of other abuses. The reforms introduced a minimum retirement age (to 58/60 for new entrants and 52/56 for existing workers) and lengthened contribution periods with a ten-year transition, raised the contribution ceiling in three yearly steps, rebased benefits on lifetime average income, and reduced replacement rates. As a result, the projected explosion of system deficits has been averted; however the deficit has not been completely eliminated nor has a renewed deterioration been avoided. More fundamental reforms will be needed. Some of these may be addressed in the planned next phase of institutional reforms, which could help to improve the incentives to both collect and contribute. This stage will require consolidating the three funds into a single well-administered scheme, separating health from pension insurance, plus personnel and management reforms. Another challenge will be to implement a private pension savings scheme in the context of adequate regulatory and attractive tax frameworks – the necessary legislation is still pending. A private scheme will help to diversify pension risks, raise incentives to stay in the formal sector, and help develop the capital market. A reduction in the high contribution rates to the public scheme (currently 33.5-39 per cent), as soon as better collections performance allows, would also improve incentives for the expansion of a private savings scheme, as well as further lowering those for joining the informal sector.

Education, skills-
and technology
development are
required for faster
growth in living
standards
and better equity
outcomes

If Turkey succeeds with its budget expenditure reforms, it can shift vital resources into areas such as *education, skills and technology development.* The need to increase spending for human development has been a consistent message of past OECD *Surveys.* An examination of the sources of growth in the past 20 years demonstrates that declining labour force participation as well as stagnating multi-factor productivity were main causes of the virtual lack of growth in per capita income. In an OECD country with robust demographics and large catch-up potential, this is surprising and unacceptable. The best way to raise the employability of the surplus labour released by agriculture is to improve its education and skills. Turkey seriously lags other OECD countries in the proportion of its resources devoted to education, despite having a much younger population. Recent efforts to improve educational standards, notably the increase in compulsory schooling to eight years, and, over the longer run to twelve years, have suffered from a lack of matching resources so that the quality of instruction has further deteriorated. Correcting this will require better funding of schools and universities, including more scholarships and new forms of financing by the private sector. Equally important will be the expansion and improvement of technical and vocational education and training at the post-compulsory stage. Such a capability, together with the quality of the university system, provides the basis for the nation's technological capacity, which is an important determinant of growth. A big problem in this respect has been the rapid expansion of public universities to meet growing social needs, but these risk becoming second-rate institutions on present patterns. The R&D intensity of business is also quite low in Turkey in general. This is quite normal for a country at Turkey's level of economic development. But if Turkey wishes to upgrade its production base and move toward a more high-tech economy, both business and government need to invest more in R&D, both to develop new products and processes, and also to gain access to technologies being developed abroad. The need to invest in education and skills more broadly is highly complementary to this effort.

The 1999 earthquakes have underlined the need for a more orderly process of urban development

The heavy human and material damage inflicted by the Marmara and Bolu earthquakes prompts important questions about the policy failures behind Turkey's lack of disaster preparedness, particularly since the earthquakes occurred along a known active fault line. Forty-three per cent of Turkey's population is living in the "first-degree" earthquake risk zone and industrial development and urbanisation are far more concentrated there than in any of the other four risk zones. A comprehensive disaster management strategy appears not to have been implemented, making for a vulnerability to shocks greatly in excess of that observed in other OECD countries subject to earthquakes. The *Survey* suggests that these deficiencies may stem from the unorganised nature of recent Turkish economic development, based as it has been on the need to assimilate a mass migration from the countryside to the cities. Against this background, the process of *risk identification* required for minimising potential losses due to earthquakes and preparing a response has been impeded. Inadequate mapping capacity is an example of this. The delineation of hazard zones indicating both soil quality and exposure to risk (earthquake zone maps) is fairly rudimentary and the cadastre has not been brought up to date. Safe urban development, including the redevelopment of the affected cities and action to "retro-fit" existing sub-standard housing in areas most at risk from future earthquakes, requires an information- and rules-based strategy for regional and urban growth. It also requires the active involvement of all parties involved, central and local governments and civil society.

Governance failures have been behind poor siting and inadequate construction practices

While a more orderly process of economic development is critical to mitigating the effects of earthquakes, *risk reduction* and *prevention measures* are key to reducing the toll of disasters and the quality Turkish urban planning has proved deficient in this respect. The combination of high property and human losses is evidence of a systemic failure to enforce building codes and implement appropriate land use and planning policies, even in relation to known risks. The governance failures behind poor siting and construction practices are complex. The laws governing such development have contained loopholes; implementation and monitoring have been deficient, while unethical practices in the construction sector and among inspectors is known to be widespread. Land use and development planning strategies require both the establishment of planning and construction standards that correspond to hazard exposure and the enforcement of these standards through adequate land use and building certification. The latter will in turn require establishing a rigorous system of training and licensing in the engineering, building and urban planning professions, as well as legal clarification of the regulatory responsibilities of the various public authorities involved. The measures being put in place to correct the deficiency in the planning and public tender legislation are both welcome and overdue. The local authorities, who operate within an overall framework of rules set at higher levels, have not exercised effective development control and may need to be empowered by greater responsibility and accountability for decision-making. Overhauling the legal and institutional framework for development control and municipal planning will be a long process and progress may be slow, but "reform fatigue" should not prevent the completion of this essential task.

Individuals need to be given greater self-responsibility for finance and insurance

Even after all possible steps are taken to minimise risk at the policy level, risk mitigation needs to be an individual responsibility and self-regulation must come to play a greater role. While aggressive education campaigns are a start, a market for *risk pricing* is needed so as to internalise risks and any residual catastrophic risk that remains will need a market for the *transfer of risk* via international reinsurance mechanisms. Insurance markets, the vehicles for the pricing and transfer of risk, are not yet developed in Turkey. Instead, the obligation of the government to rebuild damaged residences operated in the past as a disincentive to individual insurance. Insurance penetration is thus very low and the insurance industry has been unprepared to take on an active role in this respect. A mortgage market, which would serve to encourage such an insurance market, has been prevented from developing *inter alia* by endemic high inflation. The transition to a low inflation regime, now set in train, should allow such a market to develop; but it will only impact on the current housing stock with a very long lag. The government has thus introduced a new mandatory national insurance scheme, while abolishing its former guarantees in the housing area. A government-sponsored insurance pool is now being put in place, which will transfer the national risk into world-wide risk-sharing pools, managed by international reinsurance companies and backed by substantial capital resources. However, for the moment, the differentiation of risks will remain rather rudimentary and individual incentives to take precautions against earthquakes will be inadequate. The current scheme will thus need to evolve in the direction of a risk-rated system.

Greater transparency and accountability will help provide for safer and better balanced economic development

An important message to emerge from the analysis of the recent earthquakes is that their human and material effects derive from the same defects in governance and incentive structures which have affected Turkey's economic performance in general. The effective implementation of banking, privatisation and other structural reforms under the new IMF programme, better preparedness against future earthquakes and EU membership requirements all indicate the need for improved public governance and private sector incentives. In this sense, the elements of reform are inter-linked. Liberalisation of the state banks and financial sector in general will, for example, allow greater room for private sector initiative in countering future risks. And privatisation and prioritisation within the public sector will necessarily mean a closer attention to the allocation and efficient use of scarce resources, bringing into focus the need for rebalancing the regulatory and planning functions of the national and lower levels of government. Most importantly, the progress already underway within the government in enhancing transparency and accountability should both allow a more orderly, earthquake-resistant pattern of urban development than has been apparent in the past two decades and enhance Turkey's longer-run growth potential.

Summing up: there are risks, but the potential benefits of completing the current programme are great

Turkey has embarked upon an ambitious anti-inflation programme and relatively rapid GDP growth is in prospect this year and next. The immediate challenge is to overcome the risks attaching to private sector wages and the current account deficit, which may call for corrective action. In particular, further fiscal action may be needed to ensure compliance with the 2001 inflation target and to underpin the sustainability of the external account. For the longer-term, the challenge is to translate the current growth

momentum into sustained longer-term economic convergence, as a prospective basis for successful entry into the
European Union. Turkey's growth record has been rather
poor and needs improving. Pervasive state interference,
lack of budget discipline and the associated inflation pressures have helped to retard physical and human capital
development. Boosting per capita incomes requires not just
short-term measures but a major reorientation of government functions to one of guarantor of the framework conditions for a strong market economy. The new programme
recognises this and contains the necessary ingredients for
successful change in this direction, provided it is fully
implemented. Monetary and exchange rate policies are providing a nominal anchor for reducing inflation expectations
and a sounder base for non-inflationary public finance,
prospectively reducing the distortions caused by monetary
accommodation on financial and non-financial activities.
Fiscal consolidation is based on a comprehensive definition
of the public sector, bringing much needed discipline to off-
budget entities, including state owned banks. The ambitious structural reform programme contains initiatives in
nearly all structural areas, including privatisation, banking,
social security and agriculture. In parallel, the recent earthquakes have concentrated attention on the need to improve
the management and planning of urban development,
which should bring overdue changes to the structure of
fiscal federalism in Turkey. Successful completion of all
aspects of the stabilisation programme and related governance reforms is needed to ensure that Turkey enters the
21st century with a more modern, market-oriented and
efficient economy, able to provide for and meet its economic and social goals.

I. Achieving growth with disinflation

Economic confidence has increased with the change in the political landscape and the negotiation of a tough anti-inflation programme with the International Monetary Fund. A sharp decline in real interest rates, together with post-earthquake reconstruction and more favourable external conditions, should make for a sustained recovery in output over the next two years. The potential consequences of achieving the goal of disinflation are great, given that low and stable inflation is a precondition for enhancing the prospects for longer run growth and for improving the standard of living for all parts of the Turkish society. However, the tasks and challenges faced by the Turkish authorities during the implementation of the plan are as considerable as the ultimate objective is crucial to Turkey's future. This is not just because the Turkish society has developed a very sophisticated ability to live with a high and chronic inflationary environment, but also because a decade of failed attempts at stabilisation mean that any deviation from plan could quickly erode the credibility of the new effort. The chapter begins with a discussion of the current conjuncture. It then describes the essential monetary elements of the disinflation plan, identifying the areas in which the disinflation strategy differs from the failed examples of the past. The following section looks at potential problems of adjustment, and discusses the short-term outlook against the background of such problems.

From recession to recovery: an improving economic outlook

1999: a recession and failed stabilisation attempt...

The backdrop to economic policy-making was unusually difficult in the wake of the emerging-market crisis that followed the Russian default during the summer of 1998 and the political uncertainty attaching to the minority coalition government. By early 1999, exports were contracting sharply, accompanied by a marked fall in domestic demand, especially business investment, leading to a decline in GDP (Figure 1). There was thus considerable slippage in the three-year stabilisation attempt that started in early 1998, (assisted from mid-year by a self-imposed quarterly monitoring process by the IMF, discussed in the 1999 OECD

Figure 1. **Macroeconomic performance**

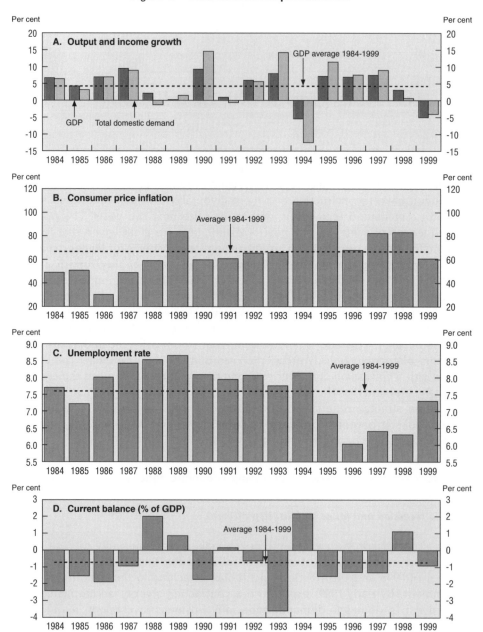

Economic Survey of Turkey). Despite an initial sharp fall in interest rates, it rapidly became clear that the assumptions underlying the programme had been too optimistic and that its basic disinflation objective, notably to reduce inflation to 20 per cent by the end of 1999 and to single digits by the end of 2000, was virtually impossible to achieve. Wage inflation, already strong in the second half of 1998, accelerated further at the beginning of 1999, driven by sharp pay gains in the private sector. Generous public sector pay concessions during the long political campaign that preceded the general elections of April also contributed to inflation; the wages of public sector workers grew by more than 40 per cent in real terms in 1999. Consumer price inflation, which had been declining through the spring of 1999, subsequently started to rise again, remaining in the neighbourhood of 65 per cent until the end of the year. Interest rates on one-year treasury bills remained well above 100 per cent throughout much of 1999 and rose as high as 143 per cent on shorter maturities.

A new, more stable coalition government was appointed in May 1999. However, while prospects for the world economy strengthened, real interest rates in the 30 to 40 per cent range caused the severe contraction in private demand to continue during the latter part of the year. With this adverse situation being compounded by the repercussions of the August and November earthquakes, real GDP declined by 5 per cent in 1999 (Table 1). The government estimates that the earthquake reduced GDP by perhaps 1 per cent. (The consequences of the earthquake and the related policy issues are discussed in Chapter IV.)

As concerns sectoral developments, it appears that lacklustre domestic demand had particularly severe consequences for construction, retail trade and the overall manufacturing sector (Table 2). Declining to about 70 per cent by the end of 1999, the rate of capacity utilisation in manufacturing was the lowest registered since the beginning of the decade, pointing to the existence of a negative gap between actual and potential output (Figure 2). Employment gains remained too modest to fully offset the effects of rising participation rates and, as a consequence, the rate of unemployment rose from 6.8 per cent in 1998 to 7.6 per cent in 1999. Especially poor labour market developments were observed for urban areas, where a significant contraction in employment was recorded. These developments widened the gap between urban and rural workers (Table 3).

... accompanied by a worsening external account

The economic recession was reflected in a significant contraction of imports, which proved to be particularly sharp in the first half of 1999. For the year as a whole, total merchandise imports fell by 12½ per cent, measured in dollar terms (Table 4). The demand for Turkish exports was also weak, however, with total merchandise exports falling by 6 per cent during the year. The full exposure of

Table 1. **Demand and output: outturn and projections**[1]

Percentage changes, volume (1987 prices)

	1997		1998	1999	Projections		
	Current prices TL trillion	Per cent of GDP			2000	2001	2002
Private consumption	19 619.1	68.0	0.6	−3.1	6.0	3.2	3.5
Public consumption	3 535.1	12.3	7.9	6.5	5.0	2.0	2.0
Gross fixed investment	7 618.4	26.4	−3.9	−16.0	16.2	7.0	5.3
Final domestic demand	30 772.6	106.7	−0.2	−6.0	8.5	4.1	3.9
Stockbuilding[2]	−377.5	−1.3	0.9	2.1	0.0	0.0	0.0
Total domestic demand	30 395.1	105.4	0.6	−4.0	8.3	4.1	3.8
Exports of goods and services	7 088.4	24.6	12.0	−7.0	15.0	6.6	7.5
Imports of goods and services	8 762.8	30.4	2.3	−3.7	18.0	4.0	5.6
Foreign balance[2]	−16 74.4	−5.8	2.6	−0.9	−1.7	0.6	0.3
Statistical discrepancy[2]	1 15.2	0.4	−0.1	0.1	0.0	0.0	0.0
GDP at market prices	28 835.9	100.0	3.1	−5.0	7.0	4.9	4.4
GDP implicit price deflator			75.7	56.0	50.1	22.4	15.8
Memorandum items:							
Consumer prices[3]			83.0	60.7	54.3	22.5	11.8
Unemployment rate			6.3	7.3	7.1	7.0	6.8
Current balance ($ billion)			2.0	−1.4	−9.1	−9.1	−8.2
Current balance (per cent of GDP)			1.1	−0.9	−4.6	−4.2	−3.4
Real effective exchange rate[4]			3.3	−1.6	10.8	8.4	5.0

1. OECD, *Economic Outlook* No. 68 projections.
2. Change as a percentage of GDP in previous period.
3. Private consumption deflator.
4. Constant trades weights with 28 OECD partners, using GDP deflator.
Source: OECD.

Table 2. **Decomposition of output growth by sector**

	1994	1995	1996	1997	1998	1999	2000[1]
Agriculture	−0.7	2.0	4.4	−2.3	8.4	−4.6	1.8
Industry	−5.7	12.1	7.1	10.4	2.0	−5.0	5.7
Manufacturing	−7.6	13.9	7.1	11.4	1.2	−5.7	..
Services	−3.6	6.0	6.6	7.4	2.4	−5.1	..
Construction	−2.0	−4.7	5.8	5.0	0.7	−12.7	3.6
Retail trade	−7.6	11.5	8.1	11.7	1.4	−6.8	..
Transport	−2.0	5.7	7.6	6.0	4.9	−4.0	4.4
GDP	−5.5	7.2	7.0	7.5	3.1	−5.0	6.5

1. First three quarters.
Source: State Planning Organisation.

Figure 2. **Industrial production and capacity utilisation**

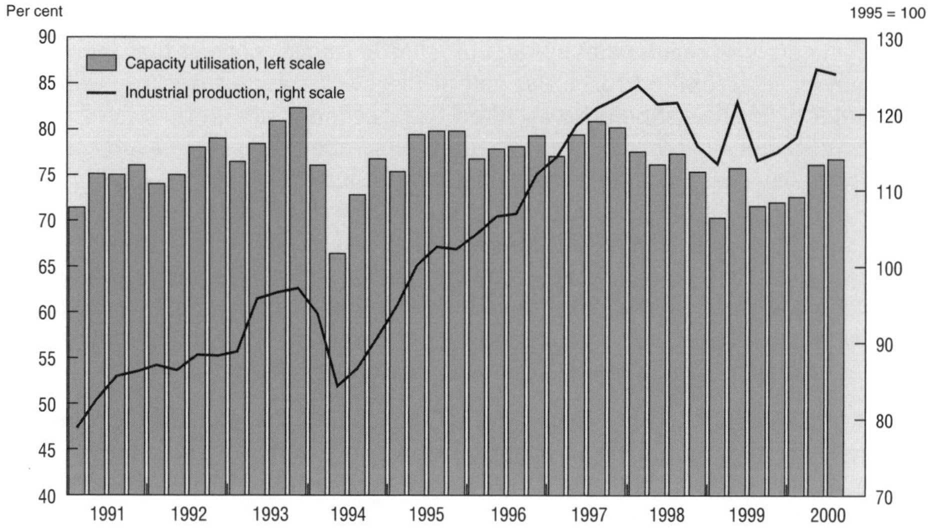

Source: OECD.

Table 3. **Labour force and employment trends**
Thousand persons, aged 15+

	1998	1999	2000[1]
Labour force	22 399	22 187	23 022
Female labour force/labour force (per cent)	27.4	28.7	26.2
Employment	20 872	21 413	20 159
Urban (per cent)	49.3	51.3	52.6
Rural (per cent)	50.7	48.7	47.4
Female employment/employment (per cent)	27.4	28.8	26.3
Number of unemployed	1 527	1 773	1 567
Unemployment rate (per cent)	6.8	7.6	7.2
Urban (per cent)	10.3	11.3	9.6
Rural (per cent)	3.1	3.8	4.2
Underemployment (per cent)[2]	6.1	8.8	8.2
Inactive labour (per cent)[3]	12.9	16.4	15.4

1. Average of Q1 and Q2.
2. Underemployment is defined taking into account two groups of individuals. The first group includes individuals who work less than 40 hours per week and are able to work more at their present job or are capable of doing a second job. The second group includes individuals who work under the same circumstances but want or are searching for a second job.
3. Inactive labour is defined as the sum of unemployment and underemployment.
Source: State Institute of Statistics.

Turkey to the loss of important markets in Russia and neighbouring countries is difficult to evaluate, reflecting the omission of a sizeable amount of trade with such countries from the official trade statistics. However, calculations for 1999 taking into account regular survey data of "shuttle trade", suggest that these markets may have accounted for about half of the overall export decline, while the remainder of the loss should be ascribed to a decline in competitiveness *vis-à-vis* emerging markets in general: Turkish exports were affected by increased competition from Asian and Brazilian producers. Many hitherto fast-growing export industries – particularly in the textiles, leather goods and steel sectors – experienced a sharp slowdown, with a resultant loss in Turkey's aggregate export market share. The invisibles balance was affected by contracting tourism receipts and weaker exports of construction services. Thus, despite falling imports, the external sector underwent a marked deterioration, and by the end of the year the overall current account had moved into a modest deficit (1 percentage point of GDP).

Notwithstanding high real interest rates, Turkey was unable to compensate fully for the capital flight experienced on the wake of the Russian crisis (Table 5). Net portfolio inflows for 1999 amounted to about $3.4 billion, significantly below the net outflow of $6.7 billion recorded for 1998. Nevertheless, total net capital movements were large enough to provide for a significant increase of foreign reserves (by about $5½ billion).[1] The expansion of capital movements concealed wide changes in the relative importance of the various components: the main determinant, portfolio investment, largely reflected the expansion of bonds issued abroad by the Turkish government as it diversified its financing sources.

2000 *sees a new stabilisation programme and strong recovery underway*

A new stabilisation programme was embarked upon at the end of 1999 by the new coalition government, supported by a stand-by arrangement with the International Monetary Fund, with the target of lowering the inflation rate to single digits within three years. In anticipation of the agreement on a stand-by, interest rates began to ease from mid 1999, and the actual announcement of the programme was associated with a sharp reduction in interest rates from 90 to under 40 per cent, reflecting both a downward revision of inflation expectations and a sharp decline in risk premia due to the ensuing boost to confidence. The Turkish economy has since entered a recovery phase. Aggregate output posted an annual real increase of 6½ per cent during the first three quarters of 2000 compared with the same period of the previous year, with both private consumption and fixed investment assisting domestic demand (Table 6). Industrial production has accelerated sharply, with service sector activity, particularly retailing, transport and communications, reinforcing the recovery. Evidence from survey data suggests that business confidence at the start of the year has not been so high since at least the late 1980s.

Table 4. **Current account of the balance of payments**
US$ million

	1993	1994	1995	1996	1997	1998	1999	1999 January-September	2000 January-September
Merchandise exports (f.o.b.)	15 611	18 390	21 975	32 446	32 647	31 220	29 326	21 112	22 800
Exports	15 345	18 106	21 636	23 225	26 261	26 973	26 588	19 249	20 010
Shuttle trade	..	..	..	8 842	5 849	3 689	2 255	1 502	2 071
Transit trade	266	284	339	379	537	558	483	361	719
Merchandise imports (f.o.b.)	29 771	22 606	35 187	43 028	48 005	45 440	39 773	28 327	38 841
Trade balance	**-14 160**	**-4 216**	**-13 212**	**-10 582**	**-15 358**	**-14 220**	**-10 447**	**-7 215**	**-16 041**
Other goods and services (net)	3 959	3 755	6 377	3 698	7 854	10 477	3 908	3 236	5 490
Private unrequited transfers (net)	3 035	2 709	3 425	3 892	4 552	5 568	4 813	3 790	3 659
Official unrequited transfers (net)	733	383	1 071	555	314	159	362	214	121
Invisibles balance	**7 727**	**6 847**	**10 873**	**8 145**	**12 720**	**16 204**	**9 083**	**7 240**	**9 270**
Current balance	**-6 433**	**2 631**	**-2 339**	**-2 437**	**-2 638**	**1 984**	**-1 364**	**25**	**-6 771**
Current balance (as a percentage of GDP)	**-3.6**	**2.2**	**-1.5**	**-1.3**	**-1.3**	**1.1**	**-0.9**	**0.0**	**-3.5**

Source: Central Bank of Turkey.

Table 5. **Net capital movements**
US$ million

| | 1993 | 1994 | 1995 | 1996 | 1997 | 1998 | 1999 | January-September | |
								1999	2000
Total net capital movements	**8 963**	**-4 194**	**4 643**	**8 763**	**8 737**	**448**	**4 671**	**1 930**	**11 123**
Direct investment	622	559	772	612	554	573	138	81	-257
Portfolio investment	3 917	1 158	237	570	1 634	-6 711	3 429	1 729	6 032
Other long-term capital	1 370	-784	-79	1 636	4 788	3 985	345	-500	2 981
Short-term capital	3 054	-5 127	3 713	5 945	1 761	2 601	759	620	2 367
Net errors and omission	**-2 222**	**1 769**	**2 354**	**-1 781**	**-2 755**	**-1 985**	**1 899**	**3 467**	**-1 955**
Current balance	**-6 433**	**2 631**	**-2 339**	**-2 437**	**-2 638**	**1 984**	**-1 364**	**25**	**-6 771**
Change in reserves[1]	**-308**	**-206**	**-4 658**	**-4 545**	**-3 344**	**-447**	**-5 206**	**-5 422**	**-2 397**

1. A minus sign indicates an increase in reserves.
Source: Central Bank of Turkey.

Table 6.   **Macroeconomic performance before and after the launching
of the stabilisation programme**

Per cent

	1999		2000		
	September	December	March	June	October
Demand[1]					
Private consumption	−2.9	−1.9	4.6	7.0	. .
Public consumption	9.1	5.7	0.3	12.3	. .
Fixed investment	−14.3	−14.6	10.6	19.8	. .
Exports of goods and services	−10.6	1.2	7.4	16.1	. .
Imports of goods and services	−2.1	5.2	25.0	14.5	. .
GDP	−5.9	−3.3	5.1	5.8	6.5[2]
Supply[3]					
Industrial production	−4.5	2.4	7.3	10.3	13.8
Capacity utilisation	71.6	72.0	72.6	76.1	76.6
Inflation[3]					
CPI	66.1	64.9	66.1	65.2	59.6
WPI	52.4	53.1	57.8	59.7	56.0
Private	55.7	71.2	90.4	97.1	83.8
Public	51.5	48.1	49.1	49.5	47.8
Interest rates[4]					
Nominal short-term	96.4	51.6	43.5	39.9	36.6
Nominal long-term	92.4	79.7	36.2	36.6	40.9
Real long-term[5]	28.9	−1.0	−8.6	−2.3	5.7
Deflated with actual inflation			−16.6	−3.3	2.0

1. Year-on-year percentage changes of quarter ending at the given month.
2. Third quarter.
3. Year-on-year percentage changes of monthly figures. Supply side figures refer to the private manufacturing sector.
4. Three and six month Treasury secondary market rates for short and long-term maturities, respectively.
5. As of 2000, deflated with expected rate of inflation, according to OECD projections.
Source: State Institute of Statistics and Central Bank of Turkey.

The role of monetary policy in the new disinflation strategy

The new stabilisation programme is broad-based, with an equal emphasis on monetary, fiscal and structural reform elements (Box 1). The three strands of policy are interlinked and mutually reinforcing. Monetary policy tightening cannot sustainably reduce inflation if fiscal fundamentals are not brought into line (discussed in Chapter II), and fiscal fundamentals depend heavily on structural policies with respect to the privatisation of state-owned enterprises, the rationalisation of agricultural subsidies, social security and banking reforms (Chapter III). However, the most important influence on short-term price, interest-rate and output movements has been the switch in monetary policy from a passive, accommodating approach to one which actively bears down on inflation expectations. Instead of allowing the Turkish lira to depreciate in line with the forecast inflation

Box 1.   The stand-by arrangement with the IMF

On 22 December 1999, the executive board of the IMF approved a 3-year stand-by arrangement with Turkey intended to support the government's 2000-02 economic stabilisation programme set out in its earlier letter of intent to the IMF.* Overall, the credit facility equals about $4 billion, an amount that excludes the $500 million released within the framework of the emergency fund created after the Marmara earthquake of 1999. Five instalments of equal amount will have been made available by end-2000, totalling $1.44 billion. The government's programme rests on three pillars: a front-loaded fiscal adjustment; structural reforms, and monetary and exchange-rate policy supported by income policies consistent with target inflation.

Fundamental goals of the programme
- To bring down consumer price inflation from over 65 per cent at end-1999 to 25 per cent by end-2000, 12 per cent by end-2001 and 7 per cent by end-2002.
- To achieve a primary budget surplus for the public sector of about 3.7 per cent of GNP in 2000 (or 2.2 per cent taking into account one-off earthquake-related expenses which are estimated at about 1½ per cent of GNP) and to sustain that level over the adjustment programme. For 1999 the public sector primary balance recorded a deficit of close to 2 per cent of GNP.
- To make fiscal adjustment sustainable over the medium-run.

Fiscal policy instruments
- To underpin the above targets for 2000 the programme requires fiscal measures worth some 7½ per cent of GNP, of which more than two-thirds result from revenue-raising initiatives and the remainder from spending cuts.
- As to the split between temporary and structural fiscal measures, permanent measures, mainly on the spending side, will be phased in more gradually and mainly from 2001 (see below).
- With a view to containing the burden of interest payments, fiscal policy is to be complemented by a more active and diversified debt management policy and the acceleration of privatisation.

Structural reforms
Consolidating the gains that can be expected from the fiscal adjustment implemented in 2000 requires structural reforms in several areas, including:
- Accelerated rationalisation of *agricultural policies*, most notably with the aim of gradually phasing out present support policies, replacing them with a direct income support system targeted on poor farmers.
- Deepening the *social security reforms* launched in 1999, both via undertaking further administrative measures to improve coverage, compliance and administrative efficiency and creating a legal framework more suitable to the expansion of private pension funds.

---

*   See Government of Turkey (1999).

Box 1. The stand-by arrangement with the IMF (*cont.*)

- Improving *fiscal management and transparency*, involving changes to the budgetary framework (preparation, execution and control) so as to broaden the effective coverage of the budget, as well as to enhance accountability in budgetary operations.
- Achieving further progress in the *reform of the tax system* and strengthening tax enforcement so as to reduce tax arrears which by 1999 amounted to some 3 per cent of GNP.
- As for *privatisations*, the government is committed to disengaging the public sector further from economic activity, while raising sizeable receipts for debt reduction, through sales in such key sectors as telecommunications and energy.
- Pushing ahead the implementation of the *reform of the banking system and banking regulation* along the lines stipulated in the banking law approved by Parliament in 1999. *Inter alia*, this foresaw the creation of a new independent supervision authority (operational from September 2000), while the government also committed itself to the introduction of measures to strengthen prudential regulation and tools to deal with problem banks.

Monetary and exchange-rate policies

Two objectives guide monetary and exchange-rate policies under the programme, notably to reduce the high degree of uncertainty underlying the stipulation of financial contracts, and the need to avoid being locked into an excessively rigid monetary framework over the long run.

- As to *exchange-rate policy*, from January 2000 the central bank abandoned its real exchange-rate targeting approach in favour of a pre-announced exchange-rate path. The lira depreciation against the exchange-rate basket (defined as $1 + € 0.77) is announced on a daily basis and is consistent with the targeted inflation rate.
- For the period *January 2000 through June 2001*, the rate of crawl remains fully determined taking into account the inflation target.
- Thereafter, the exchange-rate approach is carried out according to a *pre-announced widening of the band*, with the width of the band being 7.5 per cent by end-2001, 15 per cent by end-June 2002 and 22.5 per cent by the end of 2002.
- This exchange-rate policy is to be assisted by *monetary policy*, with net domestic assets (NDA) of the central bank not to exceed their end-1999 level(-1 200 trillion) at the end of each quarter and short-run fluctuations within quarters (with the exclusion of 3-day periods centred on religious holidays) not to exceed +/– 5 per cent of that level, over the first 18 months of the programme.
- A fixed NDA implies that any increase (decline) in the monetary base has to occur as a response to stronger capital inflows (or outflows), with *interest rates being fully market determined*.

Box 1.   **The stand-by arrangement with the IMF** (*cont.*)

Incomes policies

The disinflation process is assisted by income policies which provide a guide to the private sector as to how wage and price increases are to be set in line with the inflation target.

– Salary increases for civil servants and the increase in the minimum wage have been set in line with targeted CPI inflation. As envisaged initially, civil servants' wages were adjusted in June 2000 by the difference between inflation in the first five months of the year and 15 per cent, plus 2 per cent.

---

rate, the rate of the nominal exchange-rate crawl is now based on *targeted* inflation. This more pro-active monetary policy approach is being supported by prices and incomes policies, according to which public sector prices, rents, the minimum wage and civil servants' wages are linked to targeted rather than past inflation. Several major challenges have needed to be faced in the process of implementing the strategy, and the remainder of the chapter concentrates on the issues involved.

Problems of real-exchange rate targeting and monetary accommodation...

The background to monetary policy prior to the new approach was one where the main policy priorities of the central bank were to support international competitiveness by holding the "real exchange rate", while at the same time stabilising domestic liquidity conditions. Within this approach, open market operations were required to sterilise episodes of excessive capital inflows or, as in the wake of the Asian and the Russian crises, to inject liquidity when faced with a capital outflow, thus underwriting a substantial degree of indirect financing of the public sector deficit by granting liquidity to the banking system. Consistent with the requirements of such an approach, a key ingredient in the monetary strategy of the central bank was the control over the expansion of reserve money – in turn reflecting changes in both net foreign reserves and net domestic assets – the aim being to insulate the domestic market, as far as possible, from external instability. However, the system entrenched high inflation expectations, and did not prevent high and volatile real interest rates, a sign of inflation risk.

At the same time, the private sector found increasingly sophisticated ways of avoiding the "inflation tax" usually associated with central bank accommodation, so that the real demand for base money progressively diminished. The corresponding shift in private sector financial portfolios in response to high inflation is well illustrated by the expansion of repo transactions (Figure 3), which typically consist in the bank sale of a government security with the commitment to buy the security back at a given price. Over the past years, repos have been widely used by Turkish households as a highly remunerated substitute for time deposits and by banks to finance off-balance sheet portfolios of Treasury securities (no statutory reserve requirement governs the emission of these instruments). Nonetheless, the switch out of money remained less marked than in most other high-inflation countries – so that the seignorage revenues of the central bank did not suffer major erosion (see Annex III).

High and variable real interest rates have cramped and distorted economic activity, while increasing financial fragility. Economic agents have increasingly shifted out of real into financial investments, while banks have focused on government securities as a primary source of income, rather than on traditional lending activities. Partly as a result, the extent of traditional bank intermediation in Turkey is particularly modest by OECD standards, as revealed by the fact that total bank lending to the private sector equals only 20 per cent of GDP.[2] Instead, small and medium-sized commercial banks have exploited the interest rate premium on government securities through arbitrage activities, borrowing less costly

Figure 3. **Selected financial indicators**

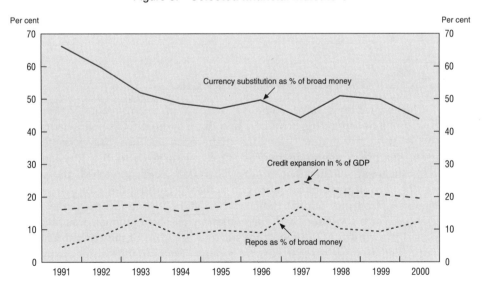

Source: Central Bank of Turkey.

foreign funds and investing them in the highly lucrative domestic government bonds. As a result, the exposure of banks to exchange-rate risk increased and this was reflected, to a large extent, in a worsened maturity mismatch between their short-term liabilities and longer-term assets (see Chapter III). Following a lowering of the prudential ceiling at the beginning of the year, the net open foreign-exchange position of the overall banking sector declined somewhat in 1999. But it remained significantly higher than the levels prevailing in the mid-1990s (Table 7).

Table 7.   **Open positions of the banking system**[1]
US$ million

	1994	1995	1996	1997	1998	1999	2000[2]
Investment and development banks	−195	−80	−13	35	88	111	73
Deposit money banks	−823	−347	−1 216	−1 918	−4 821	−4 754	−8 127
State banks	59	−213	136	287	−171	−78	−357
Private banks	−720	−206	−1 324	−2 069	−4 511	−4 408	−7 481
Foreign banks	−162	73	−29	−135	−139	−267	−289
Total	−1 018	−427	−1 229	−1 883	−4 733	−4 642	−8 054
In percentage of paid-in capital	54.7	68.2	75.5	61.7	90.7	78.7	102.1

1.   Defined as |(total assets + off-balance sheet forward purchases) − (total liabilities + off-balance sheet forward sales)| in foreign currency valued at end-period central bank buying exchange rates. Exchange-indexed transactions are not included.
2.   September.
Source: Undersecretariat of Treasury.

... were not resolved by a tighter monetary policy stance...

These problems have come to a head in recent years. Against the background of a deteriorating economic and fiscal situation, the announcement in mid-1998 of the early general elections triggered a sudden loss in confidence, evident in sharply rebounding interest rates even prior to the Russian crisis (Figure 4). In these circumstances, the new IMF staff-monitored programme engaged the central bank to be more pro-active in curbing the monetary expansion emanating from the budget deficit. While still allowing the exchange rate to depreciate at a rate consistent with past inflation, greater emphasis was placed on control over the growth of the net domestic assets (NDA) of the central bank as a means of disinflation, rather than reserve money.[3] Maintaining tighter control over the expansion of net domestic assets was meant to allow interest rates to move more freely as a means of domestic money market equilibration. However, this narrower approach to monetary targeting could only have been successfully

Figure 4.   **Interest rate developments**

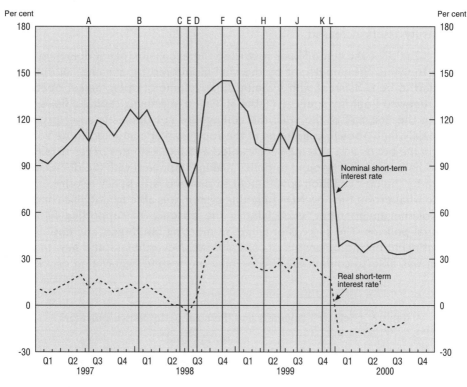

A. Asian crisis.
B. 1998-2000 stabilisation programme announced.
C. 18-month Staff Monitered Programm agreed with IMF.
D. Early general elections announced for April 99.
E. Russian crisis.
F. Yilmaz government falls.
G. Ecevit government appointed.
H. General elections.
I.   New Ecevit government.
J. First in Marmara region earthquake.
K. Second in Bolu region earthquake.
L. Stand-by agreement with IMF.

1. Deflated using consumer price inflation.

Source: Central Bank of Turkey.

pursued under a situation of relatively stable capital flows. In the event, respond-
ing to the capital outflow and liquidity crunch that followed the August 1998 crisis,
the authorities were constrained to allow the volume of open market operations to
expand, and net domestic assets surged in the latter part of 1998. This expansion
went wholly to finance the public sector, the proportion of bank deposits destined

to fund credits to the private sector falling precipitously. The reduction of bank lending was mirrored in an expansion of portfolio investment in government securities, pointing to a sizeable "crowding out" effect, as the profitability of investing in Treasury assets increased.

For 1999, the central bank restricted the expansion of net domestic assets (NDA) to within the targets set by the staff-monitored programme, an approach intended to be consistent with a diminishing volume of open market operations and a renewed liquidity squeeze (Table 8). Given improving capital inflows, especially in the first half of the year, the ceilings for net domestic asset expansion were easily met. Though conditions in the repo market continued to be volatile,[4] those in the bonds and bills market steadied and interest rates began to fall in the second half, as the background to policy-making improved with the demonstrated resolve by the new coalition government to proceed with policy reforms. It is not clear to what extent the new NDA targeting system was able to stabilise conditions in a volatile environment, especially in the absence of supporting fiscal and structural policies. The success or failure in meeting the targets still appeared to be contingent on the behaviour of capital flows. Nevertheless, the new targeting system was able to contain the rise of inflation despite aggravation of the fiscal

Table 8. **Selected monetary and financial performance indicators**

	1999		2000		
	September	December	March	June	September
Net domestic assets (TL trillion)					
Realisation	−1 494.2	−1 389.7	−1 260.2	−1 295.1	−1 307.6
Target (ceiling)	−1 000.0	−1 200.0	−1 200.0	−1 200.0	−1 200.0
Net foreign exchange reserves ($ billion)					
Realisation	17.9	16.8	16.6	17.6	17.6
Target (floor)	. .	12.0	12.0	12.8	12.8
Monthly exchange rate					
Realisation	4.2	5.1	2.1	1.7	1.3
Target	. .	. .	2.1	1.7	1.3
M2[1]	103.5	108.1	69.7	65.4	45.2
M2Y[1]	71.3	106.5	86.6	80.0	61.0
Repurchasing operations[1]	58.6	80.9	133.8	115.6	62.4
M2/M2Y (per cent)	56.9	56.3	52.3	52.0	51.3
Total deposits[1]	72.9	102.9	88.6	77.6	60.0
TL deposits[1]	113.6	100.9	68.2	61.1	43.0
Fx deposits[1]	40.1	105.1	111.7	97.6	80.4
Banking credit to the private sector	49.8	42.8	54.9	60.1	69.7

1. Percentage change, annual.
Source: State Planning Organisation and Central Bank of Turkey.

problem during the electoral campaign. In the process, the central bank seems to have increased the credibility of its anti-inflationary commitment. However, in the absence of a fiscal correction, the counterpart of reduced monetary accommodation was a surge in the level of government debt (see Annex III).

... leading to a stronger exchange-rate commitment

The strategic backdrop for the stabilisation programme in operation from the beginning of 2000 is, as noted, the acknowledgement that a strong nominal exchange-rate arrangement is critical for the credibility of the disinflation objective and the restoration of economic balance. Thus, as a means of breaking inflationary expectations, the central bank has moved from a "managed float" to a pre-announced exchange-rate path against a basket composed of a weighted average of the euro and the dollar. The first stage of the exchange-rate regime, during the period January 2000 to June 2001, which covers the first eighteen months of the programme, is a pre-announced "crawling basket peg", involving a depreciation equal to the wholesale price inflation target (20 per cent for 2000).[5]

A key medium-run issue, faced by several other countries having adopted an exchange-rate anchor, is how to minimise the loss of policy credibility that the eventual shift to a more flexible regime usually entails (the so-called "exit strategy"). The problem arises because market agents often interpret the move towards greater exchange-rate flexibility after the transition to lower inflation as a shift from a disciplined monetary approach to one where the commitment to low inflation and monetary restraint is more uncertain. As a mean of avoiding such risks, the exit strategy was announced in conjunction with the launching of the new programme. Thus, after June 2001, there will be a gradually widening symmetrical band around a central parity from 7.5 per cent by the end of 2001 to 22.5 per cent by the end of 2002. This phase is supposed to necessitate no central bank intervention.

One of the potential weaknesses of an exchange-rate based stabilisation approach is that monetary policy can become excessively expansionary if open-market operations are allowed to compensate for shifts in foreign capital inflows.[6] The new exchange-rate policy will thus be supported by a rigorous performance evaluation criterion which will provide an immediate and unambiguous signal for possible deviations from the commitment to a tight monetary policy stance. Establishing an element of continuity with the "monetary phase" of disinflation since 1998, the chosen performance evaluation item will be the net domestic assets (NDA) of the central bank. This is set to remain roughly unchanged in nominal terms at its end-1999 level during the first stage of the programme, with a floor on net international reserves (NIR). Both NDA and NIR are to be monitored on a quarterly basis during the programme. The authorities thus intend to avoid the drawbacks experienced over the medium term by a number of emerging market countries that pursued exchange-rate based stabilisation.

The implementation of monetary policy in the programme has some of the central elements of a currency board. Base money is to be created, or eliminated only in connection with balance of payments inflows or outflows, net domestic assets being thus eschewed as an instrument of monetary policy. Capital inflows/outflows will not be sterilised, so that interest rates are to be fully market-determined, thus providing for an element of automatic stabilisation. For example, "hot money" capital inflows would immediately increase the supply of funds in domestic markets and bid down the interest rate implying that further capital inflows will be discouraged. Capital outflows would, conversely, be allowed to bid up interest rates.

The adjustment process: progress and risks

Implementation of the programme is basically on track...

Monetary and exchange-rate policies were rigorously implemented in the first three quarters of 2000 and the end-quarter performance criteria for NDA and NIR of the central bank were fully met. Moreover, through mid-November the no-sterilisation policy was consistently followed, with NDA always remaining in the programme's corridor (with the allowed exception of predetermined religious holiday periods), while the observed rate of depreciation matched the (end-monthly) targets of 2.1, 1.7, 1.3, and 1 per cent for the first to fourth quarters, respectively. The third/fourth review of the stand-by agreement completed by the IMF in mid-November reiterated the conclusion of earlier reviews that the programme remains on track, the benefits thus far stemming both from the pace of fiscal consolidation (see Chapter II) and the new monetary and exchange-rate framework (Table 8). Specifically, the "no sterilisation" rule has provided additional credibility to the programme. Fiscal targets were significantly tightened for 2001, however, in order to address the concerns regarding slow convergence in inflation and higher than expected current account deficit (below).

As concerns the real economy, the early outcomes of the programme for 2000 have been largely consistent with the experiences of other countries following disinflation strategies.[7] Programmes involving a strong exchange-rate commitment are typically associated with a phase of economic expansion within the first year of implementation (Figure 5, Panel A). Programmes are often introduced after a recessionary period, indicating the existence of a considerable margin of spare capacity in the economy and providing a favourable framework for an upswing, as in the case of Turkey. Real GDP growth of around 7 per cent is estimated for 2000, well above the 5 to 5½ per cent that was originally programmed, the difference reflecting to a large extent the much larger than expected fall in interest rates at the outset of the programme.

Figure 5.   **Experiences with exchange-rate-based stabilisation programmes:
selected economic indicators**[1]

Centered on the year of stabilisation

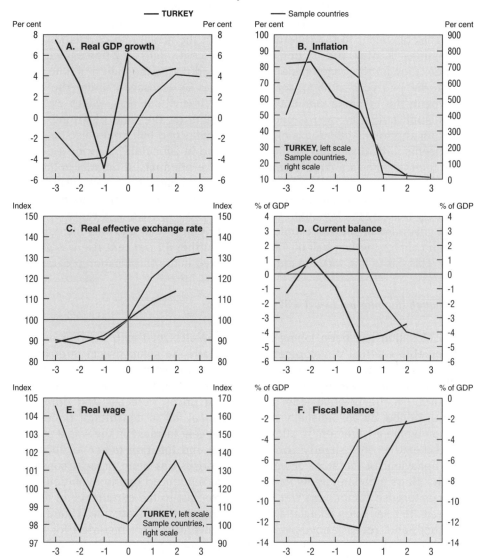

1.   Includes data for the following exchange-rate-based stabilisation experiences (year of stabilisation in parentheses):
     Mexico (87), Poland (90), Uruguay (90), Argentina (91), Croatia (93), Lithuania (94), Russia (95) and Turkey
     (2000). Figures for Turkey in the first and second year of the plan are OECD projections, except for the graph
     illustrating the fiscal balance which is based upon targets in the original letter of intent.
Source: Mussa *et al.* (2000) and OECD.

Incomes policy developments have also been relatively favourable so far for the limited groups to which they apply. Consistent with the commitments established under the 2000 budget, civil servants[8] were granted an initial wage increase of 15 per cent at the beginning of the year and were due to receive 10 per cent in the second half. An additional increase was subsequently authorised by mid-year equivalent to the difference between the actual rate of inflation in the five months to May and 15 per cent (2 per cent), plus a 2 percentage point compensation for the wage erosion that occurred during the month of June.[9] Even though the mid-year catch-up for inflation was as envisaged under the earlier agreement, the resulting cumulative increase in civil servants' wages exceeded the inflation target by over 6 percentage points (at the time of writing, it was uncertain whether an inflation compensation for second-half would also be given). As concerns individuals and families employed in agriculture, support prices on which their incomes are largely dependent have been raised broadly in line with targeted inflation. As to the non-agricultural self-employed, which include low-skilled urban workers, the most relevant figure is the minimum wage. This is statutorily fixed by the Minimum Wage Commission, consisting of representatives of the government, the trade unions and the employers, and was increased by 17.3 per cent for the first half of 2000, while a further 8.2 per cent rise was granted in July. This was in line with the targets stipulated in the stabilisation programme.

... although the inflation target will be overshot...

Inflation has been falling back since March 2000 and, in spite of some unfavourable external developments, particularly the sharp rise in international oil prices and growing euro weakness, fell to its lowest level since 1986 by mid-year. This result suggests that the programme is already impacting on price dynamics. On the positive side, decelerating prices were assisted during the summer period by an unusually strong seasonal fall in agricultural prices. The decision by the government to allow a 27.5 per cent increase in the wheat support price scheme is only slightly above the year-end inflation target for 2000. The price behaviour of the state economic enterprises has been broadly consistent with the plan's inflation targets for the year, as evidenced by the evolution of the public-enterprise component WPI index: in contrast to the experience of the last few years, this has been rising at a slower pace than the private one (Figure 6). On the other hand, recent above-average price increases were recorded for house-hold goods and cars, which suggests that the booming demand for durables has fed directly into actual inflation.[10] Fairly steep price increases were also observed for several categories of services that are typically sheltered from external competition, such as, for example, education, housing, financial services, health and personal care. Moreover, the effects of the recent law aiming to cap housing rent increases at levels consistent with the target CPI inflation rate (effective from

Figure 6. **Components of CPI inflation
and the internal terms of trade**

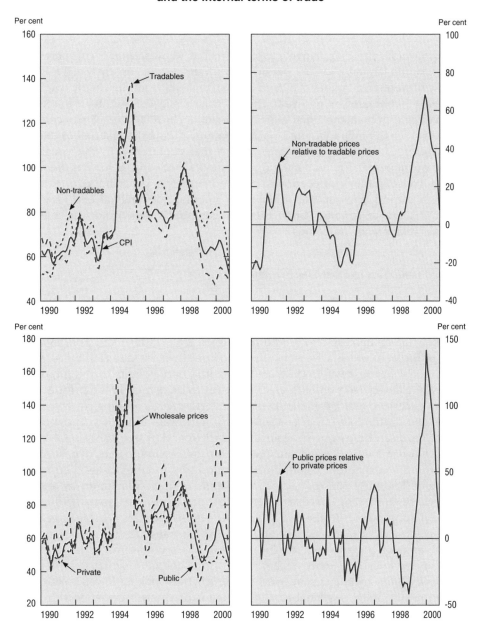

Source: State Planning Organisation.

March 2000) have been rather disappointing so far. Despite signs that compliance has been widening, the effectiveness of the new measures has been greatly undercut by a proviso limiting the extent of applicability of the rent increase ceiling to new contracts taken out after the law came into effect in February.

Overall, the cumulative increases in the wholesale and consumer price indices for the January-October period were 27 and 31 per cent, respectively, compared with year-end targets of 20 and 25 per cent, which implies likely overshoots of at least 10 per cent by end-year. OECD analysis suggest that, taking account of the overhang from higher-than-expected inflation in 2000, the 25 per cent end-year target for CPI inflation may be achieved only during the first half of 2001. The OECD (and consensus) view seems to be that confidence in the programme should be maintained even if inflation overshoots modestly, as long as the pace of budget consolidation proceeds as planned and the programme of structural reform is carried through, but a failure to maintain the original end-year target for 2001 could undermine both external competitiveness and the basis for forward-looking wage outcomes.

... while some risks and tensions are apparent

Despite its success so far, the strategy is not without risks and tensions. These are in part exogenous: from the renewed rise in oil prices, which could adversely affect inflation and feed into inflation expectations and from the weakening of the euro which adversely affects competitiveness due to the high weight of the dollar in the basket. They are also partly endogenous to the adjustment process: from wage settlements which have yet to be agreed in the private sector; from an excessive real appreciation of the currency and a growing current account deficit, and (potentially) from unwanted short-term capital inflows. The relevance of such risks can be assessed against the background of the stabilisation experiences shown in Figure 5, which illustrates the short-term outcomes of past disinflation attempts in different countries with regard to a number of key performance indicators. The early phase of adjustment tends to be accompanied by relatively generous up-front wage concessions, probably due to nominal wage rigidities, and by a real appreciation. In the first year of the adjustment this combination is usually characterised by a consumption boom, which translates into a deteriorating current account. (In this sense, the recovery of output tends to be domestic-demand led.) In the early stages, inflows of foreign capital are generally sufficiently large to finance the external deficit thus making lower inflation and strong growth jointly sustainable. But foreign capital often becomes scarce at a later stage of the programme triggering a sudden interruption of the initial booming phase, the implication being that domestic demand growth needs to be reined back to remain consistent with the exchange rate objective.

Pressures from the private sector wage round

Despite its relative effectiveness, the incomes policy is of limited coverage and the wage behaviour of the private-sector and state economic enterprises could still put inflation outcomes at risk. The background to this is an important two-year *General Protocol Agreement* signed by the government with the Public Sector Employers' Associations prior to the launching of the current disinflation attempt. This *Protocol* envisages generous wage concessions for more than half a million permanent and temporary public sector workers, which for 2000 would result in a 47½ per cent average rise of their net wage bill.[11] Besides exacerbating the inflation overhang, these precedents could have important undesired consequences for the numerous private and public sector collective bargaining negotiations scheduled for autumn 2000.[12] The evidence available so far for a number of still relatively minor agreements (such as in food, cement and rubber), suggests that, notwithstanding a less than complete emulation effect, their net wage increase for 2000 should average in the 38 to 43 per cent range. Information about the contract situation of private "white-collar" employees is scant and has to be based mainly on anecdotal evidence. However, in the major negotiations that are about to begin, unions are demanding wage increases considerably above the inflation target. Although the majority of the working population (some three quarters) does not enjoy any collective bargaining rights, if the unionised segment becomes an exception to the incomes policy, it would pose a threat both to the inflation target and to the success of the overall programme.

In recognition of these threats, a recent policy development has been the reaffirmation by the government of the need to achieve consistent price and income policies fully supported by all private and public social partners. While forward-looking indexation has been adopted for the setting of wages in the civil service, there has been as noted in the previous *Survey*, no effective institutional framework in place that would allow a forward-looking procedure to work efficiently for the private sector. This has been recognised in the attempted reinvigoration of the *Social Economic Council* as a forum for building a consensus for change among the social partners. In the area of private sector wages and prices, it is the intention that the *Council*, which was reconvened in mid-2000, should reach an agreement on a formal joint declaration in support of the government's disinflation targets and on price and wage guidelines consistent with non-inflationary growth, due account being taken of the need both to protect the purchasing power of employees and the integrity of the fiscal adjustment process.[13] Successful stabilisation strategies usually depend on the equitable distribution of the burden of adjustment which is not yet apparent.

Current account deficit and the real exchange-rate appreciation

The current account has become a major concern. The unexpected increase in international oil prices, the accelerated restocking of raw materials and unfinished products and, most significantly, strong domestic purchases of foreign durables, largely automobiles, led to a strong pick-up of imports in 2000. Import demand is being fed by booming domestic demand, in turn reflecting sharply lower interest rates, and by real exchange-rate appreciation. Furthermore, the maturity structure of public sector borrowing is such that it is generating high, if temporary, real interest earnings on past outstanding long-term government bond holdings. For the first three quarters, overall imports increased by 35 per cent in value terms over the same period a year earlier. Despite encouraging signs that the value of suitcase trade has recovered strongly over the period (by 38 per cent in annual terms), overall exports rose by only 8 per cent in the same period. Thus, a widening trade deficit was responsible for an observed large worsening of the current account balance which was only partly offset by the positive impact of the recovery of tourism receipts.[14] By September 2000, the level of the current account deficit ($6.8 billion, some 3½ per cent of GDP) was already more than four times as much the amount of the overall deficit for 1999. For the year as a whole, it is estimated to be somewhat above 4½ per cent of GDP.

The programme inevitably involves some real appreciation (Figure 7). This need not be of overriding concern, since by some estimates, the lira could probably sustain a real appreciation of 10 to 15 per cent in the course of 2000 without an unduly negative impact on the balance of payments.[15] Indeed, this "safety" margin may be higher, because of the substantial reduction in financing costs implied by the reduction in domestic interest rates, the effects of which are not easily captured in traditional indicators of external competitiveness.[16] Moreover, the adverse effects of real exchange-rate appreciation will be partly offset by accelerating global activity. Also, the real incomes of workers whose wages have been indexed will continue to fall, and competitiveness indicators based on unit labour costs have not deteriorated, on balance, over the two years to mid-2000 (Figure 7, Panel B). By next year, interest rate declines will restrict rentier income, helping to limit consumption, and hence import growth. Nevertheless, even incorporating private wage settlements in line with the programme, the normal lagged response of exports to real appreciation will add to the widening external deficit. The danger is that upcoming wage settlements could resume the earlier disadvantageous trend in unit labour costs – in the past few years, real wages per person in private manufacturing increased at a pace much stronger than productivity (Figure 8) and since 1995, relative unit labour costs have risen by almost 40 percentage points (Figure 7, Panel B) – resulting in further losses in external competitiveness.

The underlying concern here is that the import boom may not just reflect the perception of a temporarily positive income effect but also an intertemporal substitution effect (over and above the normal one in response to reduced interest rates), reflecting a rush to consume because of scepticism about future inflation and future higher interest rates. Such a concern would, of course,

Figure 7. **Exchange rate and competitiveness developments**

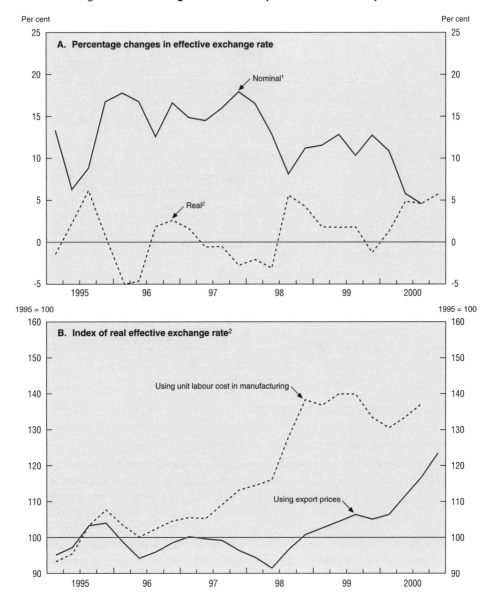

1. Using quarterly changes of the lira against the US$/Euro basket. The weights used are 1 and .77 for the US$ and the euro, respectively.
2. Weighted average taking into account 40 trading partners and deflated using export prices (Panels A and B) or unit labour costs in manufacturing (Panel B).
Source: Central Bank of Turkey; OECD.

Figure 8. **Productivity and labour costs in manufacturing**
1997 = 100

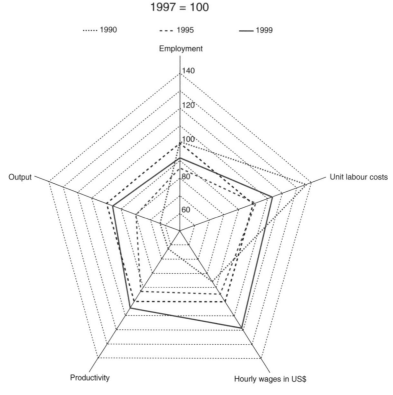

Source: State Planning Organisation.

dissipate as and when the implementation of the targeted elements of the programme remain on track. Nonetheless, the growing external imbalance could have self-reinforcing negative effects on confidence, putting the programme into jeopardy. Fiscal measures are being introduced to cool the expansion of domestic consumption so as to limit the slippage from both the inflation and the current account targets. The main measure will be higher broad-based taxes implied by the new budget for 2001, in turn suggesting a tightening of the "structural fiscal stance" in that year by some 5 per cent of GDP.[17] In addition, selected tax increases (introduced in late 2000) have been targeted at imports of automobiles, most notably an increase in the existing taxes on the extension of consumption credits (which largely go to finance car purchases) and an increase in the tax on luxury automobiles. These initiatives seem to be largely justified if evaluated against the background of risks attached to a rising current account deficit.

However, their drawback is that they could result in increasing administrative complexities and more burdensome "red tape" costs. From a structural point of view, the credibility of the plan depends on such intervention being temporary, as meeting fiscal targets should rely relatively more on lower fiscal expenditures rather than stronger revenues (Chapter II).

Encouraging long-term capital while discouraging short-term inflows

Official foreign borrowing should be roughly equivalent to the projected current account deficit in both 2000 and 2001 (see Chapter II), effectively financing the current account deficit, *ceteris paribus*.[18] But over the longer run the sustainability of the current account deficit depends on attracting long-term capital from abroad, in particular direct investment – following a long period, including notably 2000, during which Turkey has under-performed with respect to inward foreign direct investment – while discouraging short-term inflows. In fact, the "automatic stabiliser" role given to domestic interest rates in the programme will help to put a brake on hot-money inflows by increasing the interest-rate risk, insofar as interest rates are market determined. Indeed, following the introduction of the programme, the volatility of money-market interest rates has increased and this seems to have acted to discourage heavy short-term capital inflows. The "no-sterilisation" rule is thus working to smooth the operation of monetary policy while building long-term foreign-investor confidence. It will, however, be necessary to make an early decision on the monetary framework that will replace the existing one over the medium term, when the exchange-rate anchor will be phased out, in order to sustain such confidence. The government is, accordingly, studying the possibility of moving to an explicit inflation-targeting system.

Sustained capital inflows will be critical to the programme as disinflation proceeds, and as noted need to be of a long-term nature. No rapid increase has yet been observed in the demand for domestic currency, but it may be expected that as inflation decelerates the demand for money will increase, since the cost of holding money will decrease. Without corresponding capital inflows, excess demand for money could cause an excessive rise in interest rates unless private and public sectors borrow abroad. If the programme achieves its targets in the medium term, long-term foreign capital inflows should increase and the probability of sudden outflows decline. In this sense, the success of the monetary programme is endogenous to the whole process of structural reform. Indeed, reinforcing portfolio inflows and other types of capital movements, so as to ensure the financing of a possible further deterioration of the current account, requires market confidence in economic policies. A recent positive achievement is that the capital account recorded net inflows of $11 billion in the first three quarters of the year, largely of a longer-term portfolio nature (Table 5). Moreover, several rating agencies have upgraded Turkey's currency long-term credit rating. This, together with greater political and economic stability, should increase direct and portfolio investment from abroad; privatisation receipts will also help to sustain such inflows.

In this context, also, the reforms to the banking system are important, especially during a period when the banks are facing the need to adapt to a low-inflation environment and will have to learn how to intermediate additional long-term capital inflows. In any reform programme, the banking sector will have to build up its financial intermediation skills, and could be vulnerable during a period of economic adjustment. Over the 1990s, for example, in connection with large net private capital inflows, several emerging countries in the Asian-Pacific region experienced large increases in their financial sector which were manifested in a lending boom.[19] However, developments in such countries also showed that if the bank supervisory process remains weak, and the existence of a government safety net creates incentives for banks to take excessive risks, the likelihood that the lending boom ultimately results in substantial loan losses and deteriorating bank balance sheets may be considerable.[20] This makes it particularly important that Turkey implement fully the planned banking reform (see Chapter III).

Growth prospects for 2001 and the medium term

Conditions are in place for the recovery to be moderated though sustained...

The OECD central projections for Turkey assume that the external trade environment will remain supportive to economic growth during the remainder of the period covered by the stabilisation programme, with export market growth of around 11 per cent in 2001, decelerating only moderately in 2002. However, as discussed, Turkish competitiveness is expected to be eroded as the new exchange-rate regime will involve a real appreciation of the lira – by some 20 per cent over 2000-01, with a modest further appreciation in 2002 (Table 1). As a result, Turkey's share in world exports is expected to fall, although, with normal lags in the response of export volumes to relative prices, the main part of this effect will be concentrated in 2001. On the assumption that the price elasticity of exports is not very high, the projected loss in market share (goods) is 4¾, 6½, and 1 per cent in 2000, 2001, and 2002, respectively.

Domestic demand will continue to be fuelled by lower real interest rates, but is expected to decelerate markedly for three main reasons: first, as high-yielding government bonds mature during the course of 2000, their impact on spending will fade; second, the fiscal measures should restrain consumer demand, especially that oriented towards imports; and third, real interest rates are expected to re-establish themselves at more "normal" levels of 10-15 per cent, making saving more attractive. Post-earthquake reconstruction, which finally got underway in the second half of 2000 having been postponed due to the implementation of new supervisory and control measures in the construction sector (see Chapter IV), may continue to spill-over into 2001. Investment in machinery and equipment, while remaining quite strong, should decelerate somewhat owing to the rise in real interest rates. On balance, GDP growth might ease from around 7 per cent in 2000 to between 4 and 5 per cent in 2001-2002. With the growth of imports falling back in response to slowing growth and with import penetration projected to remain roughly steady at its current high level, the current account deficit should narrow to within the 3 to 4 per cent of GDP range.

... and the eventual effects of breaking inflation inertia should be to raise potential growth

For the medium term, the challenge is to raise Turkey's growth potential substantially. The reform programme creates a much more favourable climate for this to be achieved. Chronic inflation in Turkey has been accompanied by a marked under-performance in aggregate output growth, measured in terms of real per-capita income (Table 9). Real GDP per person has only managed to grow at 1¼ per cent per annum over the 1990s which is well below the average of the most successful emerging economies. Disinflation and liberalisation may be expected to change this, improving long-run economic performance and raising living standards in Turkey. Research suggests that this effect could be substantial, of the order of perhaps ¼ per cent in the growth rate per capita for a sustained 10 per cent decline in inflation. Moreover, achieving half of this overall adjustment requires between three and four quarters (see Box 2). Of major importance to this process is confidence building, with an essential element in breaking the expectations process being the lasting correction of the public sector deficit. Fiscal policy issues are discussed in Chapter II and the structural reforms needed to support fiscal consolidation are discussed in Chapter III.

Table 9.   **The behaviour of inflation and growth**

	Mean
1980-1989	
Inflation rate	51.1
Standard deviation of inflation rate	5.5
Growth rate of real per capita GDP	2.3
1990-1999	
Inflation rate	78.7
Standard deviation of inflation rate	7.2
Growth rate of real per capita GDP	1.3

Source: OECD.

Box 2. **The link between inflation and growth**

The view that inflation, even where predictable, severely alters long-run economic performance is largely accepted and supported by a wide range of empirical findings, while the past two decades have offered many examples of problems of high inflation being associated with the underperformance of output.[1] There is evidence of a similar phenomenon having been at work also in Turkey where chronic inflation has been accompanied by a marked slowdown of aggregate output growth, measured in terms of real per-capita income.

The OECD has conducted a formal econometric analysis to provide a guide as to how inflation developments are transmitted to real GDP growth per person. Annex I presents a set of estimators that have been obtained after having enriched a standard single equation growth model by adding an inflation term. All variables have the expected sign and are in general highly significant. The dynamic estimation shows that a 10 per cent increase in inflation leads to a 0.25 per cent decline in the growth rate of per-capita GDP, while achieving half of this overall adjustment requires between three and four quarters. As such, these estimates appear to be broadly in line with the findings of the recent literature that has focused on countries with a range of inflation rates similar to the ones of Turkey.[2] Aside from the standard tests, the dynamic equation was also estimated to account for the role played by inflation uncertainty, measured by the moving standard deviation of the inflation rate. The new estimates show that there is little evidence of any impact of inflation variability on the output relationship. Notwithstanding the fact that inflation has costs, economic agents in Turkey display an unusually strong capacity to adapt their habits, which prevents unexpected inflation from degenerating into episodes of extreme volatility on the real side.

_____

1. Bruno and Easterly (1995). See Braumann (2000) for a recent survey of the existing empirical evidence.
2. See Barro (1995) and Fischer (1993), for example.

II. Fiscal policy: stabilisation and reform

Introduction and overview

High and persistent fiscal deficits have been the main source of inflation inertia in Turkey, as well as being the major cause of the country's slow and erratic growth performance. As noted in Chapter I, financing the budget deficit through domestic borrowing has put pressure on the central bank to supply liquidity, underwriting inflation, and on the banking system to supply credit, depriving the enterprise sector of capital. At times when Turkey's ability to borrow abroad has been impaired, which includes the recent past, the large amount of debt redemption required under the country's very short-term maturity structure has inevitably increased the rollover risk of the Treasury, causing an unsustainable upward spiral in auction interest rates and debt service commitments. The gravity of the fiscal problem has been exacerbated by the thinness of the capital market and by major weaknesses in the budget structure, which have become extensive through the implementation of populist policies, the execution of "supplementary budgets"; the use of extra-budgetary funds, guarantees, and quasi-fiscal activities of the state banks; inefficiencies and mismanagement among the state-owned enterprises and the deficits of the social security institutions.

To restore stability and discipline, recent *Surveys* and the stand-by programme have recognised that fiscal adjustment requires not just stabilisation packages but fundamental measures to deal with the deficiencies of the system, entailing a broad range of structural reforms. While emphasising the necessity of fiscal adjustment for sustainable debt dynamics in Turkey,[21] a number of studies[22] have stressed the need to take account of all the deficit-generating parts of the public sector, not just the central government deficit. Indeed, the experience of previous disinflation attempts demonstrates that in the absence of structural reforms to deal with this issue, fiscal adjustment programmes in Turkey are not perceived as credible, given the entrenched nature of the imbalances involved. Even if there is a sharp improvement in the primary budget surplus (the balance after deducting interest payments), this is usually perceived as temporary: inflation expectations and interest rates do not respond and debt dynamics remain adverse. The current fiscal adjustment programme thus relies on two pillars: the first is the process of fiscal consolidation *per se*, needed to shift the debt dynamics onto a more sustainable path; the second is the drive for structural reform, needed to tackle the fundamental institutional weaknesses which have made for weak control over deficits. Essential elements in this process are the reform of fiscal administration and the improved transparency of the fiscal accounts.

The first section of this chapter reviews the fiscal developments in 1999, which saw an unsustainable recession- and interest rate-driven rise in public-sector liabilities, generating the necessity for a severe fiscal adjustment in 2000. The short-run requirement is for a substantial primary surplus – even allowing for the recent fall in interest rates – to achieve a sustainable path for debt dynamics. The discussion focuses on the measures being taken under the stand-by pro-gramme and the 2000 budget, with an appraisal of performance so far. The second section evaluates the current and prospective impact on debt and debt financing. The third section evaluates the overall fiscal stance and the 2001 budget. The fourth section describes policy initiatives and needs with respect to budget administration, control and transparency. The final section presents an assess-ment of the overall fiscal adjustment process.

Restoring budgetary stability

1999: *an unsustainable fiscal deterioration*

1999 was the first full budget year of the staff-monitored stabilisation programme, but in the event was noteworthy for a loosening of fiscal discipline. The original budget proposal envisaged targets for the consolidated budget deficit and the primary surplus of 7 and 4.3 per cent of GNP, respectively, to be achieved mainly through revenue increases in the form of higher tax receipts. However, Parliamentary debate on the new draft was brought to a halt by a new government crisis, which gave way to the approval of an interim budget, covering only the first half of the year. The fiscal programme agreed with the IMF on the occasion of the quarterly monitoring review process in February 1999 noted that, under current policies, the authorities were still committed to achieving a primary fiscal surplus of at least 3 per cent of GNP. However, sizeable spending overruns were already becoming apparent in the first quarter of 1999, a typical develop-ment in Turkey in the run-up to a general election, which were making the target surplus extremely difficult to achieve even before allowance for the decline in GNP.

The fiscal policy stance which actually evolved was thus basically expan-sionary. The primary surplus of the consolidated central government budget declined sharply from 4.6 per cent in 1998 to 2.1 per cent in 1999. This met the revised target announced in July (on the third review of the IMF Staff Monitored Programme). But primary expenditures reached the unprecedented level of

22 per cent of GNP, mainly due to a rise in personnel expenditures and an increase in transfers to social security institutions and extra-budgetary funds (Table 10). Higher primary spending, together with huge interest payments on

Table 10. **Consolidated central government budget statement[1]**

Per cent of GNP

	1997	1998	1999	2000				2001[2]
				Baseline[3]	Measures	Target	Estimate	Target
Revenues	19.9	22.1	23.8	20.2	5.0	25.2	26.4	25.7
Tax revenues	16.2	17.2	18.9	15.9	4.6	20.3[4]	21.3	20.7
Direct	6.6	8.2	8.6	5.8	3.2	9.0	8.9	7.9
Indirect	9.6	9.3	10.4	9.9	1.4	11.3	12.5	12.8
Non-tax revenues[5]	3.7	4.9	4.9	4.5	0.4	4.8	5.1	5.0
Expenditures	27.2	29.0	35.5			37.2	37.3	31.5
Personnel	7.0	7.3	8.8	8.4	0.5	7.9	8.1	7.8
Other current	2.4	2.4	2.8	3.1	0.2	3.0	2.9	2.3
Investment	2.0	1.7	1.8	1.8		1.8	2.0	2.3
Transfers	7.9	6.0	8.4	8.4	0.8	7.5	8.0	7.4
Social security	2.6	2.6	3.1	3.3	0.5	2.8	2.7	2.6
Extra-budgetary funds	1.3	0.8	1.3	1.3	0.2	1.1	1.7	0.6
Agricultural subsidies	0.9	0.3	0.3	0.3	..	0.3	0.3	0.7
Capital transfers	0.6	0.1	0.2	0.2	..	0.2	..	..
Transfers to SEEs	0.4	0.4	0.5	0.5	..	0.5	0.7	0.6
Banks' duty losses	0.2	0.01	0.0	0.6	..	0.6	..	..
Other	2.0	1.9	2.5	2.3	..	2.3	..	..
Primary expenditures	19.4	17.4	21.8	21.9	1.5	20.3[6]	21.0	20.7
Transfers on interest payments	7.8	11.7	13.7	..	..	16.9	16.3	10.9
Foreign interest payments	1.0	1.0	1.1	..	..	1.1	1.3	1.6
Domestic interest payments	6.7	10.6	12.6	..	..	15.8	15.0	9.3
Primary balance[7]	0.1	4.6	2.1	..	..	4.9	5.4	5.1
Overall balance[7]	−7.5	−7.0	−11.6	..	..	−12.0	−10.9	−5.8
Deferred payments	0.5	0.4	0.5	..	..	..	..	..
Advances	−0.4	−0.6	−0.6	..	..	..	..	..
Cash balance[7]	−7.4	−7.2	−11.7	..	..	−12.0	−10.9	−5.8
Memorandum item:								
Privatisation proceeds	..	..	..	..	..	2.1	1.6	2.4

1. Adjusted by special appropriations.
2. Draft budget.
3. Includes earthquake impacts.
4. Includes revenues from interest tax as 1.2 per cent of GNP.
5. Excludes privatisation proceeds, includes non-tax revenues, special reserves, funds and annexed budget revenues.
6. Includes extra 2 per cent cut from general appropriations.
7. Excludes privatisation proceeds.
Source: Undersecretariat of Treasury, SPO and IMF.

domestic borrowing due to very high interest rates, led a considerable jump in the consolidated central government budget deficit from 7 per cent of GNP to 11.6 per cent (Figure 9). For the overall public sector, based on the IMF definition, the fiscal balance exhibited a sharp deterioration, the negative impact from the central government budget being compounded by a deterioration in the rest of the public sector. The main contributing factor here was the unpaid duty losses of the state banks (see below), which increased by 3.5 per cent of GNP compared with 1998. The small primary public-sector surplus recorded in 1998 actually turned into deficit in 1999 (Table 11).

Concerning revenue developments, the most notable feature was the reversal of the 1998 tax reform in response to the adverse effects of the Russian crisis. The advanced payment period for personal and corporate income tax reverted back to semi-annual from quarterly, and the income declaration for interest earnings from deposits, repos and other mutual funds was postponed until 2002. The increase in tax revenues was also limited by the contraction in economic activity and revenue losses from the earthquake region. Towards the end of the year, a tax package was introduced to help meet the costs of the earthquake and support the disinflation programme. The first instalments of the earthquake taxes augmented tax revenues by only 0.1 per cent of GNP in 1999. Most of the measures had their major impact in 2000 (Table 12 and Box 3).

Domestic borrowing continued to be the main source of budget financing, reaching 12.4 per cent of GNP. The net foreign debt position of Turkey changed in 1999 and following four years of net foreign repayments, a small positive net foreign borrowing was realised, thanks to the help of foreign funds for earthquake assistance towards the end of the year. As in the previous two years, based on the agreement between the Treasury and the central bank, the short-term financing facility of the central bank was not used in budget financing.[23]

The deterioration of the fiscal balances led to a sharp worsening in debt dynamics in 1999. The financing requirement of a high budget deficit and principal debt redemption (Figure 10) led to a marked increase in "cash" borrowings (the direct domestic borrowings from the market for deficit financing through Treasury auctions) the stock of which increased by 8 percentage points compared to 1998, reaching 26 per cent of GNP. In addition to domestic cash borrowings, a significant rise in the stock of unpaid duty losses worsened the central government debt. Duty losses incurred through the subsidised credit lending of Ziraat Bank and Halk Bank to farmers and small-sized enterprises, respectively, rose sharply to a combined 13 per cent of GNP in 1999. Including the rest of the public sectors' domestic debt, total net domestic debt rose from 24 per cent of GNP to 41 per cent. With net foreign debt remaining almost constant, the consolidated net debt of the public sector reached 62 per cent of GNP (Table 13 and Figure 11).

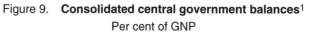

Figure 9. **Consolidated central government balances**[1]
Per cent of GNP

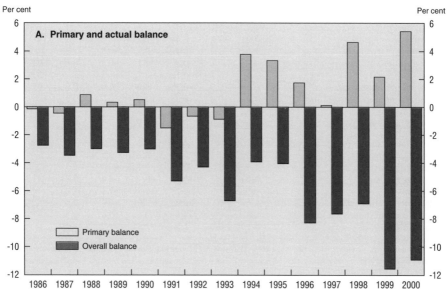

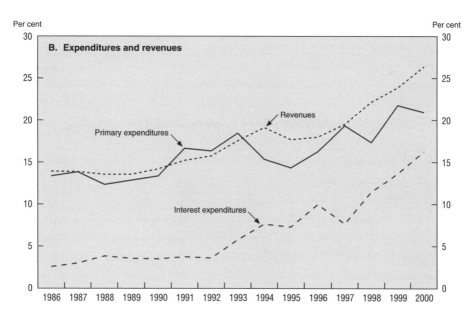

1. 2000 data refers to budget estimates.
Source: Undersecretariat of Treasury.

Table 11.   **Fiscal balances of the consolidated public sector**[1]

Per cent of GNP

	1994	1995	1996	1997	1998	1999	2000[2]	2001[3]
Consolidated public-sector deficit	−9.1	−5.2	−13.1	−13.1	−15.6	−23.3	−12.5	−5.9
Central government[4]	−4.0	−3.8	−8.5	−7.7	−7.8	−12.1	−10.9	−5.8
Extra-budgetary funds	−1.6	−0.9	−0.3	−0.5	−0.8	−1.3	1.3	1.5
Local authorities	0.7	1.1	−0.3	−0.3	−0.5	−0.8	−0.3	−0.2
SEEs	−1.9	0.7	−0.1	−0.7	−1.3	−1.4	−2.6	−1.4
Social security institutions	−0.6	−0.7	−0.2	0.0	0.0	0.0	0.0	0.0
Unemployment insurance fund	0.0	0.0	0.0	0.0	0.0	0.0		
Unpaid duty losses	−1.6	−1.1	−3.1	−3.0	−4.6	−8.2		
less: Central Bank profits	0.0	0.0	0.4	0.3	0.3	0.7		
Primary balance of the public sector	1.0	3.9	−1.3	−2.0	0.5	−1.9	3.6	5.1
Central government	3.5	3.4	1.3	−0.2	3.5	1.7	5.4	5.1
Extra-budgetary funds	−1.5	−0.6	−0.2	0.1	0.0	−0.5		
Local authorities	1.0	1.3	−0.1	−0.1	−0.4	−0.8		
SEEs	−0.3	1.3	−0.1	−0.4	−1.1	−1.2		
Social security institutions	−0.6	−0.7	−0.2	0.0	−0.4	0.0		
Unemployment insurance fund	0.0	0.0	0.0	0.0	0.0	0.0		
Unpaid duty losses	−1.1	−0.8	−1.9	−1.4	−1.2	−1.2		

1. Excluding privatisation revenues. Between 1994-1999 the IMF definition is used by adjusting interest receipts and Central Bank profits.
2. End-year estimation of the SPO.
3. Programme targets of the SPO.
4. Including interest on non-cash debt of the central government between 1994-1999, privatisation revenues are excluded for 2000 and 2001.
Source: IMF and SPO.

Table 12.   **Earthquake-related expenditures and their financing**

Per cent of GNP

	1999	2000[1]
Earthquake expenditures	0.8	1.4
of which met through:		
Central government budget	0.4	0.8
Other[2]	0.4	0.6
Earthquake financing	0.4	1.7
Revenues from central government budget	0.1	1.0
Other revenues[3]	0.2	0.0
Foreign grants and loans	0.1	0.7

1. Official estimation.
2. Funds, grants, international loans, SEEs and other public institutions.
3. Grants and insurance collection of TUPRAS.
Source: Ministry of Finance.

Box 3. The end-1999 revenue-raising measures

The end-1999 revenue increasing measures, which were taken in order to cover the losses of the two earthquakes and to support the disinflation programme, are expected to amount to 5 per cent of GNP in 2000.

Earthquake tax package, introduced on 26 November 1999

- An additional 5 per cent surcharge on 1998 assessments of earnings over TL 12 billion of wage-earners and small businesses, and of corporations.
- An additional motor vehicle and real estate tax based on 1999 assessments.
- A special communications tax of 25 per cent from each mobile operation during the year 2000.
- Special transaction tax on some banking and financial paper transactions, equal to the standard contribution made to support education.

Windfall tax measures, also introduced on 26 November

- Tax surcharge on government bonds and bills – excluding special arrangement government bonds and bonds in foreign currencies – issued before 1 December 1999 effective after 1 January 2000. The surcharges applied to zero-coupon securities as follows: 4 per cent if 1 to 91 days left to maturity; 9 per cent if 92 to 183 days left to maturity, and 14 per cent if more than 183 days left to maturity. The surcharges applied to 3-year floating rate securities at a rate of 4 per cent on coupon payments and 2-year fixed securities at a rate of 19 per cent on coupon payments. Tax is not applied to government securities issued after 1 December 1999.

Additional measures introduced in December 1999

- 2 per cent increase in the VAT rate, to 17 per cent for general goods and 25 per cent for durables and luxury goods, effective from 13 December 1999.
- 2 per cent increase in withholding tax on interest earnings: from 13 to 15 per cent on Turkish lira and foreign currency deposits, 12 to 14 per cent on repurchase agreements, and 13 to 15 per cent on gains from revenue-sharing and non-interest accounts.
- 5 per cent increase in withholding tax on rental income and self-employed earnings: from 15 to 20 per cent.
- A share from the remittances of regulatory boards' surpluses until the end of 2000.
- 25 per cent limit on adjustments in income tax brackets and special deductions.
- 25 per cent increase in fees and charges on official transactions.
- Introduction of fee on dispensation from military service.
- Reintroduction of quarterly advanced payments of the personal and corporate income tax after its suspension for the first half of 2000.

Box 3.   **The end-1999 revenue-raising measures** (*cont.*)

Implementation of the tax on corporate sector profits known as "Article 279"

- The method of "marked-to-market" in computing taxable interest receipts for all fixed income securities including repo portfolios of the corporate sector was put in place in 1998 with Tax Reform, but it was postponed due to the Russian crisis until 31 December 1999. Starting from the fourth quarter of 1999, with the reintroduction of the article, financial institutions are obliged to use this method in their securities portfolios and to pay taxes based on resulting capital gains on a quarterly basis.

The Treasury tried to manage debt in a sustainable fashion, by extending the maturity structure through the issuance of 2-year fixed-interest rate securities. Moreover, floating-interest rate securities were introduced to benefit from the possible declining trend of interest rates. Thus, the share of government bonds in the total debt stock rose significantly compared to 1998 and the average maturity of the borrowing increased from eight to sixteen months in 1999 (Figure 12). Under the pressure of a very high borrowing requirement, auction interest rates remained high, though exhibiting a downward trend throughout the year and as a yearly average 6 percentage points lower in nominal terms compared to 1998 (from 115.5 per cent in 1998 to 109.5 per cent on a weighted-average basis).

The 2000 budget and the aims of the stabilisation programme

The stabilisation programme set quarterly performance criteria for the primary surplus, with an annual target for the consolidated public sector primary surplus set at 3.7 per cent of GNP (Box 4). This is based on a broad definition of the public sector accounts, which should make for a more relevant evaluation of the fiscal stance and accurate determination of the required amount of fiscal adjustment. The broad definition includes all deficit-generating sections of the public sector: the consolidated budget of central government; extra-budgetary funds; state economic enterprises (SEEs); social security institutions and unemployment insurance funds. Also included are local government liabilities, the duty-losses of the state banks and the central bank profit-loss account in the yearly target. The target for the consolidated public sector primary surplus is net of privatisation proceeds and earthquake expenditures amounting to an expected 3½ and 1½ per cent of GNP respectively.

Figure 10. **Debt redemptions and redemption ratios**

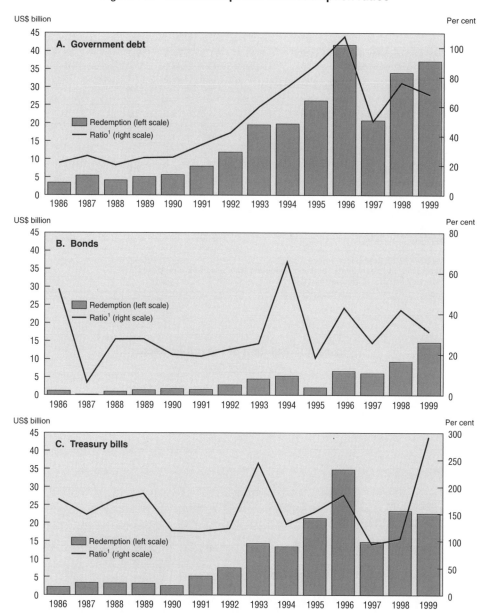

1. Defined as principal repayment as a proportion of the corresponding debt stock. For government debt, the total includes bank advances and consolidated debt.
Source: Undersecretariat of Treasury.

Table 13. **Consolidated net debt of the public sector**

Per cent of GNP

	1993	1994	1995	1996	1997	1998	1999
I. Central government debt and CBRT[1]	**30.7**	**37.8**	**34.5**	**39.5**	**37.5**	**38.9**	**52.3**
Central government debt	38.8	45.3	42.8	48.0	48.4	48.5	64.7
External debt	20.5	22.8	23.6	23.2	21.9	19.0	22.2
Cash debt	6.9	8.7	9.3	12.8	15.8	17.9	25.8
Non-cash debt	5.9	5.3	5.2	5.7	4.4	4.0	3.5
Unsecuritised debt *vis-à-vis* the CBRT	5.1	6.6	2.8	2.5	1.1	0.0	0.0
Unpaid duty losses	0.7	1.9	2.1	4.2	5.2	7.5	13.2
CBRT net assets	1.1	−0.9	1.3	3.0	7.7	8.0	11.1
Central government debt held by the CBRT	7.0	8.5	7.0	5.5	3.2	1.6	1.3
II. Rest of the public sector[2]	**4.4**	**6.9**	**6.7**	**7.0**	**5.4**	**5.5**	**9.7**
Foreign debt	5.7	6.8	6.9	6.5	5.9	6.0	7.2
Net domestic debt	−1.3	0.1	−0.2	0.5	−0.5	−0.5	2.5
Net debt of the public sector (I + II)	**35.1**	**44.7**	**41.3**	**46.5**	**42.9**	**44.5**	**62.0**
Net foreign debt	25.7	30.7	29.1	26.0	22.5	20.3	20.7
Net domestic debt	9.4	14.0	12.2	20.4	20.4	24.1	41.3

1. Central Bank of the Republic of Turkey.
2. Including extra-budgetary funds, local authorities and state economic enterprises.
Source: Undersecretariat of Treasury and IMF.

Figure 11. **Net debt of the public sector**
Per cent of GNP

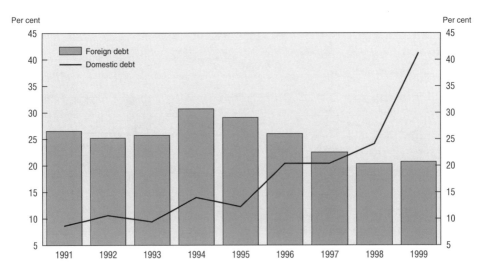

Source: IMF; Undersecretariat of Treasury.

Figure 12. **Average maturity and cost of domestic borrowing**

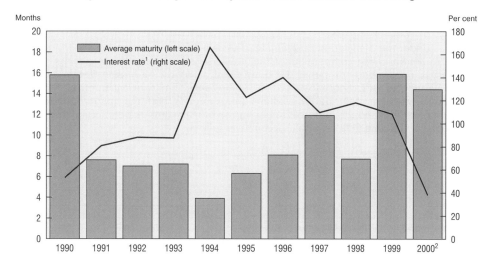

1. Compounded annual rate.
2. As of October.
Source: Central Bank of Turkey.

Based on the SPO's estimates, the consolidated public sector primary surplus will have met the programme target by the end of 2000, thanks to the good performance of central government budget, which had already surpassed its program target by August mainly with the help of the revenue-raising measures, high growth, and strict controls on current and investment expenditures (Table 10). By contrast, the deficit situation of the SEEs has worsened with the rise in oil prices and labour costs, but this has been compensated by the improving central government primary surplus and the improving position of the extra-budgetary funds, the latter thanks to the privatisation proceeds transferred to Public Participation Fund. Another positive contribution to the consolidated public sector primary budget has come from the social security institutions, which moved into collective balance in 2000, benefiting from the positive effects of social security reform on SSK's accounts, in particular the increase in the contribution ceilings.

Revenues in the central government consolidated budget

The revenue-raising measures announced in November and December 1999 contribute significantly to the achievement of the primary surplus

Box 4. The consolidated public sector accounts

Under the disinflation programme, the main objective of fiscal consolidation is to control those components of the public sector which generate deficits. To assess fiscal stance properly, the quasi-fiscal activities, off-budget items, local governments, SEEs, duty losses of the state banks should be included into the broad definition of the public accounts. Consequently, both the quarterly performance criteria and the end-year target for the primary surplus were formulated in terms of the consolidated public accounts as follows:

Quarterly performance criteria for the cumulative primary balance of the consolidated public sector (1 + 2 + 3 + 4 + 5)				End-year target for consolidated public sector primary surplus (1 + 2 + 3 + 4 + 5 + 6)
2000 Trillion TL				2000 Per cent of GDP
Q1	Q2	Q3	Q4	3.7
1 550	2 600	3 900	4 500	

1. Central government budget
2. Extra-budgetary funds (four)
    Public participation fund
    Privatisation fund
    Defence industry fund
    Mass housing fund
3. State economic enterprises (eight)
    The coal company, TTK
    Sugar company TSFAS
    Soil products office, TMO
    Tobacco and alcoholic beverages
        company, TEKEL
    State railways, TCDD
    Electricity company TEAS
    Electricity distribution company, TEDAS
    Natural gas company, BOTAS
4. Unemployment insurance fund
5. Social security institutions (three)
    SSK
    BAG-KUR
    ES

1. Consolidated central government budget*
2. Extra-Budgetary Funds
3. Non-financial SEEs
4. Local government
5. The central bank
6. Duty-losses of state banks

* Includes unemployment insurance fund and social security institutions.

targets (see Box 3). The contribution of the one-off measures in the "earthquake package" is estimated to be 0.74 per cent of GNP by the end of 2000. Other revenue measures, including a 2 percentage point increase in VAT, the windfall tax on gains on government securities, the reintroduction of the quarterly advanced payments and a recalculation of tax liabilities on interest earnings based on a "marked-to-market" valuation method are together expected to generate additional revenue amounting to 4.2 per cent of GNP for 2000. The windfall gains tax applies to government paper issued before 1 December 1999, the rate of taxation varying inversely with the residual maturity of the asset, in order to capture some of the real interest gains accruing from the disinflation programme.[24] (As such it partially offsets the high real interest payments on government debt on the spending side of the budget.) The windfall tax makes a significant contribution to tax revenues in 2000, amounting to 1.3 per cent of GNP (Table 14).

In 2000, the overall performance of tax revenues has been very successful. Tax revenues are estimated to be 21.3 per cent of GNP, 2.4 per cent above the 1999 level and surpassing the programme target. Even excluding revenues from earthquake and other "one-off" tax measures (see Box 3), which amounted to almost 2 per cent of GNP, tax performance has been good, thanks to the increase in indirect taxes receipts on foreign trade and domestic VAT, both of which have been affected positively by the economic recovery (Table 14). Towards the end of October, the government took further tax measures in order to curb domestic demand, such as an increase in the VAT rate from 24 to 40 per cent on larger-engined automobiles and an increase in levies applied on consumer loans. Thus, the ratio of consolidated budget revenues to GNP is estimated to have reached 26.4 per cent, the highest level in several decades even excluding privatisation revenues, which amounted to 1.6 per cent of GNP, and were transferred to budget as a non-tax revenue.

Expenditures in the central government consolidated budget

The stabilisation programme emphasises the need to control primary expenditures in the central government consolidated budget, given structural deficiencies implying that the deficits of the SEEs and local authorities are expected to continue in the short-term (Table 11). Consistent with the incomes policies of the disinflation programme, civil servants' wage hikes are limited to cost-of-living adjustments,[25] contributing 0.7 per cent of GNP savings to budgetary expenditures comparing to 1999. Transfer expenditures, excluding interest payments, are estimated to have declined by 0.4 per cent of GNP in 2000, mainly due to the early positive results of the social security reform on the rehabilitation of SSK financial accounts. Overall, however, despite a 0.8 per cent of GNP decline in primary spending compared with 1999, the public spending/GDP ratio still remains historically high (Table 10).

Table 14.   **Central government budget revenues**

Per cent of GNP

	1999	2000		2001
		Target	End-year estimation[1]	Target[2]
Total revenue[3]	23.8	25.2	26.4	25.7
Tax revenue	18.9	20.3	21.3	20.7
Direct	8.6	9.0	8.9	7.9
Personal income	6.3	5.1	5.2	5.5
Corporate income	1.9	2.5	1.9	1.9
Motor vehicle and wealth	0.2	0.2	0.3	0.2
Other[4]	0.2	1.2	1.5	0.3
Indirect	10.4	11.3	12.4	12.8
VAT	5.5	5.5	6.9	7.1
Domestic taxation	3.3	3.3	3.8	4.2
Foreign taxation	2.2	2.3	3.1	2.9
Petroleum excise	2.9	3.2	2.7	2.7
Foreign trade (excluding VAT)	0.3	0.3	0.3	0.3
Other	1.7	2.3	2.5	2.7
Other revenues[3]	4.9	4.8	5.1	5.0
Budgetary and non-budgetary funds	1.9	1.8	1.8	2.0
Education levies	0.5	0.5	0.4	. .
Revenue from state property	1.2	1.2	1.0	1.7
Other	1.2	1.2	1.9	1.3
Memorandum items:				
Revenue from earthquake measures:			3.0	
Supplementary taxes			0.7	
Interest tax			1.3	
Military service fee			0.2	
Extra education levies			0.4	
Revenue from regulatory bodies			0.2	
Privatisation proceeds		2.1	1.6	2.4

1. Official estimation.
2. Budget draft.
3. Excludes privatisation.
4. Includes revenues from interest tax for 2000.
Source: IMF and Turkish authorities.

The ratio of central government primary expenditures to GNP is actually relatively small compared to the average of OECD countries. The main problem arises from the burden of interest expenditures: these are by far the largest item in the budget, at 44 per cent of total central government spending in the 2000 budget. The ratio of interest expenditures to GNP is 17 per cent, rising from 14 per cent in 1999 (Figure 9, Panel B). In this context, reduced interest payments are essential for primary expenditures to be able to grow, but in the short term cuts in primary expenditures are needed to initiate lower interest rates, to reduce the debt burden on the budget in coming years. Thanks to the positive impacts of the disinflation and the monetary programme, lower interest rates will create considerable savings – almost 6 per cent of GNP for 2001 – although they have a negligible effect on interest expenditures in 2000. The savings on domestic interest expenditures should – after the achievement of the necessary expenditure reform – help in the necessary reallocation of the expenditures towards education and health, which have a relatively low share in budgetary appropriations.

Risk factors

While the consolidated central government budget has performed better than initial expectations, the poor performance of some SEEs has created risks for the overall balance of the public sector in 2000. At issue here, and inherent in the disinflation programme, is a potential conflict between the inflation and fiscal targets, due to the rise in oil prices. The adverse impact of the recent increase in world oil prices on the fiscal accounts comes through deterioration in the financial performance of the SEEs, especially of those operating in the energy sector. According to the disinflation programme, energy price increases are to be aligned to targeted inflation, which is not sufficient to cover operating and transmission costs, due to the large rise in world crude oil prices as well as the inefficiencies in the energy system. A further deterioration in the SEEs fiscal balances is thus unavoidable if precedence is given to the inflation target rather than fiscal balance targets. The collective deficit of the non-financia l SEEs is expected to exceed its deficit limit of 1.2 per cent of GNP, by 0.8 per cent of GNP, this amount constituting an extra burden on the primary surplus of the consolidated public sector (Table 11).[26] The imbalance could be corrected by generating a higher primary surplus from the central government budget. Recently, increases in energy prices were introduced for residential users and some adjustments were agreed between the Treasury and state entities in the energy sector in order to solve their financial problems. However, the long-term solution to the need for rehabilitation of the SEEs operating in the energy, agriculture and transport sectors lies in their structural reform and privatisation (see Chapter III).

Other adverse effects of the rise in oil prices on the central government budget have been seen on current expenditures and the sacrifice of tax revenues to contain inflation. In order to mitigate the effects of world oil prices on domestic prices, the government made adjustments to the oil consumption tax. Starting from February 2000, the automatic oil pricing mechanism was changed from proportional taxation to fixed amount taxation in order to smooth out the effects of rising world oil prices on domestic inflation. Recent adjustments have demonstrated the authorities' concern about both inflation and the fiscal targets, as they have compensated for tax losses by increasing the VAT on liquid petroleum gas as an alternative source of power used in cars, and by raising the oil consumption tax when the dollar price per barrel declined. However, the inflation and fiscal balance targets remain in potential conflict. Indeed, so far, the developments in petroleum consumption tax revenues imply that the targeted level will be difficult to achieve in 2000.

Debt developments and budget financing

The high primary surplus, successful implementation of the privatisation programme, external borrowing facilities and lower interest rates are expected, collectively, to help to roughly stabilise the net public sector debt-to-GNP ratio in 2000, at around the 1999 level of 62 per cent of GNP. A gradual decline is also expected over the following two years of the programme.

Stabilising the debt ratio: more favourable debt dynamics

So far, macroeconomic developments have been consistent with the objective of stabilising the debt ratio at the 1999 level. As noted in Chapter I, real GDP growth seems likely to be near to 7 per cent. Moreover, the use of an exchange rate basket as a nominal anchor has contributed to the virtual elimination of foreign-exchange risk and promoted a sharp reduction in interest rates (Chapter I). As of October, interest rates on government securities averaged 38 per cent, having declined from 109 per cent on average in 1999 (Figure 12). The combination of faster growth, falling real interest rates and the higher primary surplus has brought a marked improvement in debt dynamics. A renewed ability to raise funds from abroad (see below) has also helped in this respect.

Privatisation revenues are an important tool in the debt-reduction programme, the target being $7.6 billion in 2000 (see Chapter III). According to the 2000 Budget law, the proceeds of privatisation, such as from the sale of 20 per cent of the equity in Turk Telekom, licence sales and the sales of operating rights in energy generation and distribution facilities, can be recorded as non-tax budgetary revenue in the central government budget. The proceeds from the privatisation of assets from the portfolio of the Privatisation Administration (PA) are not recorded as revenue to the budget. However, after deducting the necessary operational costs and other expenses, the PA transfers the proceeds to the Treasury via the Public Participation Fund (PPF) as part of its liabilities, which accumulated from previous Treasury-guaranteed foreign debts (see Table 24 below). The Treasury could use these revenues directly in debt reduction. As of November, the PA had raised $2.7 billion from the sale of enterprises in its portfolio (including Tüpras, Poas and some smaller enterprises), of which $2.5 billion was transferred to the budget. Another $300 million in privatisation receipts (going directly to the budget) came from the transfer of operating rights of power plants, and $500 million from the first instalment of the sale of the GSM licence. Thus, an estimated $3.5 billion in privatisation receipts has been collected in all. With $2 billion from the sale of the GSM licence deferred to early 2001, the total amount receivable for privatisation deals in 2000 amounts to $5.6 billion, as much as collected since the privatisation programme began in 1986.

Despite this setback, since the beginning of the year, the stability programme has been considered as credible by both domestic and international markets. Following the upgrading of Turkish debt rating by the credit agencies, Turkey has had easier access to international markets and the external borrowing target of $6 billion was already surpassed in the first half of the year and reached $7.5 billion by early November (Table 15). With the support of privatisation revenues, foreign borrowing enabled the Treasury to borrow less than its redemptions from the domestic market. In the first ten months of 2000, the Treasury refinanced almost 73.6 per cent of its redemption from the domestic markets, which contrasts with over 100 per cent in 1999, and as a consequence the rate of increase in the domestic debt stock of the central government slowed sharply from May onwards. OECD calculations show that the domestic cash debt to GNP ratio is likely to have declined by 2 per cent comparing to 1999. The non-cash debt-to-GNP ratio is also estimated to have declined by 1 per cent in 2000, excluding the government

Table 15.   **External borrowing in 2000**

		Bond issues in 2000		
Issue date	Amount (million)	Maturity (years)	Yield to investor	Coupon rate (per cent)
10 January	US$ 1 500	30	UST + 525 bp	11.875
26 January	Euro 750	10	BUND + 385 bp	9.25
8 January[1]	Euro 250	10	BUND + 383 bp	9.25
18 February	Yen 35 000	3	Yen Libor + 271 bp	3.50
30 March	Euro 600	5	BUND + 301 bp	7.75
2 June	Euro 500	3	Euribor + 225 bp	Euribor + 2 per cent
8 June	US$ 750	10	UST + 575 bp	11.75
15 June	Yen 55 000	4	Yen Libor + 225 bp	3.25
13 July[2]	Euro 533	7	BUND + 325 bp	8.125
19 July[3]	US$ 500	9	UST + 501 bp	12.375
1 September[4]	Euro 200	7	BUND + 300 bp	8.125
5 September[5]	US$ 750	10	UST + 529 bp	11.75
3 November	Yen 50 000	3	Yen Libor + 219 bp	3.00
Total	US$ 7 478			

1. Increase to 26 January 2000 dated US$750 million euro bond issue.
2. This issue will be added to the issue of DM 1.5 billion in 1997 maturing on 22 October 2007 as of 22 October 2000 and will be viewed as one issue at a total of euro 1.3 billion.
3. Second issuance of the 18 June dated Global US$ bond issue.
4. Re-opening of euro 533 million bond issues on 13 July 2000.
5. Re-opening of US$750 million global bond issued on 8 June 2000.
Source: Undersecretariat of Treasury.

paper which will be transferred to Banking Regulation and Supervision Agency (BRSA) to replace the bad loans of the transferred banks. Including the latter bond issues, which are expected to amount to some 3 per cent of GNP, the overall net debt to GNP ratio should approximately stabilise.

Debt management: towards a more diversified structure

Debt management is also intended to play an active role in the stabilisation process. In financing the 2000 budget, the Treasury is attempting to diversify between domestic and foreign borrowing. Starting from 1994, up to the final quarter of 1999, net domestic borrowing had been used for both budget financing and for making net repayments of the foreign debt. In the 2000 budget, the ratio of net foreign borrowing to GNP is expected to be 1.4 per cent, which facilitates a decline in the amount of domestic borrowing for budget financing of 4.5 percentage points compared to last year. Government bonds have been heavily used in the financing of the cash deficit, which is expected to reach 9 per cent of GNP by the end of year (Table 16).

Table 16.   **Consolidated central government budget financing**

Per cent of GNP

	1999	2000 End-year estimate
Foreign borrowing, net	0.6	1.4
Receipts[1]	3.6	4.3
Payments	−3.0	−2.9
Domestic borrowing, net	12.4	7.9
Government bonds, net	15.6	8.7
Receipts	21.6	16.0
Payments	−6.0	−7.3
Treasury Bills, net	−3.2	−1.3
Receipts	8.7	4.2
Payments	−11.9	−5.6
Receipts from on-lending[2]		0.5
Central Bank advances	0.0	0.0
Other	−1.3	0.1
Total financing[3]	11.6	9.3

1. As of October 2000, privatisation proceeds of the Privatisation Administration amounted to $2 454 million, $1 872 million of which has been transferred to the Public Participation fund (PPF) due to law out of this sum, PPF transferred $140 million to the Treasury for the reduction of the guaranteed external debt of PPF which had been serviced by the Treasury. This amount is included in the total figure of receipts from on-lending of foreign debt.
2. PPF transferred $1 385 million to the Treasury for the reduction of the guaranteed domestic debt of PPF which had been serviced by the Treasury.
3. Equals consolidated central government cash balance shown in Table 10, inclusive of privatisation receipts.
Source: Undersecretariat of Treasury and SPO.

The composition of the domestic debt stock has continued to move in favour of government bonds, the share of which increased from 74 per cent at the end of 1999 to 84 per cent in October 2000. Nevertheless, the average maturity of the domestic debt stock declined from 15.9 months to 14.4 months over the same period (Figures 12 and 13), even though the maturity of new issues lengthened. Debt management policy in 2000 has relied on a more diversified policy to extend the maturity of the debt, mainly by issuing long-term floating rate government bonds rather than using a fixed coupon, which carries a potentially excessive burden in a disinflationary environment.

Fiscal restraint and the 2001 Budget

How restrictive is the fiscal stance?

Assessing the extent of the restraint is made difficult by the widely diverging trends in the primary budget balance and debt interest payments. From 1994, a surplus has been generated in the central government primary budget, but the conventional deficit has continued to widen as the interest rate component has risen. However, in a high inflation environment, the measure of the conventional budget deficit may be a misleading measure of fiscal effort, because a large, and varying, part of the high interest payments appears as a compensation of inflationary erosion of the real debt stock. The concept of the "operational budget",[27] attempts to correct for this factor by incorporating only the effects of real interest payments; it thus serves as a more accurate indicator of the fiscal stance under a high inflation environment than either the primary or overall budget balance (Figure 14).

The correction is particularly important at a time of structural transition in inflation. An expected consequence of the disinflation is that government real interest payments will rise in the first year of the programme, even though a "windfall tax" has been introduced on government securities to compensate some of the real interest gains accruing from the disinflation programme. Taking the maturity of Treasury borrowing as, on average, one year or a little longer, real interest payments will have a significant stimulating effect on domestic demand via a "wealth effect". This means that with the help of the high primary surplus, the operational balance improves to a great extent for the consolidated public sector but still continues to be in significant deficit this year due to the impact of declining inflation on interest payments (Figure 14). In 2000, therefore, fiscal policy may be reinforcing the impact of lower credit costs on domestic demand – or, conversely, helping to offset the squeeze on demand from the recent tax packages and income policies (see Chapter I).

The 2001 Budget

The 2001 budget was submitted to Parliament on 17th October 2000. The budget assumes that growth in real GNP slows to 4.5 per cent from 6 per cent, with

Figure 13.   **Debt indicators**

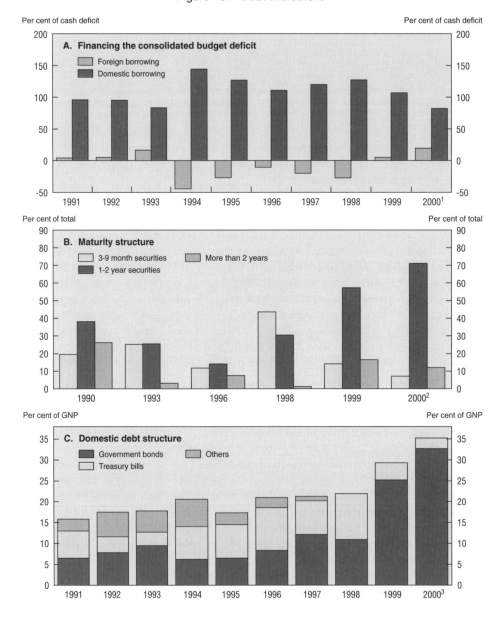

1.   Budget estimates.
2.   As of October.
3.   January-September data.
Source: Central Bank of Turkey, Undersecretariat of Treasury.

Figure 14.   **Operational budget balance**[1]
As a percentage of GNP

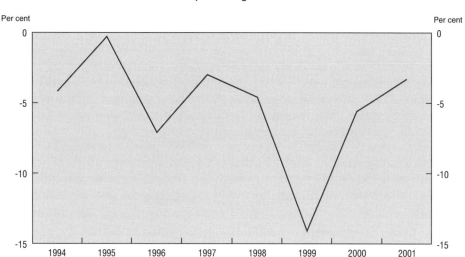

1.   Consolidated public sector.
Source: IMF.

an 18 per cent increase in the GNP deflator. The projected budget deficit exhibited a marked improvement, due to the savings on interest payments. The primary surplus of the central government was planned to be 5.1 per cent, excluding privatisation revenues, representing a slight reduction in the primary surplus compared to 2000. Excluding privatisation revenues, the budget expected the ratio of central government programmed budget revenues to GNP to remain below its 2000 level, after taking account of the impact of slowing the growth of the economy and the termination of one-off taxes and other revenue measures.

However, after the submission of the budget draft, the government decided with the IMF on a further fiscal tightening of 2 per cent in order to curb domestic demand. To this end, in early November, the government sent a "supplementary tax draft" to the parliament. The draft includes: *i*) the extension of special communication taxes, transaction taxes, basic education levies and a continuing share from the regulatory boards' surpluses until the end of 2002, while giving authority to the cabinet to increase special transaction taxes and basic education levies by up to ten times; *ii*) the granting of authority to the cabinet to increase the annual motor vehicle tax rate and the motor vehicle purchase tax rate by up to 50 per cent (over the normal inflation adjustment) on an across-the-board basis and on top of this to increase the amount by up to 20 times for certain types of vehicles (such as those using LPG), and finally to increase the supplementary motor vehicle purchase tax rate on luxury cars, which is 24 per cent at present, up to 36 per cent; *iii*) and the re-imposition of the "standard of living" tax for self-employed business.[28] Besides these measures, the cabinet decided to increase VAT rates on (non-mobile) telephone services from 17 to 25 per cent and on natural gas from 8 to 17 per cent, and prepared a draft law on tax exemptions for bank mergers.[29] With these tax arrangements, which come into effect on 1st January, the government expects to get almost 2 per cent of GNP additional revenues in 2001. The government is thus relying on tax measures rather than radical cuts in primary expenditures for further fiscal contraction. The privatisation process is expected to speed up in 2001 with receipts targeted at some $6-7 billion (3-3½ per cent of GNP), taking into account privatisation receipts expected in 2001 from deals concluded in 2000. All these receipts, whatever their source, will be transferred to the Treasury for debt reduction, apart from $1.1 billion that will be used by the PA for operational costs and transfers to the SEEs.

Central government expenditures are expected to decline by more than 5 per cent of GNP, but largely due to savings in domestic interest payments. Primary expenditures are projected to remain almost constant (a slight decline of 0.3 per cent of GNP compared to 2000). To this end, incomes policy will continue to be based on a CPI inflation target of 12 per cent. Civil servants' wage hikes will be 10 per cent for the first half of 2001, subject to the same conditions as were imposed in 2000 regarding *ex post* compensation for excess inflation and welfare bonus. While transfers to the social security institutions will remain virtually unchanged, agricultural transfers are planned to increased by 0.4 per cent of GNP, due to the costs of switching to income support for the agricultural sector.

Correcting deficiencies in fiscal management

Improving transparency

Effective fiscal management requires strong control over the budget aggregates. However, as noted, many quasi-fiscal activities in Turkey are performed outside the central consolidated budget via extra-budgetary funds, state banks, and state economic enterprises. The introduction of the broad definition of the consolidated public accounts is thus one of the most important features of the structural issues in fiscal policy (see Box 4).

Off-budget and quasi-fiscal activities

The extra-budgetary funds, which includes both budgetary and non-budgetary funds, operate outside the central government budget and are not subject to parliamentary review, leading to a loosening in budget discipline.

Hence, in order to enhance the control of developments outside the budget, four extra-budgetary funds are included in the consolidated public budget definition and quarterly performance criteria, namely the pubic participation fund, the privatisation fund, the defence industry fund and the mass-housing fund (which has the ability to borrow abroad). As part of the process of improving fiscal management and transparency of the budget accounts, the creation of extra-budgetary funds is no longer allowed and some of the non-budgetary funds are planned to be closed by June 2001. By May 2000, 25 budgetary and two non-budgetary funds had already been liquidated. However, three non-budgetary funds and 20 budgetary funds, which were planned to be closed by the end of July and August respectively, had not been closed as of November. It has been announced by the government that all the extra-budgetary funds will be liquidated in the first half of 2001 (Box 5).

Duty losses of the state banks

Under the disinflation programme, control of the quasi-fiscal activities of the state banks also plays a crucial role in enhancing budget transparency and accountability. The "duty losses" of the state banks, incurred as a result of quasi-fiscal operations performed on behalf of the government (subsidised lending, etc.) reached 8.2 per cent of GNP in 1999 and was one of the main contributing factors to the deterioration in the consolidated public deficit (Table 11). The cost of credit subsidies became enormous for state banks, due to the large differences between the subsidised rates and market rates. To relieve the burden of the duty losses, under the new procedure, the subsidised rate is based on the 12-month (average or closest maturity) bond auction rates in the preceding three months, multiplied by 1.05. Starting from the beginning of 2000, thanks to the decline in the interest rates, this method of calculation has implied that there are no duty losses resulting from subsidised credits. For 2000 as a whole the cost of credit subsidies is expected to decline to just 0.1 per cent of GNP.

Besides the attempts to rehabilitate the subsidy scheme, settling the government's outstanding obligations with respect to duty losses has also been of concern to the authorities. With the objective of controlling the outstanding stock of unpaid duty losses and its pressures on the financial markets, for the first time, appropriations were included in the 2000 budget for direct cash payments to state banks in order to compensate for the duty losses incurred in 2000. Until the end of March, a small portion of this appropriation was used, since then duty losses stemming from credit subsidy disappeared and the rest of the appropriations were not allocated. Moreover, the Treasury issued special non-cash bonds in both 1999 and 2000, equivalent to 15 per cent of the stock amount at the end of the previous year, to state banks in order to liquidate the stock of their unpaid duty losses. Thus, the stock of duty losses is expected to decline by 1.8 per cent of GNP in 2000, to 11.4 per cent.

Box 5.   Extra-budgetary funds

Extra-budgetary funds operate outside the basic budget legislation under their own expenditure and revenue regulations and operating procedures. Funds are non-profit institutions, so serving as a protection for and inducement to economic activities. The main rationale for the massive number of funds operating outside the budget has, indeed, been that they facilitate rapid disposition of funds without being subject to basic state fiscal legislation: *i.e.* that they provide flexibility to the political authority in achieving certain objectives in variety of areas, such as implementation of mass housing, support of foreign trade and agriculture, defence contracts, education and health etc.

In 1999, there were 74 *extra-budgetary* funds of which 61 were *budgetary* and 13 were *non-budgetary* funds. The type of regulation applied to revenues and expenditures determines the type of funds. While the budgetary funds transfer all their receivables to the central government budget and make expenditures through budgetary appropriations, non-budgetary funds are not obliged to transfer the revenues if it is not specified by any law. Also, the expenditure of the non-budgetary funds is not met through central government budget.

Besides the violation of budgetary principles in terms of proceedings and allowances, extra-budgetary funds destroy fiscal discipline by borrowing from abroad with a state guarantee. Moreover, in auditing of funds, legal holes appear in the system.* Extra-budgetary funds are not subject to budgetary review, but based on their establishment regulations, funds are audited by different institutions such as Sayistay (Court of Auditing), High Auditing Board, Banking Auditors, Special Committees, Ministry of Finance, Treasury, Prime Ministry, etc. Due to the size of funds, auditing takes time and becomes inefficient, leading to a waste of resources.

In the stabilisation programme, the liquidation of the extra-budgetary funds was foreseen. 25 budgetary and 2 non-budgetary funds were already closed by May 2000. 20 more budgetary funds were originally planned to be liquidated by the end of August 2000 and the rest by June 2001. Three more non-budgetary funds were planned to be closed in July, and two more by February 2001. The remaining six non-budgetary funds were to be subject to further review. The government has more recently announced that all the budgetary and non-budgetary funds would be definitely closed by the first half of 2001. However, as of November 2000, the foreseen liquidation of 20 budgetary and three non-budgetary funds since May were not realised. Until the elimination of the privatisation, defence industry and mass-housing funds, these are integrated in to the broad definition of public accounts in order to assess the overall balance of the public sector correctly.

---

*   Saygili (2000).

Treasury-guaranteed debts, which arise mainly through the borrowings of local governments and SEEs from international markets, also have adverse effects on fiscal management. Again with the objective of increasing the transparency of the fiscal accounts, the government has made public the stock of its contingent liabilities, which reached $5.8 billion at the end of 1999, and plans to put limits on the issuance of new guarantees.[30]

In creating a fiscal structure which will assert fiscal discipline, it is crucial to bring the problem-generating parts of the fiscal system into the open. Thus, consistent with the fiscal restructuring and transparency requirements of the fiscal adjustment programme, the government has declared that a "Public Finance and Debt Management Law" will be submitted to the Parliament soon. Under this law, a framework will be created for dealing with all the above issues in fiscal policy, covering a redefinition of the borrowing rules and strategies of the public sector; cash management regulation; a widening of budget coverage by including quasi-fiscal operations; the abolition of off-budgetary activities; establishment of new accounting standards; achieving summary and clarification of the budget and limiting Treasury-guaranteed debts.

Improving tax policy and administration

The effective implementation of the tax reform, which aims to simplify the tax system and expand the tax base, so helping to prevent tax evasion and reduce the size of the informal economy, requires consistent and stable tax laws, together with an efficient tax administration. However, following the Russian crisis and the earthquakes, the reform process experienced some reversals in 1999, as steps were taken to support economic activity by either abolishing or postponing certain innovations in the 1998 reform (see above). Under the stand-by programme with the IMF, the government took revenue measures to meet fiscal targets and gave an emphasis to structural issues in improving tax policy and administration. Progress has been made in many areas, but there are still some issues needing to be resolved.

The Ministry of Finance has been conducting several projects to expand the tax base and increase the efficiency of tax collection. Basically, these comprise an increase in use of tax identification numbers; the full automation of tax offices; the introduction of management-information and decision-support systems; the establishment of a "third party information centre" and six "regional auditing centres", and the setting up of a system for monitoring tax arrears. The 1998 tax reform introduced the requirement for a tax identification number in auto and real estate transactions, with the aim of expanding the tax base by bringing informal economy into the formal one. It has been widely used and the number of tax identification numbers issued reached more than 14 million as of June 2000, compared with 5 million in 1998. However, using tax identification numbers in banking and other financial activities is necessary to capture the bulk of the informal sector.

The new strength of the tax administration lies in the completion of the first stage of the automation project in March 2000. This minimises the lags in tax collection by monitoring almost 95 per cent of the daily tax revenues to the head office. Even small-sized tax offices in the smaller regions have the ability to use internet facilities in processing tax identification numbers and transferring daily tax collections to the head office. Moreover, high monthly charges are applied to discourage delays in tax payments. While the automation system helps to increase efficiency in the operation of tax offices and to allow time for more inspections, the management-information system and decision-support system increase the efficiency and speed of the decision making at the top-management level. The "third party information and auditing centres", which is an important stage in improving the efficiency in tax inspection, has started to be used widely to check the consistency with income tax returns and the information gathered from the tax identification number and the use of credit cards. Thus, with this system tax evasion can be more easily detected.

An important source of revenue weakness is the tax arrears mainly related to the unfulfilled tax liabilities of public entities such as SEEs and local administrations due to their financial problems and the effects of past tax amnesties, which have encouraged arrears by raising expectations about the future amnesties. The size of tax arrears has reached 4¾ per cent of GNP, around half of which is due to public entities. The Ministry of Finance has set up a quarterly monitoring system to follow and reduce the tax arrears. To encourage compliance, the government has announced that it will not allow any further tax amnesty in Turkey.

Assessment of the fiscal consolidation process

The necessary measures have been taken to restore short-term fiscal sustainability, correcting the explosive debt dynamics which hit the budget in 1999. Discretionary steps have been taken to increase taxes and to reduce primary expenditures, which, with privatisation revenues, should generate a primary surplus sufficient to stabilise the debt/GDP ratio. However, the largest contribution to stability is coming from the boost to confidence and ensuing decline in real interest rates which has come as a result of the comprehensiveness of the overall programme of fiscal adjustment. The record of past failed stabilisation attempts is that if they are not accompanied by structural reforms, they are ineffectual. The stand-by programme thus correctly emphasises the need for measures to tackle deficiencies in the budget system along a wide front.

Perhaps most crucial to the programme's success is the improvement in transparency and accountability which should result from the budgetary integration of the hitherto off-budget sources of public spending and inflation: the integration of the extra-budgetary funds into the budget; the elimination (at least on a flow basis) of the "duty" losses of the state banks; and closer monitoring of the financial impact of SEE deficits. The correction of the fiscal balance of the overall public sector, rather than the central government narrowly defined is probably the most radical and essential part of the programme and the factor that distinguishes the current adjustment programme from previous efforts, underpinning its credibility. This means that the debt dynamics are a function of confidence in the whole adjustment programme, which is both a strength of the current programme and a source of vulnerability.

Elimination of deficit finance being, to some extent, a function of a widening of the tax base, tax reform, structural and administrative, is an essential element of the disinflation strategy. There has been significant improvement here, especially with respect to tax administration, which has been reflected in the improvement of the tax revenues. Nevertheless, tax arrears remain a significant problem and the tax and social security systems still have to achieve a design that will allow the informal economy to be absorbed into the formal one. Further implementation of fiscal transparency and improvement in the tax administration are vital for achieving a sustainable fiscal progress.

On the spending side, a radical overhaul is still required, and will become more feasible as the macroeconomic situation stabilises and sustainable growth is restored. Better control over pension spending and agricultural subsidies (see next chapter) should help in releasing inefficiently used resources for education and health programmes, both of which have suffered under the system of inflationary finance. Meanwhile, the legislative steps being taken to bring the main features of fiscal policy within the framework of "fiscal law" should permit the better functioning of fiscal institutions, acting as a safeguard against populist policies.

Perhaps one of the greatest threats to the programme comes from the continued inefficiency of the state-owned enterprises. The emphasis on transparency and accountability should, in principle, result in greater operational and financial efficiency of the SEEs, as well as more efficient costing and control of the subsidised lending of the state-owned financial institutions. But some SEEs will run higher deficits in 2000 than allowed for. Because of buoyant general revenues, the fiscal target seems attainable despite such an overshoot. Oil price increases may prove temporary. But widening financial losses among the Turkish state economic enterprises can to a great extent be explained by a lack of operational and organisational efficiency rather than short-term factors. Without restructuring and privatisation (or corporatisation), public sector enterprises remain the most important potential source of budgetary weakness. The success of the disinflation programme depends on structural reform measures which inject more market-based incentives into hitherto state-sponsored economic activities. Structural reform developments are the topic of Chapter III.

III. The structural reform programme

At the heart of past fiscal excess, and hence the source of inflation and weak growth, has been the pervasive involvement of the government in the economy. Structural reforms to unwind this presence will entail a public divestiture of productive assets and a withdrawal of subsidies and administrative guidance in favour of market signals to allocate resources. The main sectors undergoing restructuring are agriculture, energy and communications, banking, and the social security system. The government's role is moving toward one of guarantor of the framework conditions for a strong market economy, which will reduce the need to provide public support to inefficient activities, while also boosting productivity, growth and living standards by allowing higher savings and its more efficient allocation to investment. The government's efforts in the structural reform area are being assisted and guided by the World Bank in the context of an Economic Reform Loan and forthcoming Financial Sector Adjustment Loan – the structural adjuncts to the stand-by programme. Another powerful incentive to structural reform has emanated from the recent decision by the EU to admit Turkey to candidacy status, which will require that Turkey move its economic and political structures toward the EU model (Annex II). This chapter discusses the main issues and reform agendas in each of the areas undergoing restructuring, after giving an overview of the supply side of the Turkish economy. A final section on human capital reviews the progress and main outstanding needs in this area.

Growth, the labour market, and income distribution

Over the past decade, per capita growth in Turkey has been below the OECD average, and markedly slower than its most successful development phases in the past. Table 17 shows that Turkey's growth over 1989-99 has fallen short of that of Spain and Korea during their "take-off" periods. GDP growth in Turkey has barely kept up with population growth, so that living standards have stagnated. Per capita income growth has also been considerably lower than in the fastest growing upper middle income countries with which Turkey is classified by the World Bank (Figure 15, Panel A). As noted in Chapter I, high inflation has tended to stunt the development of credit markets (Figure 15, Panel B), preventing the mobilisation of resources for the efficient financing of investments. The consequence has been

Table 17.   **Comparison of growth performance**
Annual average growth rate

	Turkey		Spain	Korea
	1989-99	1988-98[1]	1964-74	1979-89
Real GDP	4.4	5.2	6.4	9.7
Agriculture	1.6	1.3	2.5	3.3
Industry	4.4	6.2	9.1	13.1
Services	5.4	5.8	5.4	9.1
Per capita real GDP	1.9	2.4	5.2	6.5
Real value added per worker				
Agriculture	1.2	0.4	8.4	19.0
Industry	1.9	2.9	8.7	16.3
Services	2.0	1.7	2.7	12.5
Real wages in manufacturing	−0.8	1.1	8.8	5.9
Memorandum item:				
Starting per capita GDP[2]	2 512	2 561	5 662	2 797

1. Excludes the severe recession in 1999, partially due to impacts of earthquakes in that year.
2. At the price levels and exchange rates of 1990 in US dollars.
Source: World Bank (2000) and OECD.

stagnant private investment, outside housing, which has remained at around 10 to 12 per cent of GDP. Public investment has declined due to repeated stabilisation episodes, while infrastructure investments by the state economic enterprises have stagnated as a result of pricing policies often dictated by social concerns.

Low business and infrastructure investment has been reflected in slow growth of both productivity and employment. As seen in Table 17, productivity growth in Turkey was far slower than in Spain or Korea during the comparison periods. The differences in industry have been largest, but they have also been significant for agriculture. A (notional) decomposition of productivity growth into its capital intensity and total factor productivity components by the OECD suggests that growth of capital intensity was relatively low, hence a major constraining factor (Table 18). TFP growth – the main presumed source of catch-up – appears to have been sharply trending downwards, suggesting inadequate human capital investment at home and insufficient technology transfer from abroad.

A second main factor dampening growth was a falling employment rate, reflecting in turn declining labour market participation and, to a lesser extent, rising unemployment. This fall outweighed the benefits of a rising share of the working-aged in the overall population. The main explanation for low and declining participation was the high rate of exit of women from the labour market due to rural-to-urban migration (Table 19). The urban unemployment rate among men is

Figure 15.   **Inflation, growth and credit-market development**
Average 1990[1]-99

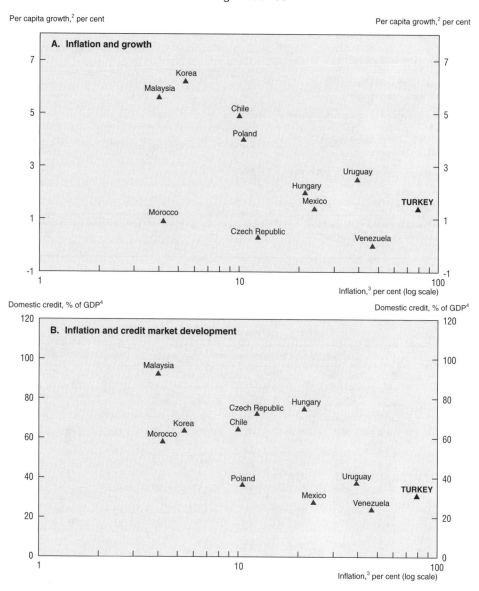

1.   Or first year available in 90s.
2.   Growth of GDP at constant prices per capita.
3.   Growth of the consumer price index.
4.   Consolidated monetary authorities' and deposit money banks' data.
Source: SPO; Central Bank of Turkey; IMF, *International Financial Statistics*; OECD, *Main Economic Indicators.*

Table 18.   **Decomposition of real income growth**
Annual average growth rate

	1980-1989	1990-1999
Growth of real GDP per capita	2.3	1.3
of which:	2.8	1.9
Productivity (GDP per worker)	2.8	1.9
of which:		
Capital intensity effect[1]	0.5	1.2
Total factor productivity	2.3	0.7
Employment rate (employment/working population)	−1.0	−1.0
of which:		
Unemployment rate (inverse)	−0.1	−0.2
Participation rate	−0.9	−0.8
Demographics (working age population/total population)	0.5	0.4
Memorandum item:		
Growth of real GDP	4.8	3.1

1.   Capital stock assumed to depreciate by 5 per cent per annum for the machinery and equipment component and by 3 per cent for the building component.
Source: OECD estimates.

Table 19.   **Indicators of labour supply**

	Labour force participation rates[1]						Female economic activity rate		
	Per cent			Index 1980 = 100			Rate 1997	Index 1985 = 100	As a per cent of male rate
	Male	Female	Total	Male	Female	Total			
Turkey	74.4	27.8	50.8	88	61	78	34.9	114.9	59.6
Greece	62.9	36.2	48.9	84	134	98	31.3	146.2	57.3
Hungary	60.4	42.8	51.2	83	85	84	40.5	101.0	73.6
Italy	61.2	34.8	47.5	89	108	95	32.9	128.2	58.1
Korea	75.6	49.5	62.2	99	116	105	41.2	129.4	70.1
Mexico	84.2	39.3	60.7	99	130	106	25.7	146.6	47.0
Portugal	67.2	49.4	57.8	84	112	95	42.4	119.8	71.9
Spain	63.6	37.5	50.2	85	138	100	31.1	150.1	55.5
Malaysia	80.8	46.8	63.8	98	114	138	30.5	116.9	60.6
Lebanon	76.0	27.2	50.5	102	138	82	19.2	152.6	38.7
Argentina	76.2	41.3	58.2	95	143	108	24.9	120.0	45.3
Brazil	82.0	51.4	66.1	95	153	111	32.1	144.7	53.4
Chile	74.6	35.1	54.4	106	133	115	25.9	145.7	47.5

1.   1997. Brazil, 1995; Argentina, Lebanon and Malaysia, 1995.
Source: ILO, *Key Indicators of the Labour Market*; UNDP, *Human Development Indicators*, 2000 Report.

high, moreover (see Table 3). The inability of the urban/industrial sector to absorb the surplus workers released by agriculture seems to be, apart from the insufficiency of capital-widening investments, a function of generally low education levels of such workers (see Box 6).[31]

In addition, high labour costs may have stunted labour demand in the formal sector, pushing perhaps 40 to 50 per cent of the workforce into the informal sector where labour costs are lower but social insurance and safety standards are absent (see OECD, 1999). Reflecting the narrow tax base, the tax wedge for Turkey was 40 per cent in 1998, compared with 15 per cent in Korea and 22 per cent in Mexico – countries with similarly low rates of government spending in GDP (Table 20). Labour costs also suffered from excessive real wage growth within the public enterprise sector, encompassing almost one-third of the labour force in manufacturing and reducing competition in the labour market as a whole (Table 21). Real wage growth has also been quite volatile, as public-sector and civil service pay, together the minimum wage, have tended to spike in election years (e.g., 1999) and contract sharply in post-crisis stabilisation periods (e.g., 1994-95). Eliminating labour market distortions thus requires the subjection of state-owned enterprises to competition, via privatisation, a reshaping of the tax system and a parallel strengthening of social security administration.

The low employment creating potential of growth is closely associated with a high poverty rate and a low "elasticity" of poverty with respect to growth (Box 6). This is partly related to the need for human capital development via increased educational investment to improve labour supply and for reforms to smooth the intersectoral shift from agriculture to industry and services. But poverty is also related to the structure of government spending, which is severely regressive in nature: whereas in other OECD countries, government tax and transfer policies tend to smooth inequalities in market income, in Turkey they have the opposite effect, in particular as regards social security and agricultural support policies. Remedying this bias will require – besides overall deficit reduction – an overhaul of all social spending to make it better targeted to those in need.

Agricultural reform

A costly and counterproductive system of agricultural support

The present system of agricultural support has been in place since 1932 and is in need of rationalisation. Support to farmers has been provided through price support and input subsidies, with the government heavily involved in the marketing of crops. Administered prices for cereals, sugar and tobacco are complemented by import tariffs of 50 per cent and above. Credit and other input subsidies, particularly for fertilisers, have been significant. Agricultural SEEs serve

Box 6. Poverty in Turkey

Income growth, besides being insufficient, is also unequally distributed. The skewed nature of the income distribution suggests that average per capita income is not a very good indicator of living standards in Turkey. Income differentials across regions and social groups are wide and persistent. Poverty is concentrated in the Eastern provinces, and regional disparities are growing. Moreover, broader indicators of human development, including access to medical care and educational services, lag severely in the rural and poor regional areas. Income inequalities are increasing in a country that has the second widest (after Mexico) income dispersion among the OECD countries: the bottom 20 per cent of households account for only 5 per cent of the disposable income. Based on a country-specific minimum food basket, 7½ per cent of the population are in absolute poverty. Many more are economically vulnerable, i.e. barely above the poverty line: 36 per cent of the population are unable to purchase the basic needs basket including non-food items. A dynamic view of the income distribution and poverty over the period 1987 to 1994 is given by a recent OECD study (Förster 2000). Five relevant facts for the Turkish economy stand out:

- the distribution of disposable income widened significantly among working age and retired persons;
- the income share of the highest quintile of the distribution increased by 5 percentage points while that of all other quintiles fell;
- child and prime-age poverty rates decreased, while those of the elderly increased;
- the share of children in the poor population fell, while remaining one of the highest in the OECD, at 47 per cent;
- poverty increased among workless households with children, jobless single persons and lone parents, although the share of these groups is smaller than in the other OECD countries.

In a major poverty study for Turkey, the World Bank (2000) has found that inequality and economic vulnerability are largely tied to human capital endowment and opportunities in the labour market, with education shown to have a particularly high correlation with poverty risk. This seems to be consistent with studies of poverty in the OECD in general.* Furthermore, unlike in most other OECD countries, there is very little redistribution via the tax and transfer system. The pre-transfer distribution of incomes is, in fact, quite similar to that of France or Italy. This may be surprising in light of high inflation in Turkey, which the Bank report attributes to the fact that people have been able to protect themselves against inflation with a variety of indexing mechanisms. Thus, it appears that present social transfer spending, in particular social security and agricultural support, has not only failed to act in its normal capacity of smoothing the market distribution of incomes, but has actually aggravated it, According to the OECD Social Expenditure Database, public support to low-income households amounts to a mere 0.15 per cent of GDP while spending on family benefits equalled 1 per cent of GDP in 1997. At just over 11 per cent of GDP in 1997, public social expenditure is low in comparison with the other OECD countries. Moreover, almost half of all public transfers go to the three top declines (Förster 2000).

Box 6. **Poverty in Turkey** (*cont.*)

In conclusion, while higher and more stable growth will help to raise living standards, eradicating poverty will require that the "elasticity" of poverty with respect to growth also be raised by means of structural changes such as more investments in education, especially for poor children, and removal of barriers to the demand for labour. These will need to be accompanied by better mechanisms of post-market income distribution, including better targeted assistance and a reasonable safety net.

---

* OECD studies on poverty transitions and duration in some other OECD countries (see Oxley *et al.* 2000) show that there is a greater tendency for the uneducated to fall into poverty than the well-educated and they also tend to exit poverty less.

both as direct purchasing agents and as agro-processors. Ziraat Bank administers credit subsidies. The government also controls and provides special privileges and budget support to Agricultural Sales Co-operative Unions (ASCUs) which help farmers to process and market commodities, acting to prop up the prices of other crops not under official price support schemes.

The overall value of the support to agriculture was equivalent to 8.7 per cent of GDP in 1999 – a large jump from just five years ago and far above the OECD where support levels have been declining, to a current average of 1.5 per cent (Table 22). The difference with the OECD mainly reflects the larger weight of agricultural production in GDP in Turkey (17 compared with 2½ per cent), as the

Table 20. **The tax wedge on labour: international comparison**
Single worker, no children, 1998

	Turkey	Mexico	Korea	Spain
As a percentage of gross labour cost				
Tax wedge	40	22	15	39
Gross labour cost	113	125	110	131
Gross wage earnings	100	100	100	100
Net take-home pay	67	97	94	80
Memorandum item:				
Government spending as a percentage of GDP	20	22	25	40

Source: OECD.

Table 21. **Real wage index**

Per cent change year over year

	Manufacturing[1]			Total economy[2]			
	Public	Private	Total	Public workers[3]	Private workers	Civil servants	Minimum wage
1990	..	..	..	18.4	16.3	15.0	13.3
1991	35.2	41.3	39.7	43.6	37.1	7.2	13.0
1992	16.9	−1.5	4.4	6.0	6.0	13.8	9.1
1993	3.7	5.0	3.9	8.0	1.7	2.1	5.8
1994	−16.2	−24.4	−21.6	0.0	−18.2	−21.9	−15.9
1995	−15.9	−6.0	−12.1	−17.1	−8.3	−4.8	−6.7
1996	−5.2	2.9	−0.5	−25.0	1.9	7.6	18.5
1997	13.6	1.6	3.1	19.2	−3.0	16.5	9.6
1998	4.3	−0.9	−0.3	−1.3	17.0	−1.3	−4.9
1999	19.3	8.2	11.0	42.0	12.9	4.5	35.3
2000[4]	18.4	−19.1	3.9	7.6		−11.2	−13.5

1. Hourly.
2. Real net wages.
3. Includes local administration employees.
4. First half for manufacturing workers.
Sources: State Planning Organisation; State Institute of Statistics; and Turkish Employers' Union.

rate of producer support remained somewhat lower (36 compared with 40 per cent as a percentage of farm receipts). About one quarter of the overall cost was borne by taxpayers in the form of net budgetary transfers to producers. The remainder was borne by consumers in the form of higher prices for agricultural products, these being on average 68 per cent higher than the border (world) price. The trend has been sharply upward, with real prices rising by 50 per cent in the past decade. At the same time, substantial variability in the levels of support for the various crops has reflected shifting political pressures.

There is also an important element of indirect fiscal cost, namely the burden of the debt incurred to finance initial costs in the form of debt write-offs, coverage of duty losses, loan guarantees and equity injections to agricultural SEEs and Ziraat Bank. According the IMF, this indirect fiscal cost has risen from an estimated 2 per cent of GDP in 1997 to over 5 per cent in 1999 (Table 22). By far the largest and fastest-rising component has been the interest charged on unpaid duty losses (credit subsidy costs) of Ziraat Bank, reflecting mainly the sharp increases in market interest rates. Adding this to the OECD estimate of primary fiscal cost implies an overall budgetary burden related to agricultural support schemes of 7½ per cent of GDP in 1999.

Agricultural support policies have not only been costly, but also counter-productive. First, they exacerbate regional and individual income disparities. Benefits have tended to flow mainly to better-off farmers in richer regions. Small

Table 22. **Estimates of support to agriculture**

	1986-1988	1997	1998	1999	1999
	Per cent of GDP				In US$ million
Total support estimate (TSE)	**4.5**	**6.8**	**8.9**	**8.7**	**16 141**
(OECD)	**2.3**	**1.4**	**1.5**	**1.5**	**361 493**
Uses of TSE					
Producer Support Estimate (PSE)	4.1	5.4	7.1	6.5	11 935
Market price support	3.0	4.3	6.1	5.8	10 633
Payments based on output	0.0	0.1	0.1	0.1	113
Payments based on input use	1.1	1.1	0.9	0.6	1 189
General services support estimate (GSSE)	0.4	1.4	1.8	2.3	4 206
of which: Marketing and promotion	0.1	1.3	1.7	2.2	4 081
Sources of TSE					
Transfers from consumers	3.2	4.9	6.6	6.5	12 058
Negative of consumer support estimate (CSE)	3.1	4.7	6.3	6.2	11 505
Excess feed cost[1]	0.1	0.2	0.3	0.3	554
Net transfers from budget	1.3	1.8	2.2	2.3	4 083
Transfers from taxpayers	1.4	2.1	2.4	2.5	4 649
Budget revenues[2]	−0.1	−0.3	−0.2	−0.3	−566
Rates of support					
Percentage PSE[3]	19	31	36	36	
(OECD)	40	31	36	40	
Percentage CSE[4]	−17	−30	−40	−40	
(OECD)	−34	−23	−28	−31	
Memorandum items:					
Cost of debt service[5]	..	1.9	3.2	5.2	10 281
of which: Ziraat Bank interest charge component	..	0.9	2.1	4.2	8 413
Total value of production (at farm-gate)	21.4	16.5	18.5	17.1	31 526
(OECD)	4.7	3.1	2.8	2.5	617 337

1. This is deducted from the market transfers from consumers to producers to obtain the CSE, as it represents the producer contribution to the market price support on crops used in animal feed.
2. Represents transfers back to the budget on the share of consumption that is imported (tariff payments).
3. Ratio of PSE to the value of total gross farm receipts, measured by the total production (at farm-gate prices), plus
   budgetary support.
4. Ratio of CSE to the total value of consumption expenditure on commodities domestically produced, measured by
   the value of total consumption (at farm gate prices), minus budgetary support to consumers.
5. These represent the indirect fiscal cost (as estimated by the IMF) of the burden of accumulated debt that has been
   incurred to finance the initial cost, such as interest penalties on tax arrears in agricultural SEEs, the carrying cost of
   large stocks of unsold surplus production, or imputed interest on the stock of unpaid duty losses of Ziraat Bank.
Source: OECD (2000); Moalla-Fetini (1999).

farmers (two-thirds of output and have better access to, and more intensive use
of, subsidised resources such as water, machinery, fertiliser, and chemicals. On the
farmers owning five hectares or less) benefit less as they often produce for their
own consumption and are too poor to use purchased inputs. Large farmers sell

their consumption side, the tax equivalent of price supports is a highly regressive one, as food commands a much larger share of (urban) poor than of richer household budgets. Second, the transfers associated with these policies impose a heavy burden on the economy. There is a dead-weight cost due to the high operational costs of SEEs and to storage and debt service costs accumulated as a result of past policies. High price supports and input subsidies limit the influence of world market signals on production decisions. Also, the volatility of politically-determined price support levels makes it very difficult for farmers (and budget managers) to plan rationally. Benefit claims are subject to abuse, and there is an incentive to over-use subsidised inputs. As a result, waste and carrying costs of unwanted production are high, efficiency is low and public and private resources are misallocated. Agricultural productivity, farmers' incomes, and budget outcomes would all clearly benefit from a consolidation of agricultural-support measures into a transparent and well-targeted scheme.

The reform programme

In the context of the agreement with the IMF, the government has developed a strategy to phase out the current mechanisms of production-oriented support and to substitute these by direct income payments. The reform will proceed on three parallel tracks:

- A unified national programme of direct income support will be introduced over the 2000-02 period. In the first year, implementation will start on a pilot basis for four selected regions. The task of the pilot programme will be to prepare a farm registry and to ascertain the best method to distribute the income support (to the owners of the land or the sharecroppers). In the second and third years, the results of the pilot scheme will be applied nation-wide.

- In parallel, price supports and input subsidies will be phased out. The fertiliser subsidy will continue to be held constant in nominal terms as it has been since 1997. Subsidised credits via Ziraat have effectively ended in March 2000 (see Chapter II), preventing the further build-up of debt. Agricultural support prices will be linked to market prices by steadily reducing the premium, with the aim of eliminating it by 2002.[32] At the same time, import tariffs will decline.

- In the longer run, most agricultural state enterprises will be privatised. In preparation, the government is hardening budget constraints, via limits on Treasury loan guarantees, equity injections, and budget transfers, and establishing the legal framework for privatisation.[33] ASCUs, which are nominally private, will have complete autonomy, with credit subsidies being eliminated and those agencies that are viable being restructured into private co-operatives.

The planned agricultural reform is perhaps the most radical and most difficult part of the programme, touching the lives of 40 per cent of the population.
From a social point of view, the shift is astounding in both its magnitude and proposed speed. If it is implemented as planned, by 2003, almost $5 billion in fiscal
support to agriculture (credit and fertiliser subsidies, subsidies to agricultural
SEEs and ASCUs) will have been replaced by under $2 billion in direct income
payments (Table 23), while some $12 billion in transfers from consumers via higher
prices (Table 22) will simply disappear. This implies a reduction in the level of
support from almost 9 per cent of GDP to 1 per cent within the space of just three
years. However, the counterpart benefits of higher agricultural productivity will
take time to appear. In the meantime, formerly supported crops may become
unprofitable, putting certain farmers out of business, and many workers in the
agricultural SEEs (currently numbering about 50 thousand) are likely to become
redundant.

The transition period is thus critical. Under the World Trade Organisation
framework, transfers may, in the short run, purely compensate for the decrease in
price support to allow for a relatively smooth transition. But over time, these

Table 23.   **Budgetary expenditure associated with the agricultural reform programme**
US$ million

	2000, no reform	2000	2001	2002	2003
Credit subsidy	1 400	140	0	0	0
Fertiliser subsidy	201	201	210	0	0
Price support					
Cotton	267	267	172	0	0
Oilseeds	44	44	40	0	0
ASCUs	860	658	202	0	0
Wheat (TMO)	792	624	562	0	0
Tobacco (TEKEL)	371	320	156	144	0
Sugar (TSFAS)	874	770	714	0	0
Subtotal	4 848	3 023	2 055	144	0
Direct income payment[1]	0	2	950	1 900	1 900
Total	4 848	3 025	3 005	2 044	1 900

Note: Exchange rates:
         1999 – $1 = TL 417 758.
         2000 – $1 = TL 622 750.
         2001 – $1 = TL 714 000.
1. Assumptions:
    Subsidy of $80 per hectare per year (for the pilot $50 per hectare) and a maximum of 20 hectares per owner
    to be subsidised.
    All farmers are beneficiaries from direct payments in 2001, but the first tranche will be paid within the year.
    8 000 farmers are considered in calculations in 2000 (pilot programme).
    8 million hectares are used in calculations in 2001 (90 per cent of this area is under 20 hectares).
    16 million hectares are used in calculations in 2002 and 2003 (90 per cent of this area is under 20 hectares).
Source: Turkish authorities.

payments should be more targeted toward the poor and integrated into the overall safety net, being gradually redefined on the basis of considerations of regional development or, in general, socio-economic factors. Under current plans, no compensation for declining price supports is foreseen while (much lower) cash payments are based on the amount of land owned (Table 23). While the absence of any transitory, production-based compensatory payments is understandable given the stringent fiscal constraints of the stabilisation programme, such payments are probably inevitable and they should be properly planned for and budgeted in order to sustain confidence in the agricultural reform. Moreover, it is not clear how efficient the distribution of cash support will be, given the very fragmented land and ownership structure; many farmers are sharecroppers owning no land at all. To target income support to farmers, there is a need not only to register farmers *ex ante*, as is being done under the pilot scheme, but also to more effectively monitor closely the social impact of the reform. Equally important will be research, education and training programmes, including extension services, perhaps provided in the context of the redefined SEEs and ASCUs, to assist farmers affected by structural change.[34] The result will also depend on faster growth of industrial and service sectors, to increase the demand for surplus labour.

Privatisation and liberalisation in the utilities sectors

Turkey sorely needs more efficient infrastructure, and in particular energy and telecommunications capacity, in order to eliminate bottlenecks which have constrained growth. The government's primary objective in these areas is to accelerate privatisation, by both eliminating barriers to entry and allowing private participation in existing facilities, in parallel with reform of the legal and regulatory frameworks needed to support the medium term transition to competitive market structures meeting EU standards. OECD experience shows that liberalisation and privatisation of the utilities sectors can bring important benefits for efficiency and consumer welfare if sufficient attention is paid to ensuring competitive outcomes (Box 7).

Energy

The domestic energy supply-demand gap is projected to widen sharply over the coming decade, increasing the country's dependence on imported primary energy sources, notably oil and gas but also increasingly coal (Figure 16). This points to both sluggish domestic energy supply and inefficient use as major problems. The energy sector is mainly state-owned, with the government heavily involved in the management of the SEEs operating in this sector. The resultant inefficiencies mean that TEAS, the state electricity generation and transmission company, and TEDAS, the state distribution company, have a poor collection performance and register losses on their operations. The government has generally maintained prices below the level at which SEEs could make the necessary

Box 7. **Liberalisation and privatisation of network industries: lessons from OECD countries**

Network industries such as telecommunications (fixed telephony), electricity, and railroads are characterised by high fixed costs, in which non-competitive and competitive market segments co-exist. For example, the local loop in telecommunications, electricity transmission and distribution, gas and water pipelines, and rail track, are all characterised by economies of scale which give rise to a natural monopoly – a "market failure" which justifies the need for either public ownership or a regulated private monopoly. Mobile telephony and air travel also have network elements and sizeable fixed costs, but are largely competitive industries.

Liberalisation (of prices and access to markets previously restricted by legal and regulatory barriers) and privatisation have been undertaken by OECD countries in a wide range of network industries, and has led to important welfare and efficiency gains.* The general movement to reduce barriers to entry and private ownership has been strongest in telecommunications, with a slower pace of liberalisation in electricity and railways. Due to privatisations, OECD public enterprise sectors are less than half the size they were at the beginning of the 1980s. Privatisations have generally led to improved company performance and, in industries with non-competitive segments, better regulatory supervision. However, where privatisation revenue has been a prime concern, insufficient attention to the market power of the firms being privatised has led to inefficient outcomes. Moreover, especially in some new member countries, the benefits of change of ownership have sometimes proved disappointing, due to weaknesses in the legal, institutional, and market environment.

Experience shows that privatisation – if carried out and subsequently regulated with a view to circumscribing market power and limiting informational asymmetries – can reinforce competition policy. New entry is unlikely in a market that features a state-owned incumbent with a soft budget constraint, because the incumbent can credibly deter entry through predatory pricing. The recent experience of OECD countries abounds with examples of vertically-integrated public enterprises which were found to abuse their dominant position in an upstream market to foreclose entry of new competitors in liberalised downstream markets. Privatisation may also enhance competitive developments through the horizontal and/or vertical unbundling of the activities owned by the former state monopoly and their separate sale to different private investors. In the electricity industry, for example, transmission should be separated from generation in order to eliminate the incentives for the transmission-grid owners to discriminate in favour of self-owned generating capacity. Generating capacity should also be split among a sufficient number of independently owned companies so that it would be difficult to suppress competition among them through either collusion or consciously parallel pricing etc. It also helps if at least the larger municipal electricity distribution grids are placed under separate ownership and required to apply the same accounting rules. Regulators can then apply "yardstick" regulation to compare each municipal electricity distribution company with the others and set permitted tariffs at levels strongly encouraging all distributors to lower their costs to industry best practice levels.

---

* See Gonenc *et al.* (2000).

Figure 16.   **Energy balances**[1]
Mtoe

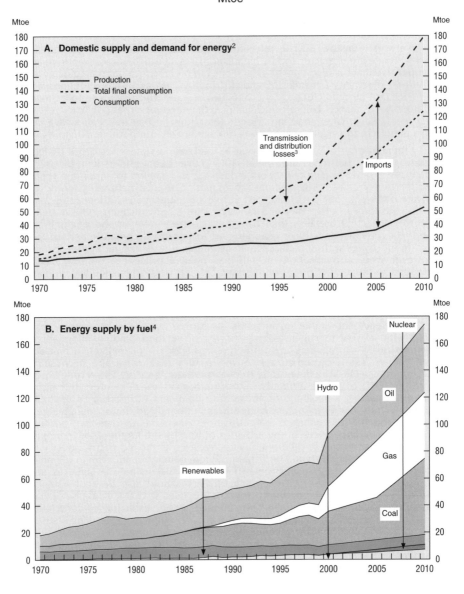

1.   Data for 2000, 2005 and 2010 are IEA projections. Between these years data have been interpolated.
2.   Last available year 1998.
3.   Includes statistical differences.
4.   1999 data are preliminary.
Source: IEA.

investments, and as a consequence the latter have been dependent upon capital transfers from the Treasury and state guarantees for investment. This pricing policy has had an increasingly negative impact on the economy. It has increased the budget deficit and encouraged the inefficient use of energy. Turkey has the highest transmission and distribution losses of any IEA country, at 2.5 and 13.5 per cent respectively.

The creation of an efficient energy industry requires privatisation of the state-owned enterprises – or at a minimum corporatisation – together with clear and stable market rules. The government has accordingly undertaken to move toward a "market model". In such a model, prices would reflect costs, which in turn should with greater efficiency be lower, and state subsidies would be eliminated. Price reform would also increase the confidence of private investors. Despite reformist intentions and some private investments (mainly domestic) within the scope of the BOT/BOO and TOOR schemes ("Build-Operate-Transfer/Own" and "Transfer of Operating Rights" – see Box 8), progress has been slow. The main stumbling block has been the lack of clear legal framework for private participations, in particular the lack of recourse to international arbitration which deterred foreign investors. According to provisions of the Turkish constitution, the Council of State, or Danistay, had a final say over investment approvals as well as any disputes involving foreign private investors in the public services sectors, and it had blocked approval for most BOT contracts.[35] Frequent changes in model design as the government tried to get around these constraints only served to increase investor uncertainty.

The current reform programme attempts to accelerate this shift to the "market model". A first major step involved clarifying and stabilising the legislative framework for the privatisation process. In August 1999, Parliament approved a long-awaited set of constitutional amendments which: i) create a constitutional basis for privatisation and allow the government to determine by law which investments and services carried out by public entities can be contracted out or transferred to private agents, ii) provide for international arbitration to settle disputes arising from concession contracts and other legal agreements concerning public services where there is a foreign element,[36] and iii) limit the Danistay to an advisory role with respect to concession contracts and other legal agreements pertaining to public services.[37] These amendments were implemented in early 2000 by making the necessary changes in existing laws. With the legal conditions for the transfer of rights and BOT/BOO schemes thus clarified, entrepreneurs are able to evaluate their investments better. This should help to unlock significant financing in the energy sector from international markets.

However, the contracting method in this sector has been problematic. Until recently, long-term BOT contracts between private firms and TEAS have been concluded in the absence of an independent regulator and have made

Box 8.   **Private energy investments under the market model**

The government's strategy to move to a market model in the energy sector has the following key points:

Electricity

– In the electricity sector, the government has undertaken a financing programme, *Build-Operate-Transfer/Own* (BOT/BOO), to increase generating capacity in the electricity sector via new private investments. In a typical BO project, the private owner is responsible for construction and operating costs but signs a long-term power purchase agreement with TEAS, in which the latter commits itself to buy the output of the firm over a (usually 20-year) period at a fixed price in foreign currency. Backed by Treasury guarantees, the government thus retains the commercial risks of demand and exchange rate, or even fuel supply, fluctuations over the life of the contract. This implies significant off-budget and contingent liabilities for the public sector. The government is also engaging in *transfers of operating rights* (TOOR) of the existing generation plants of the state electricity-generation and transmission firm TEAS and the distribution facilities of the state distribution firm TEDAS.

– Despite earlier problems with implementation, the BO schemes (as well as some "auto-generation" schemes) have already served to expand energy supply: in 1998 around 65 per cent and in 1999 around 50 per cent of the installed capacity was added through *investments of the private sector*, which presently account for over 20 per cent of all electricity generation. The clarification of the legal framework in 1999 should serve to boost supply capability in the future. However, insufficient attention has been paid to market competition in the design of price purchase guarantees for BO schemes, giving rise to concerns about the implied long-run costs to consumers and taxpayers. Few of the TOOR projects have been concluded, moreover, as private investors have for the most part not been able to make the required up-front payments.

– To address the serious problems in the electricity sector, the government is moving toward a *market model* that is consistent with EU principles. The government's stated objective is to meet the nation's incremental power needs after 2005 on a market basis without guarantees, thus transferring risks back to the private sector in the case of BOT/BOO schemes. Also, the TOOR model will give way to outright sale of the underlying generation and distribution assets, and in parallel, TEAS and TEDAS are being restructured in preparation for eventual privatisation. An independent regulator will be set up to establish a clear set of rules for third party access to transmission and distribution lines, and ensuring tariffs are fair and transparent.

– In a liberalised market, BO plants can sell their electricity directly to consumers, there will be an increased choice of suppliers and a *competitive element* which could serve to increase efficiency and reduce costs. Private companies can also accelerate the pace and lower the cost of construction, helping address the urgent need for new facilities. The government estimates that Turkey needs to add 3 500 to 4 500 MW production capacity annually until 2020, requiring an additional $4.5 to $5 billion in annual investments in the electricity sector.

Box 8. **Private energy investments under the market model** *(cont.)*

Other energy sectors

- Consumption of natural gas has grown rapidly and the government is considering the possibility of *liberalising natural gas imports* and implementing third party access in the transport and distribution of gas. An independent regulator will be set up to handle access to pipelines and pricing issues.

- Given its large potential as a transit country for Caspian oil, Turkey has been actively involved in proposals for projects to build oil pipelines through its territory. In mid-1998, the government issued a *price formula to link oil product prices to international prices*, prior to *privatisation* of the public refiner Tüpras (whose prices may have been too low in the past) and the public distributor POAS.

- In spite of efforts to reduce costs, *hard coal production is still subsidised*, leading to distortions in inter-fuel competition. The government is planning a regional development project in hard-coal producing areas.

- The government is to encourage *a shift to renewables in the primary fuel supply for electricity generation* such as wind power, solar, hydro and nuclear. However, tenders for the proposed nuclear power plant had to be postponed recently due to the difficulty of providing guarantees under current budgetary conditions.

---

limited use of competitive bidding. The lack of transparency and competition has resulted in expensive agreed prices for purchased power over the length of the contract (whose average remaining length is 20 years), creating large implicit and contingent liabilities for the government (Box 8). As these prices are generally above authorised retail prices, TEAS faces major losses;[38] the absence of competition also acts to perpetuate its own operational inefficiencies. If the marginal costs of generating power by entities benefiting from the guarantees turn out to be higher than the long-run incremental costs of more efficient generators – as would seem likely due to the incentive effects of guarantees – there could also be important inefficiencies for the sector as a whole. In that case, national welfare would be increased if the inefficient generators were simply paid the profits they were implicitly guaranteed, and competition among efficient generators were permitted to set prices for power sold to the transmission company.

In other respects, the sector is being liberalised. TEAS has been separated into legally-distinct generation, transmission, and wholesale sale-purchase functions in order to make costs and prices more transparent, out of which separate companies were formed (Transmission, Generation, and Trading Companies).[39] This sets

---

the stage for an electricity reform law, establishing an independent electricity sector regulator to regulate and oversee the market and eventually allowing distribution companies to buy from any generator (not just TEAS) and generators to sell to any distribution company (not just TEDAS). The law is to be sent to Parliament by end-2000 and to come into operation in 2002. Complementing these efforts, the privatisation programme in 2000 will focus on implementation of the TOOR programme to improve management of TEAS facilities. The programme was originally targeted to raise $1.1 billion in revenue (see Table 24); however, due to lack of financing for the projects, only part ($300 million) of this amount will be realised. Those TOOR projects which do not find financing within a specified time period will lapse. For distribution companies which remain under state management, the government will launch a new approach starting in January 2001 based on privatisation of the underlying assets. In the gas sector, legislation (a set of draft amendments to the Petroleum Law) has likewise been prepared to establish the framework and time-table for deregulation. An independent regulator will be established. The government expects the regulator to be functional by end 2000 and the market to begin operating by 2001. BOTAS, the state gas company, will also be split into distinct transmission, distribution, and trading companies. The gas distribution companies will be privatised.

Table 24. **Privatisation programme for 2000**

US$ million

	2000				
	Q1	Q2	Q3	Q4	Total
Proceeds from the PA's portfolio[1]	75	1 100	925	1 000	3 100
To be used by the PA	28	84	232	422	766
To be used by the PPF	14	168	180	94	456
To be used by the Budget	33	848	513	484	1 878
Proceeds from energy and telecom	0	1 000	367	3 133	4 500
GSM licences	0	1 000	0	0	1 000
Turk Telekom	0	0	0	2 400	2 400
Power plants/distribution grids	0	0	367	733	1 100
Total	75	2 100	1 292	4 133	7 600
of which: To the Budget	33	1 848	880	3 617	6 378

1. There is a complex accounting mechanism for the privatisation receipts of the Privatisation Administration (PA), arising from institutional arrangements in the past. The PA transfers its proceeds to the Public Participation Fund (PPF) after keeping some money in its own accounts for necessary expenditures (e.g. administrative costs, clean-up of pre-privatisation firms, and severance payments for workers). Since PPF has liabilities to Treasury, mainly due to the issuance of public participation shares and highway contractor's liabilities, PPF has to transfer the proceeds to Treasury after deducting some amount for necessary expenses. As of October 2000, PA privatisation proceeds totalled $2 454 million, of which $582 million was used by PA. The remaining $1 872 million was transferred to PPF; of which $347 million was retained by PPF for investment expenditures. The remaining $1 525 million was transferred by PPF to Treasury, all used for the reduction of debt ($1 385 domestic and $140 external).
Source: Government of Turkey (1999).

Telecommunications

Despite impressive progress in recent years, Turkey remains behind the average for OECD in terms of the development of telecommunication infrastructure as measured by access lines per 100 inhabitants and in terms of mobile diffusion. Reform of the telecommunications sector should therefore be a priority but has been relatively slow compared to most OECD countries. However, at the national level, relative to other sectors such as energy, reform has been much more rapid as technical and legal preparations were advanced enough for a telecommunications reform bill to be approved in January 2000. The new legislation enabled Turk Telekom (TT) to be converted into a joint stock company subject to the commercial code in order to open its capital to private participation, established an independent regulatory authority for telecommunications and enabled private provision of value added and wireless services. The legislation paved the way for a market structure for the telecom sector over the medium term, with a four-year transition. Under this transition, TT will be partly privatised and restructured: the company's cable TV and wireless operations will be placed into separate subsidiaries in accordance with EU standards. It will be allowed to maintain its monopoly over fixed line services up to the end of 2003. However, fairly stringent conditions have been maintained for new entrants after 2003, which will require not less than 51 per cent equity by Turkish citizens in value-added services (although being a regulation of the Ministry of Transport, this could be amended over time).

The privatisation process enabled by the new legislation has unfolded as follows. In early 2000, a tender for two GSM licences was made, of which one was sold at a price of $2.525 billion, against initial expectations of around $1 billion from the sale of both licences. (The bulk of the receipts of the licence sale, around $2 billion, will not be received until early 2001, however.) The high price discouraged bidding for the second licence (which was constrained to be equal to or higher in price than the first), and it did not sell, although it could be reopened with future legislation. To increase its future attractiveness to private investors, TT was awarded a wireless licence at the market price established by the auction. With two pre-existing licences, this brings the number of operators to four (with a fifth slot empty). As to the privatisation of TT, a first block sale of 20 per cent to a strategic investor planned for the autumn of 2000 had to be postponed to 2001 due to potential investor concerns over management rights, as well as to deteriorating market conditions (the sale was to have raised some $2.4 billion; see Table 24). Following planned completion of the block sale and an opening of the company's capital to the public in 2001,[40] the objective is to leave the Treasury with a 51 per cent holding.

In managing the transition to the market model, it will be important that the new independent regulator force TT to increase its efficiency. The usual cross-subsidisation of under-priced local services by over-priced long distance services needs to be ended, while taking care to stimulate growth of the internet by establishing a separate numbering for internet and local voice calls (as some European countries have done). The extended period of monopoly rights will retard the disciplining effect of market forces but has no doubt been granted, in part, because the network has not yet been completed, and private investors are needed to share in these up-front expenses. However, the issue of minority rights in a government majority-owned company has become a larger concern. To resolve this problem, the government is considering increasing the size of the block share along with the management rights attached to it. It is within the jurisdiction of the Council of Ministers to amend the relevant decree to allow an increase of the stake to up to 34 per cent (beyond this limit, legislation would be required). The drawback of this option is that it risks lowering the amount of capital to be opened to the public, inhibiting development of the local capital market, unless subsequent legislation were to allow the government's share to fall below 51 per cent. Once the transition period has been completed, moreover, continuing efforts by the regulator will be needed to restrict TT's market power, including clear regulation of access to fixed networks.

As far as wireless services are concerned, there is some debate as to whether the structure of the auctions of licences was sufficiently conducive to competition, as purchasers of the first licence had an incentive to over-bid in order to pre-empt sale of the second licence. Charges to consumers could also be pushed up by the high combined start up costs of licences and infrastructure. The regulator will need to be vigilant in this sub-sector as well. Experience in other countries has also shown that the independent regulator should have greater scope to manage the transition to the competitive model; relying on legislation for every step greatly slows down the process. Thus, the Ministry could for example be empowered to reopen the bidding for the second auctioned licence upon the recommendation of the authority.[41]

The privatisation programme

The overall privatisation programme is committed to raising $7.6 billion in 2000 (equal to 3½ per cent of GDP). By comparison, only $6 billion was raised over the entire previous decade, in part due to inappropriate market conditions but also due to weak political will, non-transparency, and failure to create public confidence in the process. The 2000 programme represents a fresh start, specifically geared to overcoming such difficulties, and has three main parts: telecommunications, energy, and the privatisation portfolio of the Privatisation Administration (PA) (see Tables 24 and 25). The enterprise privatisation programme managed by the PA is targeted to raise $3.1 billion in cash, and has made a promising start. As of October, privatisations worth $2.7 billion in deals were at the approval stage and $2.5 billion in cash had been received. Important benchmarks were established by

Table 25.   **Privatisation programme under the Privatisation Administration, 2000**

As of August 2000

Q1	Q2	Q3	Q4
Deniz Nakliyat[1] (Turkish cargo lines)	Poas[1] (petroleum distribution)	Ataköy Marina and Hotel (tourism)	Erdemir (IPO) (iron and steel)
Orüs[1] (asset) (forestry product asset)	Tüpras[1] (IPO) (petroleum refining)	THY (block) (airlines)	Tüpras (block/IPO) (petroleum refining)
Etag[2] (wood product)	Petkim Yarimca (petrochemicals)	Tügsas[3] (2nd quarter) (fertiliser)	Petkim (block/IPO) (petrochemical)
Ankara Sigorta[1] (insurance)	Isdemir[3] (iron and steel)	IGSAS[3] (2nd quarter) (fertiliser)	Ataköy Tourism (tourism)
Güven Sigorta[1] (insurance)	KBI[2] (block) (copper)	Stock market shares	Participations[3]
Asil Çelik[1] (iron and steel)	SEKA[3] (asset) (pulp and paper assets)	Participations[3]	
Ebas[1] (asset) (meat processing plants)	Sümer Holding[3] (asset) (textile plants)		
KBI[1] (asset) (copper plants)	6 ports[3] (maritime)		
Taksan[2] (small machinery)	Tümosan[3] (motor equipment)		
Turban[1] (asset) (tourism)	Participations[1]		
TZDK[1] (asset) (agricultural machinery)			

1. Completed.
2. No bids.
3. Tenders – negotiations – contract.
Source: Privatisation Administration.

the Tüpras (petroleum refining) 31.5 per cent of equity public offering, and the POAS (petroleum distribution) 51 per cent block share sale, which respectively raised $1.1 and $1.3 billion. Some of the additional large-scale company privatisations originally planned for 2000 have been shifted to 2001: Turkish Airlines, a major iron and steel complex, a petrochemical company, and further tranches of Tüpras and POAS.[42] A number of smaller scale enterprises privatisations are continuing in parallel. The PA is working to maintain an appropriate balance between large and small scale privatisations with a view to ensuring the maximum positive impact on the private sector. It may also have to be prepared to deal with issues of corporate governance such as those that arose with the attempted sale of the 20 per cent block share of Telekom.

There is a trade-off involved in any privatisation between maximising revenues and promoting competition. Privatising market power allows higher privatisation receipts. However, pre-privatision restructuring designed to increase post-privatisation competition serves to generate higher consumer welfare and more output (hence tax receipts) in the longer run (see Box 7). The government has, in fact, been taking many important steps in this direction, *i.e.* unbundling of core services and corporatising/restructuring the separated companies prior to privatisation. It is also encouraging that the Competition Authority has been given the right to review privatisation plans and bids in all sectors,[43] and it is essential that it use these powers assertively as it is the principal party within government likely to be interested in long-term efficiency issues and not overly concerned about short-term budgetary impacts of privatisations. Once the new independent regulators come into operation, it will be important that they be as well informed as possible, in large part by minimising market power and the possibilities for collusion at the outset, and that regulation diminish as competition in the sector increases.

Banking sector reform

Inflation and banking sector distortions

The problems suffered by the banking system as a result of high inflation were noted in Chapter I. Profits to be made from government paper, increasingly based on foreign borrowing, have crowded out private sector operations. The country was opened to capital flows in the late 1980s prior to establishing adequate regulatory safeguards, in part because it needed the foreign capital to finance rising fiscal deficits in the face of diminishing seignorage from the inflation tax. A subsequent inflow of "hot" money allowed banks to capture high real interest rates (reflecting inflation risk and the pressure of public debt) through the use of the net open position – borrowing from abroad at much lower interest rates without hedging the exchange risk and using the proceeds to buy government bonds. There was a limit on such positions, but it was circumvented by booking them in affiliates established in off-shore centres. Domestic trading in government paper, in the form of "repos", became another major bank activity. Table 26 shows that between 1990 and 1999, the share of securities in bank assets rose sharply to the detriment of the loan portfolio, while on the liabilities side, dollar-denominated deposits crowded out TL-denominated deposits and time deposits steadily replaced demand deposits. Off-balance sheet, open positions in foreign exchange and repos surged. Uncovered arbitrage led to important profitability gains, at least ½ per cent of GDP and probably more per year.[44] However, both on- and off-balance sheet risks increased. The expanding repo position was associated with maturity mismatch between bank assets and liabilities, creating a balance-sheet vulnerability to short-term interest rate increases: by the end of 1999, government bonds had an average maturity of one year, while deposits

Table 26.   **Selected banking statistics**

	State banks		Private banks		Foreign banks	
	1992	1999	1992	1999	1992	1999
Structural data:						
Number of banks	8[1]	7	38[1]	52	22[1]	22
Assets (per cent of GDP)	17.2	25.2	18.3	35.8	1.5	3.8
Number of branches	2 875[1]	2 877	3 238[1]	3 976	106[1]	124
Number of employees	78 090[1]	76 343	63 405[1]	93 393	3 562[1]	4 252
Distribution of bank assets						
(as a percentage of total)	48.4	38.3	47.8	50.4	3.9	5.6
Balance sheet data:						
Deposits (as a percentage of total assets)	63.6	76.2	58.3	62.7	26.0	34.8
Demand deposits	18.0	12.7	17.9	11.0	12.8	7.5
Time deposits	45.6	63.5	40.4	51.7	13.2	27.3
Denominated in TL	45.5	60.5	27.6	17.8	12.6	12.1
Denominated in US$	18.1	15.8	30.7	44.9	13.3	22.7
Loans (as a percentage of total assets)	41.1	24.3	39.8	33.5	14.7	31.3
Securities (as a percentage of total assets)	12.8	10.7	10.6	20.9	34.5	16.5
Capital/asset ratio (per cent)						
Investment and development banks	11.9	19.7	8.4	22.0	11.4	6.5
Commercial banks	6.4	4.1	10.0	12.9	13.3	12.6
Profit as a percentage of total assets	1.7	1.2	2.5	4.4	6.6	6.8
Non-performing loans						
(as a percentage of total loans)	19.4	12.1	6.0	4.5	3.0	3.5
Off-balance sheet data (in millions of US$):						
Open position of deposit money banks	−660	−78	−1 944	−4 408	−12	−123
Commitments						
Repo transactions	195	3 595	1 062	8 448	217	1 710
Reverse repo transactions	80	36	583	1 452	121	402
Other commitments	600	4 764	837	2 429	18	761

1.   1995 figures.
Source: Association of Turkish banks.

were around three months. A 100 per cent state guaranty on savings deposits, in place since the 1994 crisis, together with a lax supervisory regime, provided an incentive for less sound banks to assume excessive risks. The exchange-rate risk associated with the growing (non-transparent) open position was implicitly contained by the real exchange-rate targeting regime, but balance sheet weaknesses have implied that the banking system remains extremely vulnerability to liquidity squeezes associated with the pursuit more recently of the nominal exchange-rate target.

Because credit markets were thin, competition deficient, and the macroeconomic environment volatile, domestic interest margins (loan-deposit spreads) were high in internationally relative terms.[45] Banks also enjoyed high yields from the "float" income earned on demand deposits held at no interest. The demand for real base money fell as inflation ratcheted up in the 1990s. Between 1987 and 1998, base money as a share of GDP (the base of the inflation tax) continued to decline, falling from over 10 per cent in the early 1970s to 6½ per cent in 1986 and further to 4½ per cent in 1998. Nevertheless, compared to other countries that have gone through episodes of high inflation, Turkey is unique in the slow pace at which the demand for real base money has been eroded by inflation.[46] Even adjusting for the higher transactions costs associated with inflation, float income may have amounted to ½ per cent of GDP in 1999, not far from earnings on uncovered arbitrage (see Annex III). Banks also benefited from high services income, given the high velocity of money transactions and frequent demand for financial services that is typical to high-inflation economies. However, the booming demand for bank services also led to over-branching and over-manning, especially among state banks but also in private banks (Table 26), with inefficiencies being masked by easy profits. Moreover, the opening of new branches was made easy and closure of less sound banks difficult by weak and heavily-politicised control over the issuance and withdrawal of licences. The number of banks (81) is perhaps double what would be expected given the size of the sector.

The prevailing corporate culture may have reinforced distortions in the supply of credit. Many banks, especially the larger ones, are part of extensive family-dominated holding groups, so that established banking relationships, in the context of complex ownership structures and cross-holdings, have tended to be the dominant mode of finance. Small and mid-sized banks have in numerous cases lent to "related parties". Such arrangements clearly exclude small or new firms and individuals. To help small investors, the government has intervened in the form of specialised public banks offering subsidised credits for housing, small business, and agriculture (respectively by Emlak, Halk, and Ziraat banks). Public banks accounted for almost 40 per cent of total banking sector assets in 1999 (Table 26). However, as a result of their quasi-fiscal operations, very large "duty losses" have accumulated on the books of two of these banks (Table 27). To deal with the result-

Table 27.   **Duty losses of the state banks**
End of period

	In US$ billion[1]		In per cent of GNP	
	1999	2000[2]	1999	2000[2]
Ziraatbank	11.3	11.8	7.8	6.4
Halkbank	7.8	9.2	5.4	5.0
Total	19.2	21.0	13.2	11.4

1. Exchange rate: 540 098 TL/$ – end-1999; 676 800 TL/$ – end-2000.
2. Estimated.
Source: Undersecretariat of Treasury.

ing cash flow problem, these banks had to bid up interest rates in order to attract an ever-growing deposit base, distorting the sector as a whole. But even in sectors favoured by these specialised public banking institutions, relationships and influence appear to have mattered for access to credit.[47] Enterprise entry and expansion – the basis of economic growth – was on the whole inhibited by the dearth of arms-length external financing sources, having to rely mainly on family finance and retained earnings. The lack of mortgage finance, moreover, exacerbated distortions in housing and land markets (see next chapter).

The impact of disinflation

The stabilisation programme will change the banking climate dramatically, but only with a delay. Profits will increase strongly in 2000 as sight deposit rates fall immediately in line with market interest rates, while high returns on government securities portfolios – the average maturity of which is around one year – continue to accrue despite the windfall gains tax. Indeed, banks apparently accelerated their arbitrage activities once interest rates started to fall, as net open positions almost doubled in the first nine months of 2000 (Table 7), magnifying the windfall though exacerbating the exposure to exchange risk and the associated maturity mismatch. The windfall should provide banks with a "breathing space" during which they need to prepare to switch to traditional lending activity for profits. The danger is that a scramble by banks to replace paper trading and inflation profits by new loan business could lead to a rise in non-performing loans if proper credit risk assessment procedures are not applied. Turkish banks thus far have greatly expanded their consumer lending, helping to finance the boom in consumption and imports, but also increasing the exposure to default and interest rate risks.

At the same time, demand for bank transaction services will decline in a low inflation environment and control of costs will be much more important than previously, so that banks will need to revisit what they consider to be the optimal number of branches and staffing levels. Bank consolidation also may be needed to cut down on the number of banks by merging poor performers with stronger ones. Well-prepared banks have moved forward on bank automation and internet services to cut costs, and the closing of superfluous branches. They are developing both wholesale (industrial) and retail (customer) banking capabilities, but with an emphasis on the latter where monitoring of credit quality is easier and because of the expected expansion of consumer demand in the early stages of the stabilisation programme. A low inflation environment will give banks substantial new income earning opportunities. Banks have begun to offer mortgages, although at the higher end of the market where margins are higher and risks are lower. Banks are also positioning themselves to enter investment banking services, stimulated by growth of the stock market, initial public offerings and privatisations. These innovations should lay the foundations for stronger economic growth via a healthier balance between bank and non-bank forms of finance.[48]

The reform programme

Rehabilitating the banking sector was at the top of the agenda of the coalition government when it took office in June 1999. In the same month, a new banking act was passed, ushering in the "first phase" of the reform which seeks to bring the regulatory and supervision regime for the Turkish banking sector up to the level of international norms and best practice. The law created a new regulatory agency operating under the governance of an autonomous Bank Regulation and Supervision Board, and combining the supervisory responsibilities previously split between the Central Bank and Treasury. The agency became fully functional in September 2000. In December 1999 and June 2000, the law was significantly strengthened by a series of amendments and decrees, which:

- widened the authority of the Banking Board, giving it complete independence over entry and exit of banks (bank licensing), and over decisions on the take-over of failing banks and on changes to prudential regulation;

- tightened the prudential regime: banks' financial statements were to be reported on a consolidated basis, with capital adequacy and open position ratios calculated on this basis;[49] and loan-loss provisioning rules were redefined and clarified, reversing the relaxation of loan classification rules introduced under the July 1999 emergency stimulus package;

- imposed tighter limits on connected/insider lending; bank shareholders and managers were to become personally liable for the mismanagement and abuse of bank resources;

- removed unlimited deposit insurance coverage, while bringing such coverage into line with EU standards by 2002, thereby reducing moral hazard and promoting competition and discipline in the banking sector;[50]

- required banks to establish internal control and risk management systems, with market risk charges to be included in the calculation of the capital adequacy ratio in line with the Basle standards.[51]

The effectiveness of the new supervisory authority will, in particular, be enhanced by its independence from political influences (a major factor which hampered bank supervision in the past). Even so, a further strengthening of accounting standards may be warranted, to allow the new authority to undertake "prompt corrective actions" in order to prevent incipient bank problems from developing into insolvency. In particular, the consolidation of accounts may not be complete, and may need to include integration of accounts with related leasing companies and life insurance firms, while prudential standards will need to be toughened to include risk-adjusted capital adequacy ratios.

Once the framework conditions have been established, the reform seeks to guide the consolidation of the private sector ("second" phase). Following enactment of the banking law amendments at the end of 1999, the Saving Deposits

Insurance Fund (then under the Central Bank) launched a problem bank resolution operation by taking over five small insolvent banks, on top of the three that had been taken over previously. In October 2000, the new Banking Board authorised the take-over of two more mid-sized banks with weak financial structures, bringing the total number of banks controlled by the Fund to ten, representing 5 per cent of total banking sector assets. These banks' problems stemmed mainly from lending to related parties; losses from risky open and repo positions may also have played a role. Resolution of the bad bank problem has taken longer than hoped, however, and delay has been costly, as the troubled banks have been asked to carry on business, attracting high-interest deposits. The process has been less than fully transparent, especially insofar as carrying costs have not been made public. Criminal investigations into some of the banks in receivership have magnified uncertainties. The new Board has provided greater transparency in announcing that the total non-performing loans of the ten bailed-out banks amounts to $10.8 billion, while preparing an "action plan" for the rehabilitation of the ten banks. Concurrently, the government has prepared a draft corporate tax law allowing tax exemptions for mergers and acquisitions in the banking sector, so as to assist voluntary bank consolidation.

The third phase of reform will deal with the long-standing problem of the state banks. This will require developing and implementing strategic corporate plans, including plans for the operational, financial, and capital restructuring of the public banks, in preparation for their eventual privatisation. This restructuring should make state banks subject to competition, imparting stability to the banking sector. As noted in Chapter II, important steps have already been taken to stem the flow duty losses and to issue government bonds to compensate for 15 per cent of the outstanding ($20 billion) stock of duty losses. Over the medium term, the government plans to fully privatise three state banks, Halk, Emlak, and Ziraat Banks, as well as to divest its minority holding in Vakif Bank.[52] However, it is of some concern that the enabling legislation for privatisation has, at the time of writing, not yet been enacted, delaying World Bank approval of a $777 million Financial Sector Adjustment Loan. The privatisation of Ziraat may take longer because of its size and the complexity of its quasi-fiscal operations (besides extending subsidised credits, it also acts as a tax-collecting agency and banker for the government).

Social security reform

Pension and health reform

Budget reform requires addressing the glaring inefficiencies and distortions in the national social insurance system for pensions and health (see the 1999 Survey for a detailed discussion). A landmark social security reform bill was passed by Parliament in September 1999. The reform has two phases, short and medium term. The first involves the so-called "parametric" reforms to re-establish balance in the public PAYG system (Table 28), the changes being as follows:

- *Eligibility for retirement*: the imposition of a minimum retirement age, 58/60 for women/men for new entrants and 52/56 for current workers with a 10-year transition period; an increase in the minimum contribution period to 20-25 years for new entrants and 17 for current workers (from 14 years previously) with a 10 year transition.

- *Benefit determination*: a reduction in benefit accrual rates for the private sector schemes, averaging 3 per cent versus 4 per cent previously and declining steadily as the number of years worked increases; automatic indexing of pension benefits to the CPI, as opposed the discretionary formula of the past, which normally indexed to civil servants' wages.

- *Reference period for benefits*: an extension of the reference period for calculating pension benefits for the private sector schemes from a recent period to the full working history.

- *Contributions*: an increase in the ceiling on premiums from less than two times the "minimum pensionable wage"[53] to three times in January 2000, then to four times in August 2000, with the Council of Ministers authorised to increase it further to five times. The health insurance contribution rates for the self-employed and farmers were also increased.

The reform will prevent the severe deterioration in social security balances that would be expected on unchanged policies, from a deficit of 3 per cent of GNP in 1999 to some 16 per cent by 2050. However, it is not enough to eliminate system deficits or to prevent an eventual renewed deterioration. Figure 17 suggests that the deficit will steadily decline to 1 per cent by around 2015, but then rise again to around 6 per cent by 2050.[54] Part of this U-shaped pattern reflects that, in the near term, pension system balances will improve owing to the increase in the ceiling on contributions,[55] whereas in the more distant future, the same policy change must be reflected in higher benefit pay-outs. Further increases planned for 2001 and 2002 may be expected to accentuate this U-shaped pattern.

A higher contribution ceiling will help to maintain public pension incomes in light of the reductions in replacement rates and the longer reference period for benefits.[56] On the other hand, the reform may be going too far in this direction and in doing so runs up against serious drawbacks: *i)* it obviates the need for more fundamental reform by keeping the system "immature" through steady expansions of coverage; *ii)* it leaves less scope for contributions to a private funded pillar; and *iii)* it extends the regressive and high tax wedge to a more heavily populated part of the wage distribution, accentuating the high cost of labour and increasing the incentive to operate in the underground economy. The disincentive to stay within the formal system may be further aggravated by the rather sharp

Table 28. "Parametric reform" of the social security system
September 1999 reforms

Fund	Coverage	Contribution rate[1]		Eligibility for retirement		Reference period for benefits		Benefits determination for regular pension	
		Old	New	Old	New[2]	Old	New[3]	Old	New
Sosyal Sigortalar Kurumu (SSK)	Private-sector employees and public-sector workers except civil servants	33.5 *percent* 20 per cent for pensions; 12 per cent for health care; and 1.5 per cent for other benefits[2]	Unchanged	*Regular pension* 5 000 days (13.9 years) *Partial Pension* 3 600 days (10 years) if age 55 – men; 50 – women	Age: 58 Female 60 Male and *Regular Pension* 7 000 days (19.4 years) *Partial Pension* 12.5 years	Last 5 years for those paying at less than the contribution ceiling; last 10 years for those paying at the contribution ceiling	Full contribution period	60 per cent for 5 000 days plus 1 per cent for each additional 240 days	3.5 percent accrual rate for first 10 years; 2 per cent for next 15 years; 1.5 per cent for each additional year
Emekli Sandigi (ES)	Civil servants	35 *percent* combined for pensions and health care	Unchanged	25 years – men 20 years – women	58 Female 60 Male and 25 years	Last month's wage; last six months' wage if the worker has recently been promoted	Unchanged	75 per cent plus 1 per cent for each additional year	Unchanged
Bag-Kur	Self-employed urban workers and farmers	32 *percent* 20 per cent pensions; 15 per cent health care for self-employed; 15 per cent health care for farmers	35 percent 20 per cent pensions; 20 per cent health care	*Regular pension* 9 000 days (25 years) – men 7 200 days (20 years) – women *Alternative* 15 years if age 55 – men 50 – women	Age: 58 Female 60 Male and *Regular Pension* 9 000 days (25 years) *Partial Pension* 15 years	Last 1 year	Full contribution period	70 per cent plus 1 per cent for each additional year	3.5 percent accrual rate for first 10 years; 2 per cent for next 15 years; 1.5 per cent for each additional year

1. The wage on which contributions are based was previously capped at 1.8 times the minimum pensionable wage. Following the reform, the maximum contribution ceiling was raised to three times the statutory pensionable minimum wage in January 2000 and then to four times in August 2000.
2. For new entrants. Days (years) refers to the minimum contribution period. For current workers, there will be a 10-year transition period to the new eligibility requirements.
3. There is a transition to the new lifetime contribution base by means of a pro-rata system.
Source: IMF (1999); OECD.

Figure 17.   **Impact of social security reform**
Overall social security balances as a percentage of GNP

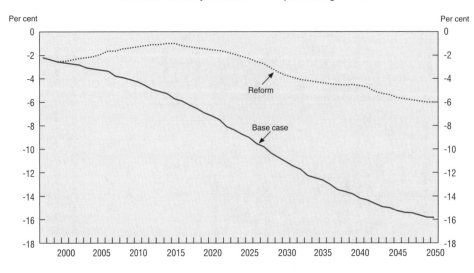

Source: World Bank (2000*b*).

drop in benefit accrual rates as the number of years worked increases (Table 28), in combination with the still-low minimum contribution periods. On the other hand, the switch to lifetime averaging should reduce abuses that had their counterpart in the black economy, so that the net effect of the reform is in this respect uncertain. Finally, the key reform – the minimum retirement age – is lower while the transition to it is longer, than recommended in last year's *Survey*. While this is probably the most that was politically feasible[57] – and indeed great progress has been made – it does mean that more reforms will be required later on (as substantiated by Figure 17).

The second and future phase is intended to implement a programme of administrative streamlining and institutional reforms of the social security system to improve coverage, efficiency, and transparency. Consistent with the recommendations made in the previous *Survey*, this envisages the integration of the social insurance functions of the three schemes under a single agency and a clear separation between pension, health, and unemployment insurance, with harmonisation of the contributions and benefits for each. Compliance should improve though better enforcement and management, in turn allowing a reduction of contribution arrears and thereafter, a cut in contribution premiums. However, no detailed action plan is yet available and it is not clear to what extent these efforts will be co-ordinated with the tax reform. The authorities also intend to introduce full health care coverage by means of a system of universal health insurance, although no detailed plans are yet available and the costs of the programme are not yet known. The latter might be considerable, given that a substantial part of the population is currently without insurance while demand for health care among the insured (currently less than adequate in rural regions) is likely to grow. This will – like other major gaps, *e.g.* in education – require further prioritisation of expenditures and increase in the tax base. In any event, reforms to the pension and health care systems will continue to be pressing policy needs.

A major challenge in the second phase remains the creation of a legal and regulatory framework for private pensions, which are needed in order to diversify the sources and risks of pension income, to improve (formal) labour market incentives, and to stimulate the development of the capital market. The authorities have prepared legislation for the introduction of privately-managed supplementary individual pension schemes, with expected enactment in 2000. However, further legislation will be needed to deal with tax treatment and prudential regulation of the new pension schemes. In this respect, the World Bank has recommended that the government undertake a broader view of tax benefits for financial investments in Turkey (including life insurance) which would correct distortions in the existing tax structure and make the private pension schemes more attractive. It should also be noted, though, that the still-high benefit accrual rates on public pensions, together with very significant growth in the contribution base, will not allow for much reduction in replacement rates, limiting incentives and means to put savings into a private scheme. The government should thus consider lowering contribution premia and accrual rates, while flattening the rates in order to reduce distortions in the labour market. Making the individual savings schemes mandatory should also be considered, in connection with a limited PAYG scheme (foregoing future planned increases in contribution ceilings).

Strengthening the social safety net

An unemployment insurance scheme was introduced in parallel with the social security reform, effective from June 2000. This is a compulsory scheme which covers private dependent workers[58] and mandates an additional social insurance contribution of 7 per cent of the pensionable wage – 3 per cent by the employer, 2 per cent each by the employee and government. Although the tax wedge will rise, the new charge replaces contributions to the mandatory savings scheme, which has been abolished.[59] After 20 months of contributions, workers will become eligible for unemployment benefits equivalent to 50 per cent of the average of the last four months' insurable net wages for a period of six months and benefits cannot exceed the minimum wage. The existing system of severance payments will be retained, however. This covers only workers hired under one year or longer contracts, and encourage firms to dismiss (mainly unskilled) workers before they attain sufficient seniority to qualify for benefits and later rehire them. The two schemes together have the potential to exacerbate such distortions and the implementation of the new scheme needs to be closely monitored from this perspective. Experience from other countries shows that, while a well designed UI scheme can increase labour participation in the formal sector;[60] the introduction of a poorly designed one would exacerbate the expected rise in unemployment. As far as the repercussions of the stabilisation and reform programme are concerned, the new UI scheme is unlikely to be of much help to groups which will be adversely affected, as it will require almost two years of contributions before pay-ing out benefits. Dealing with the distributional consequences of reform requires the development of a minimum social assistance scheme for vulnerable elements of the population, including a monitoring system to track the impacts of the reform programme on these groups. To be implemented quickly, this would require initial financing and technical expertise from donors such as the World Bank.[61]

Human capital development

Education policy

Previous *Surveys* have stressed the need to raise both the quantity and quality of schooling, in the process earmarking efficiency savings from structural reforms to raising health and education standards, especially for the poorest elements of society. Insufficient progress – even backtracking – has occurred in this regard. Macroeconomic crises and stabilisation attempts have tended to shrink the resources available for human development. Table 29 shows that between 1990 and 1996, public spending for education in Turkey shrank by nearly 15 per cent,[62] whereas that in Mexico and Portugal expanded by 40 to 50 per cent. The level of public education spending in 1997 ended up at just 2¾ per cent of GDP, only around 60 per cent that in countries like Hungary, Mexico, Korea and Spain. If an adjustment were made for the proportion of the population between five and nineteen, spend-ing would need to rise to 6 per cent of GDP, *i.e.* almost tripling, in order to match Korean levels. As with health, there is a severe gap in access to and quality of edu-cation services between urban and rural areas, so that the increase in the flow of resources to the latter would need to be much greater still.

Educational standards have improved in a longer term perspective. Table 30 shows that since 1980, Turkish literacy rates have increased markedly, though from relatively low levels while remaining quite low among older women. This in turn reflects that, over the past three decades, female enrolment rates increased to near 100 per cent in the compulsory years of primary schooling, and both female and male secondary school enrolment rates jumped (Figure 18). Turkey's catch-up process is now set to accelerate with the 1997 law to raise the number of years of compulsory education from five to eight. Implementation is virtually completed with enrolment rates of 90 to 100 per cent (depending on

Table 29. **Expenditure on education**

	Demographic indicators, percentage of the population, 1998 for OECD and 1997 for non-OECD, aged			Direct public expenditure, per cent of GDP,[1] 1997	Expenditure by resource category, per cent of total expenditure,[2] 1997		Change in public and private expenditure index, 1996, 1990 = 100[3]		
	5-14	15-19	20-29	1997	Current	Capital	Public	Private	Total
Turkey	21	11	19	2.7[4]	87	13	86[4]	136[4]	98[4]
Greece	11	7	15	3.5	87	13	..	..	..
Hungary	12	7	16	4.5	92	8	61	122	66
Italy	10	6	15	4.6	97	3	82		
Korea	14	9	18	4.4	86	14	..	..	..
Mexico	23	11	19	4.5	93	7	137	..	..
Portugal	12	7	16	5.8	95	5	147	..	..
Spain	11	7	17	4.7	95	5	119	154	124
Malaysia	23	10	18	4.4	89	11	..	..	..
Argentina	19	9	16	3.7	92	8	..	..	..
Brazil	22	11	18	4.8[5]	93[5]	7[5]	..	..	..
Chile	19	8	17	3.2	94	6	..	..	..

1. Educational expenditure for all levels of education combined.
2. Covers expenditure by public expenditure in primary, secondary and post-secondary non-tertiary education. For Korea, Portugal and Spain covers expenditure by public and private institutions. For Turkey, Greece, Argentina and Chile excludes post-secondary non-tertiary education.
3. Between 1990 and 1996. Covers all levels of education.
4. Estimated by splicing national series to latest (1995) OECD published data.
5. 1996 data.
Source: OECD, Education at a glance (various issues); data provided by Turkish authorities.

gender and region) registered for the twelve to fourteen age group in 1999. However, sufficient resources have not been allocated to match increased needs. As a result, classroom bottlenecks and teacher shortages have sharply worsened. The government intends to move eventually to twelve years of compulsory schooling, with preparations to be completed within five years, in line with EU standards. It will be essential not only that current bottlenecks be addressed before then, but also that a further build-up of capacity be allowed to prevent serious new bottlenecks from emerging. The university system needs to turn out many more high-quality teachers, especially in science and English-language areas, and enrolments should be encouraged by means of scholarships and better wages in the teaching profession. In addition, at the upper secondary level, there is a need to provide more vocational and technical qualifications for the labour market, with corresponding training programmes offered to adults with sufficient levels of basic education. These will be needed for the shift to higher technology and growth.

Table 30. **Estimated adult literacy rates**

1997, per cent

	Age 15 and over						Age 15-24					
	Total	1980 = 100	Male	1980 = 100	Female	1980 = 100	Total	1980 = 100	Male	1980 = 100	Female	1980 = 100
Turkey	83.4	127	92.5	114	74.1	149	95.6	112	98.4	104	92.7	123
Greece	96.7	107	98.3	102	95.2	111	99.7	101	99.7	101	99.8	101
Hungary	99.3	100	99.4	100	99.1	101	99.8					
Italy	98.3	102	98.8	102	97.8	103	99.8	100	99.8	100	99.8	100
Korea (1995)	96.9	104	98.8	102	95.0	107	100.0					
Mexico	90.4	109	92.6	107	88.4	111	96.5	104	97.2	104	95.8	105
Portugal	91.0	111	93.8	108	88.4	114	99.8	102	99.8	102	99.8	102
Spain	97.3	104	98.4	102	96.3	105	99.8	101	99.7	100	99.8	101
Malaysia	85.7	123	90.3	113	81.2	136	96.8	110	96.8	105	96.9	114
Lebanon	92.3	127	95.9	116	88.9	141	97.5	111	99.2	106	95.8	117
Argentina	96.6	103	96.6	102	96.5	103	98.5	102	98.3	102	98.7	102
Brazil	84.1	113	84.2	110	84.0	115	91.7	106	89.9	105	93.5	107
Chile	95.3	104	95.5	104	95.0	105	98.6	102	98.4	102	98.8	102

Source: UNESCO, *World Education Report*, 2000 and 1999 *Statistical Yearbook*.

Science and technology policy

Building on the foundation of a literate and adaptable workforce, Turkey's transformation into a high growth industrialising economy will require more rapid advances in the area of science and technology. Under conditions of global competition, science and technology are fundamental instruments for creating new industries, expanding existing ones, creating jobs and providing the higher wages that raise overall economic conditions and living standards. OECD studies have shown that government spending in the R&D area can bring significant externalities for industry in part by stimulating greater university-industry linkages, while R&D spending in the economy as a whole is an important determinant of growth performance.[63] However, the R&D intensity of Turkey's business sector is quite low in general. The OECD in 1995[64] recommended that general expenditures on R&D (at that time less than ½ per cent of GDP against an OECD average of 2½ per cent) be doubled within the next four or five years. However, as of 1999, the ratio was essentially unaltered (Table 31). If Turkey wishes to upgrade its product specialisation and raise multi-factor productivity, both business and government will need to invest more in innovation and R&D, both to develop new products and processes and also to help gain access to technologies being developed abroad.[65] The requirement to invest more in R&D must be accompanied by investment in the necessary education and skills, as outlined above.[66]

Figure 18. **Age-specific enrolment ratios**[1]
Per cent

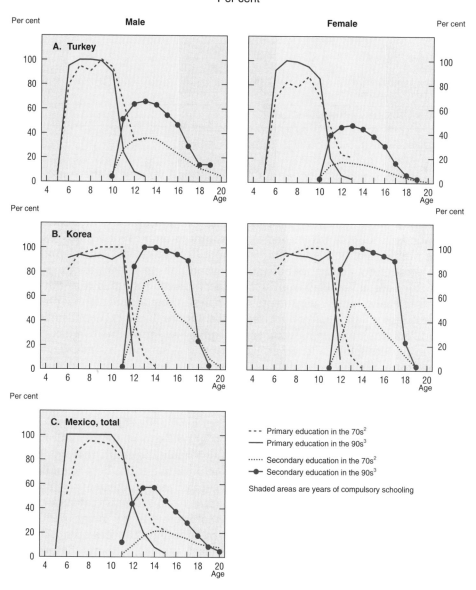

1. The age-specific enrolment ratios are measured by relating the enrolment of a given year to the population of
    the same age and year.
2. Turkey, 1973/74; Korea, 1972/73; Mexico 1970/71.
3. Turkey, 1994/95; Korea, 1995/96; Mexico 1993/94.
Source: UNESCO (1997), *Primary and Secondary Education: Age-Specific Enrolment Ratio, 1960-1996.*

Table 31. **R&D spending**

As a per cent of GDP

	Turkey		OECD	
	1993	1998	1993	1998
General spending on R&D	0.44	0.49	2.2	2.2
of which:				
Financed by business	0.14	0.20	1.3	1.4
Financed by government	0.29	0.26	0.77	0.68

Source: OECD, *Main Science and Technology Indicators.*

Turkey is well positioned for a technological take-off in the sense that it has under-utilised potential. Intellectual R&D capacity is underused, often due to lack of good equipment and poorly-paid and under-motivated technical personnel. The new public universities, being built at a very fast pace to meet increasing social needs, risk becoming second-rate institutions on present tendencies which include problems of both underfunding and politicised central control. And while Turkey possesses a number of outstanding institutions in science and technology – including several first-class universities, government institutes (*e.g.*, TÜBITAK), research-intensive industries, and research parks – there are substantial problems and weaknesses. The mission of these institutions has not been sufficiently clarified; linkages between industry and university research remains weak; R&D in software, biotechnology and other "new economy" services is underdeveloped and that for agriculture severely underdeveloped; and financing for innovation and entrepreneurial activity is largely missing.

An area of serious concern in Turkey is the "brain drain", as many good scientists leave for other countries, where they have better opportunities and are paid better. One way to tackle this problem might be to focus some public funding on so-called "centres of excellence" where high quality scientific research can be conducted. This makes staying in Turkey more attractive to the best scientists and is also more likely to be produce scientific research that of sufficient quality to be useful to Turkey. The evidence for other countries also suggests that such centres may be important to gain access to technologies that are being developed abroad. These might also attract private co-financing. The example of highly successful private not-for-profit universities (such as Bilkent) shows the potential role that private funding can play in alleviating public resource constraints in human capital development.

A summary of the progress being made under the government's structural reform programme along with recommendations for further steps is provided in Table 32.

Table 32. **Progress and recommendations on structural reforms**

Area/objective	Recent/planned action	Recommendations for further steps
A. Competition and product-market reform		
Agriculture		
Replace production-oriented support by targeted direct income scheme	Develop income-support scheme: Set up a pilot programme in 2000 to register farmers and distribute cash benefits; extend the results nation-wide during 2001–02	Implement as planned
	Phase out existing production support policies by 2002; move prices to world levels and reduce import tariffs	Compensation payments need to be fully transparent, with phase-outs
	Privatise ASCUs and SEEs, putting into force legislation passed in 2000	Convert privatised entities into research, marketing and educational facilities for farmers, close down non-viable ones
Energy		
Increase efficiency and capacity via privatisation and liberalised pricing and entry	Legal framework reforms in 1999/2000: key constitutional amendments permitting privatisation and international arbitration in 1999; laws establishing regulatory framework for electricity and gas sectors by end-2000	Regulatory/competition authorities will need to monitor privatisation process, ensuring adequate number of players to prevent emergence of collusive market structures
	Move to market model over medium-term: vertical unbundling of SEEs, private participation via transfer of operating rights, asset sales and BOT/BOO investments	Develop new alternatives to allow existing contracts with price/purchase guarantees to be made consistent with market model
	Financial recovery plans for State enterprises, TEAS, TEDAS, BOTAS	Greater SEE efficiency will require more competition in the sector (see above)
Telecommunications		
Privatisation of Turk Telecom (TT), open market for wireless and value-added services to private sector	Passage of Telecommunications Act in early 2000, splitting up and commercialising TT, establishing new legal and regulatory framework and setting timetable for move to market model over 4 years	Regulatory/Competition Authorities will need to monitor transition to market model; TT must reduce costs and realign prices; assure full competition in value-added services; Regulatory Authority could be given more power
	Sale of one of two GSM licences auctioned in early 2000; third license awarded to TT	Unsold second licence should be re-opened to ensure more competition

Table 32. **Progress and recommendations on structural reforms** (*cont.*)

Area/objective	Recent/planned action	Recommendations for further steps
State Economic Enterprises		
Privatise state companies in wide range of sectors (beyond energy and telecoms)	Sale of block share of TT to a strategic investor postponed in late 2000, pending a probable increase in size of share from 20 to 29-34 per cent; 14 per cent international IPO planned for 2001	Need to attach more management rights to minority private shareholders; consider removing majority government ownership in TT
	Current privatisation programme has following targets: 2000: $7.6 billion; $5.6 will probably be reached by end-2000;[1] 2001: $6 billion;[2] 2002: $4 billion[2]	Maintain balance between large and small-scale privatisations; give more attention to corporate governance (management rights) issues
Re-examine enterprises in Treasury portfolio	Regional development projects prepared for hard coal-producing areas	Impose hard budget constraints; give managers necessary scope and incentives to operate along commercial lines; consider closing down non-viable operations (with safety net); find other ways of meeting social objectives (transparent transfers or subsidies)
		Prepare other enterprises for eventual inclusion in PA portfolio
B. Financial sector adjustment		
Banking		
Bring supervisory, regulatory, and accounting framework in line with EU standards	Bank Act and Amendments of 1999 created new supervisory authority (BRSA) and independent board (BRSB), fully operational 1 September 2000	Ten problem banks need to be resolved
		Board must act independently and with full transparency about banking system problems
	New accounting standards (*e.g.* consolidated accounts) and prudential regulations	Complete the modernisation of accounting standards; consider integrated accounts between banks and related leasing and insurance companies; implement regulation of risk exposures (capital adequacy including market-risk and risk-management procedures)
	Total of ten problem banks transferred to the Savings Deposit Insurance Fund by October 2000	Sell or close problem banks quickly making carrying costs until such resolution transparent
	Plans to restructure and privatise state banks over medium term	Financial recovery plans, balance-sheet clean-ups (*e.g.* unpaid duty losses of Ziraat) are needed

Table 32. **Progress and recommendations on structural reforms** (*cont.*)

Area/objective	Recent/planned action	Recommendations for further steps
Capital markets Develop and deepen local capital markets	Introduction of primary dealers in early 2000	Allow sufficient opening of capital to public in SEE privatisations; allow holding of domestic equity in future private pension funds
		Develop venture capital arrangements for innovating small firms
C. Reform of social transfer policies		
Social security Make the public pension system solvent and complement it with a private pension scheme	Social security reform of September 1999: parametric reform of the PAYG system to restore balance	Contribution period should be increased further; eliminate drop in benefit accrual rate as working period lengthens; speed transition to new retirement age/contribution period
	Plans to raise contribution ceiling further to 5 times minimum pensionable wage	Consider replacing further ceiling increases with more fundamental reform (above) and quicker move to private pension leg (below)
	Reform of the Social Security Institutions in 2001-02, including separation of pension and health insurance and administrative streamlining	Address personnel and management incentive issues; consider co-ordinating with tax reform effort
	Creation of the legal framework for private pensions	Favourable tax incentives and regulation to both address prudential concerns and allow scope for well-diversified portfolios
Health care Move to system of universal healthcare insurance	Social security bill included some increases in health insurance premia and new co-payments	Legislation for universal health care needs to be drafted and put to Parliament; improve facilities and access for rural poor
	Building of a national healthcare database has started	Continue upgrading health database, use it to define best practices and control costs
D. Improving labour markets and developing human capital Build unemployment insurance scheme	Social security bill introduced an unemployment insurance scheme as of mid-2000	Maintain strict time limit (6 months) on receipt of UI benefits; eliminate present distortionary system of severance payments
		Monitor social impacts of reforms through surveys and other studies

Table 32. **Progress and recommendations on structural reforms** (*cont.*)

Area/objective	Recent/planned action	Recommendations for further steps
Raise demand for and supply of labour in the formal sector	Above reforms of product markets and social insurance will help to achieve this goal	Work on eliminating work-place and socio-cultural biases against women
Raise human capital	Compulsory schooling will be raised from 8 to 12 years, with preparations to be completed by 2005	At least double public education spending as share of GDP; targeting rural poor; increase quantity and quality of teacher training; increase vocational and technical skills training at secondary level; develop adult education programmes to reduce illiteracy and teach skills
Increase multi-factor productivity growth		At least double R&D spending by government as share of GDP; focus some public funding on "centres of excellence" where high-quality scientific research can be conducted
		Better and new forms of funding of public universities, with more decentralised control attract private co-financing of higher education
E. Making the policy-making process more transparent		
Build internal evaluation and adjustment mechanisms into the reform	Budget reforms of 2000 to improve fiscal transparency	Develop multi-year budgeting capability; continue to increase transparency in all aspects of government as the country moves towards EU accession status
Improve the social consensus for reforms	Re-convening of Social and Economic Council	Need to engage unions in more constructive role by "selling" benefits of reform

1. Information from PA.
2. Letter of intent.
Source: OECD.

IV. Policy implications of the 1999 earthquakes

In August 1999 the Marmara area of Turkey was hit by a severe earthquake and this was followed by a further large shock in the Bolu area in November. The earthquakes struck an economy facing severe macroeconomic and structural policy challenges, with implications for both. The affected area constitutes the industrial heartland of Turkey and the associated economic and financial shock has had to be absorbed at the same time as the country is undergoing a major disinflation programme and associated structural reform process. In the event, as the previous chapter has shown, the policy issues highlighted by earthquakes, in conjunction with the target of sealing eventual EU accession status, have offered an opportunity to accelerate and reinforce the impetus to reform. More fundamentally, Turkey's vulnerability to earthquake damage, along a known active fault line, has direct implications for the modernisation process by underlining the need to correct the factors which have contributed to an exaggerated toll in terms of mortality and material damage. This vulnerability may be linked to the nature of Turkish economic development in recent decades, which has been based on the need to assimilate a mass migration from the countryside to the cities: a process which has been informal rather than rules-based. This needs to be superseded by a more orderly system of development, which requires not just an overhaul of governance structures, including better central-local co-ordination and urban planning procedures, but also the introduction of financial market mechanisms for assessing and controlling risks.

In the light of the above, the aim of this chapter is to draw out the implications of the 1999 earthquakes and of Turkey's susceptibility to high rates of material damage, especially to residential infrastructure, for the budgetary and structural policy reform issues discussed in the previous chapters. The chapter has the following structure. The first section presents the general factual background, including geological characteristics and impact effects of the earthquake. The second section investigates the economic and budgetary costs of the earthquakes and their implications for economic growth and the budget. Understanding such costs is necessary for near-term budget planning and the longer-term re-allocation of national resources. The third section describes the regulatory and governance factors behind the country's vulnerability to heavy earthquake damage, including factors related to building codes and zoning requirements. Co-ordinating central and local government roles here is obviously essential. But achieving the ultimate goal of damage minimisation also implies changing private-sector behaviour and culture through a combination of education, regulatory reform and private incentives. In this context the fourth section looks at the policy issues surrounding better private sector risk management, through the development of the insurance and mortgage markets. The final section contains an assessment of the catastrophe, and the main lessons it holds for enhanced disaster preparedness.

Background

Geological background to the earthquakes

The earthquakes struck western Turkey on one of the world's longest and best-recorded strike- slip (horizontal motion) faults: the east-west trending North Anatolian fault. This fault is very similar to the San Andreas fault (Map 1), which has led to active scientific collaborations between scientists in Turkey and the US aimed at understanding the hazards both countries face.

Turkey has a long history of large earthquakes, which have occurred in progressive adjacent historical phases. The August 1999 event was the eleventh, with a magnitude greater than or equal to 6.7, of a sequence of major earthquakes which started in 1939. By 1944 the earthquake locations had moved westward, rupturing 600 km of contiguous fault. An additional adjacent 100 km of fault then ruptured in the events of 1957 and 1967. The August and November 1999 events filled in a 100 to 150 km long gap between the 1967 event and two smaller disturbances which took place further west during 1963-64 (Map 2). The severity of the first, magnitude 7.4, earthquake is underlined by the fact that there was as much as five metres of horizontal fault slip and two metres of vertical slip. Geologists now expect that Southern Istanbul will, with very high probability, experience an event with significantly larger intensity of ground shaking than in the Marmara, within at most 30 years and probably within the next decade.

Despite the fact that the epicentre of successive earthquakes seems to be moving westward along the North Anatolian fault with a high degree of regularity, a comprehensive national study of disaster risk is currently unavailable. The scientific study of the geological fault lines in Turkey has only been undertaken in recent decades and geological surveys conducted by professionals who follow established international practice apparently exist for certain localities only. Geological mapping has suffered from a lack of coherent direction, unreliable compilation, inadequate financing, and a shortage of trained personnel. A national assessment of areas of risk has been undertaken using proxy data, including the recorded levels of earthquake frequency and intensity in recent decades. This

Map 1. **Comparison of the North Anatolian and San Andreas Faults**

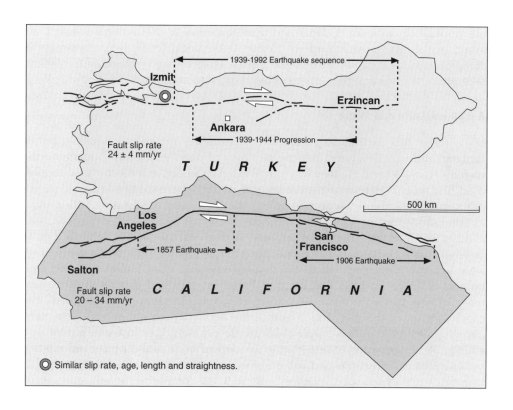

Map 2. **The known faults**

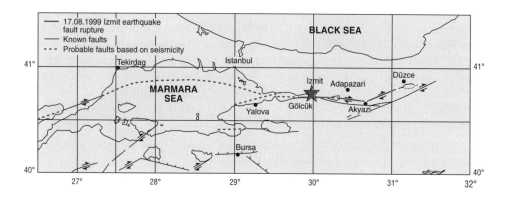

generated a 1996 map by the Ministry of Public Works, which divides the country into five zones. This division is not detailed enough to distribute insurable risks (except over entire regions) or determine land use plans, although more than half the population, numerous dams and three-quarters of the nation's industry are found in the two most hazardous zones. At the local level, risk assessment is compromised by a gap in coverage at a scale large enough (minimum 1: 1 000) to take property lines and the outline of buildings into account.

A high mortality and injury rate

The two earthquakes caused considerable damage to housing, public facilities and infrastructures, but the numbers of dead and injured dominate the tragedy (Table 33 and Figure 19). Over 18 thousand people are estimated to have died, and around 50 thousand were injured, of which perhaps two-fifths will be left permanently disabled. Large portions of the area were devastated, with around 113 thousand housing units and business premises completely destroyed, and another 264 thousand damaged to varying degrees. Numerous schools, health facilities, roads, bridges, water pipes, power lines, phone lines, and gas pipelines were severely damaged. Up to 600 thousand people were forced to leave their homes, of which perhaps half became homeless and had to stay in tents, and many of the survivors, especially children, were left deeply traumatised. The characteristics of this population and of the survivors are not known: how many parents lost children, how many children are orphaned, or lost one parent or a sibling, etc. Information of this kind is needed to understand better the relation between the constructions and vulnerability (e.g., what types of household tend to live on what types of structure), as well as long-term health and social welfare costs.

As in any natural disaster, the level of the earthquake's destructiveness reflected not only the intensity of the shock, but also the vulnerability of structures subjected to this shock. The maximum intensities of ground shaking in Turkey were less than what was recorded in the earthquakes in Northridge, California in 1994, and Kobe, Japan in 1995, yet the loss of human life was at least an order of magnitude higher.[67] Since population density was similar, this reveals the far higher vulnerability of structures in Turkey. Surface fault opening, ground shaking, and soil-liquefaction caused structural damage that was dramatically exacerbated by poor construction quality. Expert evaluations of the post-earthquake devastation confirm that much of it could have been avoided with proper siting and construction practices (Box 9).

In most other OECD economies, good construction techniques, enforcement, land use planning and emergency planning usually mean that injuries and deaths are low, while property losses can be very significant. Property losses have been rising throughout the 1990s, at least in part because natural disasters in

Table 33. **Major disasters in OECD countries with implications for regional development**

Date	Place	Agent	Deaths	Damage cost	Additional comments
1906	San Francisco	Earthquake	2 000	$6 billion in 1987; $500 million in 1906	
1908	Messina, Italy	Earthquake	150 000		
1923	Kanto Plain, Japan (Tokyo)	Earthquake	140 000 +		
1939	Erzincan, Turkey	Earthquake	32 000		230 000 homeless
19-20 September 1985	Mexico City, Mexico	Earthquake	7 000 +	$4 billion	40 000 injured 30 000+ homeless. General hospital collapsed, burying 600 staff, patients, widespread *ad-hoc*, collective solidarity efforts. Reconstruction fostered outer-edge development at expense of city centre
10-17 September 1988	Gulf of Mexico	Hurricane Gilbert		In US, $10 billion In Mexico, $880 million	400 000 homeless in Mexico
15 September 1989	Texas	Hurricane Hugo		$5 billion	
7 October 1989	California (Loma Prieta)	Earthquake	61	$7 billion	Collapse of Cypress Freeway in Oakland
28 December 1989	Newcastle NSW, Australia	Earthquake	12	Australian $1 billion	Reconstruction to take 5 to 10 years; 10 000 houses damaged in city of 300 000 people
1990	Sicily	Earthquake	20 +	$10 to 15 billion	
25 January-26 February 1990	NW Europe	Storms, Gales, Daria, Vivian	120	$10.5 billion	
13 March 1992	Erzincan, Turkey	Earthquake	540	$1.5 billion	180 000 homeless, 3 850 injured
23-26 Aug. 1992	Florida	Hurricane Andrew	34	$16 to 30 billion	Reconstruction changed socio-economic structure of many south Florida communities; greater segregation and polarisation by income, race, ethnicity

Table 33.   **Major disasters in OECD countries with implications for regional development** *(cont.)*

Date	Place	Agent	Deaths	Damage cost	Additional comments
July-August 1993	Midwest, US: Mississippi Valley	Flooding	50	$12 billion	100 000 evacuated; 150 000 homeless; 40 000 business or homes damaged or lost; changes afterward in settlement pattern
17 January 1994	Northridge, CA	Earthquake	56	$30 billion	25 000 homeless; 8 500 injured thousands without water or power; Major disruption to highway system (detours cost $1 million/day in congestion, accidents)
17 January 1995	Kobe, Japan	Earthquake	6 000 +	$100 billion (+)	Massive devastation to port city, trade disrupted. 50 000 injured, 300 000 homeless. City rebuilt with new infrastructure for economic activities, social integration, disaster preparedness
February 1995	NW Europe	Flooding	40 +	$3 billion	250 000 evacuated. Flooding raised questions about land-use changes and planning practices, which increased vulnerability and intensity. Worst storms in the Netherlands since 1953, after which the Dutch initiated a major civil engineering project of protection. In 1953, 2 000 drowned, 300 000 displaced people
7-10 October 1997	Mexico	Hurricane Pauline	230 +	$100 million insured value	50 000 Homeless. Worst affected were Acapulco, Guerrero, Oaxaca
17 August 1999	Izmit, Turkey	Earthquake	18 000 +	$5 to 14 billion	50 000 injured; 600 000 homeless. Death and damage include impact of second shock on 12 November 1999 in Bolu province
26 December 1999	France	Wind storm	80-90	$8 to 10 billion	Major damage to electricity distribution network, railroads and forestry industry

Notes: All dollars ($) are US$ unless otherwise stated.
        Major emerging risks:
          • Urbanisation in coastal zones.
          • Increasing gap between value of losses and insurance cover.
          • Lack of capacity to plan for reconstruction within a strategic vision for regional development.
Source: OECD.

Figure 19.   **The extent of the damage**[1]

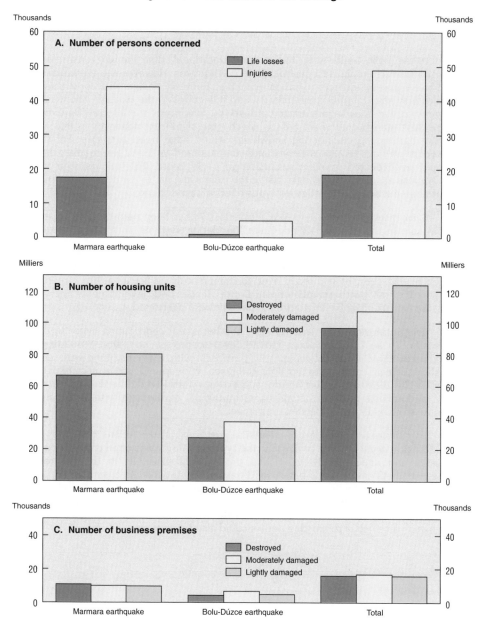

1.   Excluding infrastructure.
Source: Turkish authorities.

Box 9. **Engineering, construction and siting errors
in the earthquake zone**

In the past, builders in Turkey used traditional, time-proven construction
methods which minimised destruction in earthquakes. However, the earthquakes
revealed several defects in urban planning, building design and construction
which may have amplified the material and human toll of the disaster. The resulting loss of life is especially tragic because the majority of the affected buildings
were less than twenty years old, by which time significant advances in international earthquake engineering knowledge would have been available. For the
30 years previous to August 1999, Turkey had suffered far fewer earthquakes than
would be expected from its seismological track record. This lull reduced the
awareness of seismological risks just at the time when huge numbers of buildings
were being erected. The following types of error were common:

Siting on liquefiable soils: large-scale urbanisation has been permitted on liquefiable soil. In the absence of adequate foundation systems, this was a primary
cause of the destruction in cities like Adapazari.

Siting on the fault line: many other structures were also destroyed by virtue of
their having been built directly over, or immediately adjacent to, the ruptured
segment of the North Anatolian Fault. Entire villages and developments (including the Gölcük naval base) straddling the fault were destroyed.

Construction engineering problems were another major contributing factor to the
disaster. These included weak ground level stories of multi-storey buildings,
related to their usage for commercial purposes, with fewer retaining walls and
higher ceilings, causing ground floor collapses. Widespread use of unreinforced
hollow clay tiles to construct interior and exterior walls had deleterious effects on
the performance of the structural frame during the earthquake, with an ensuing
failure to provide adequate shear resistance.

Poor construction materials and construction errors: visual inspections of collapsed
buildings suggest that the concrete in the typical building was often of a very poor
quality and unacceptably weak. The presence of seashells in the concrete
suggests that contaminated beach sand was used in the mix. Also, smooth (unde-
formed) steel reinforcing was used; causing degradation of the bond between the
concrete and the steel reinforcing, which is not permitted in much of the world
especially in construction expected to withstand the shock of an earthquake. Poor
or incomplete use of reinforcing details could also be observed.

Source: Wiss, Janney, Elstner Associates, Inc. (1999); BBC *Science News* (15 November 1999).

highly urbanised regions have been more frequent and more intense. In both developed and developing countries, some social groups, and especially the poor, are most at risk, their exposure often being a function of the location and quality of housing. However, most of the people affected in the Turkish earthquakes were not the poor but the middle class. The earthquakes occurred in a fast-growing region with high per capita incomes, and where population growth had been managed through the construction of multi-storey housing which had replaced traditional buildings. The ratio of numbers of deaths to numbers of houses destroyed in August (over 17 000 deaths and over 60 000 houses destroyed) is exceptional when compared to other earthquakes in OECD Member countries (Table 33).

... and an initially difficult relief effort

A contributory factor in the heavy loss of human life may have been the difficulties in mounting a timely and effective official emergency response to the first earthquake. To a large extent, this was due to the fact that it struck at 3 a.m. in a heavily populated and large area. Many people were asleep and trapped inside collapsed buildings, including the officials responsible for implementing emergency response efforts.[68] Emergency response resources were largely destroyed or damaged. In the critical first hours, rescue efforts were provided by on-site survivors mobilising themselves in an *ad hoc* way. Telecommunications, transport, and electricity infrastructures were severely damaged by the earthquake and initially overwhelmed by outsiders trying to phone or drive to the region.[69] This in turn prevented the arrival of civil defence rescue units and medical teams (dispatched by Ankara) until early evening. Even after arrival, the lack of non-telephone communications (radios) hampered the effectiveness of the rescuers. Full telecommunications and electric power was restored only two to three days after the earthquake.[70]

Economic impact of the disaster

Sectoral impacts

The region affected by the earthquake is both geographically extensive and economically dynamic. It forms the industrial heartland of Turkey. The major industries are autos, petrochemicals, manufacturing and repair of motor (and railway) vehicles, basic metals, production and weaving of synthetic fibres and yarns, paint and lacquer production, and tourism.[71] The four districts most severely affected (Kocaeli, Sakarya, Bolu and Yalova) contribute over 7 per cent of the country's GDP and 14 per cent of industrial value added (Table 34). Per capita income is almost double the national average. Though containing only 4 per cent of the nation's population, the region contributes over 16 per cent of budget revenues. The immediately surrounding districts (of Bursa, Eskisehir, and Istanbul) have been

Table 34. **Selected indicators for the earthquake region**[1]

	Population	Share in GDP	Share in industrial value added	Per capita income	Share in budget tax revenues	Share in bank deposits	Share in banking credits
	Thousands	Per cent		US$	Per cent		
Kocaeli	1 177	4.8	11.3	7 845	15.8	1.4	0.9
Sakarya	732	1.1	1.1	2 734	0.4	0.5	0.2
Yalova	164	0.4	0.7	4 966	0.1	0.2	0.1
Bolu	553	0.9	0.7	3 104	0.3	0.3	0.2
Bursa	1 959	3.5	5.0	3 434	3.0	2.4	3.2
Eskisehir	661	1.2	1.1	3 335	0.8	0.7	0.7
Istanbul	9 199	22.8	26.8	4 728	37.5	44.1	41.0
Kocaeli + Sakarya + Yalova + Bolu	2 626	7.2	13.8	5 243	16.6	2.4	1.4
Total of 7 Cities	14 444	34.7	46.7	4 581	58.0	49.6	46.3
Turkey	62 866	100.0	100.0	3 031	100.0	100.0	100.0

1. 1997 or 1998.
Source: Turkish authorities.

mainly affected indirectly by their close economic linkages with the former area, *e.g.*, industries and small businesses supplying services or material inputs to each other's production processes. They also are subject to a shared seismic risk and so face magnified uncertainty for the future as a fall-out of the recent events. Taking all seven cities together, the wider earthquake region accounts for 35 per cent of national GDP and almost half of the nation's industrial output.

Damage to economic infrastructure

Heavy damage was sustained in the energy, transport, and communications sectors. In electricity, an estimated 3 400 distribution towers and 490 km of overhead lines were damaged or destroyed, and there was extensive damage to underground cable lines. Oil and gas production facilities suffered extensive damage, though the fiscal cost has been held down by insurance coverage of fire damage to the Tüpras oil refinery. Modest oil and gas pipeline damage was sustained to municipal distribution systems, and there were clean-up costs due to oil and chemicals discharged into the Sea of Marmara. Telecommunications damage included ruptured transmission lines, station damages, buildings and network facilities. Office buildings, water pipes and supplies, wastewater treatment, sewerage systems and other structures accounted for additional damage to municipal infrastructure.

Damage to the transport infrastructure included 60 km of the Ankara-Istanbul highway, the Gebze-Izmit-Arifiye railroad, the railcar factory in Adapazari and rolling stock, Derince Harbour, local streets and provincial highways. Traffic on the railway and motorway connections between Istanbul and Ankara was restored quite quickly. Damage to the industrial facilities and port or jetty structures located along the northern shores of the Gulf of Izmit was concentrated and varied from small displacements to settlement and total collapse. With immediate inter- vention, a large part of these infrastructure facilities were soon serviceable again. However, SPO estimates that at least $500 million will be needed both to repair damage and to meet the infrastructure requirements of new construction, without counting the cost of relocating cities.

Effects on the enterprise sector

Private and public sector estimates of the damage to the enterprise sector as a whole range from $1.1 to $4.5 billion (Table 35 below). The agricultural sector suffered little damage (SPO estimates $25 million in financing needs in the sector). In manufacturing, damage to large enterprises was lighter than in smaller enterprises, though by no means trivial (SPO estimates an $880 million total loss just for the 19 affected state-owned enterprises in the region). Human capital losses sustained by industry have been more serious, but harder to estimate. Besides immediate disruptions to labour supply due to deaths, injuries, and trauma, SMEs and large enterprises in the region are concerned about possible out-migration of qualified employees. Consequently, many of the larger enter- prises are participating in the provision of shelter, care, and housing for their employees, which appears to have persuaded many to stay in the area. The tourism industry (based in Yalova) has been virtually destroyed and tourists may not return for many years, so that a fundamental restructuring will be needed.

Microenterprises (retail shops, artisan workshops, and services employing up to ten people) suffered the most, losing most of their working capital and premises (often situated on the ground floors of collapsed buildings, see Box 9), and key family workers. They accounted for the major part of the more than 15 000 destroyed and nearly 31 000 damaged business premises (Figure 19). Smaller firms were also hurt by close economic linkages with larger firms.

The government has attempted to help businesses in two ways. First, it has announced the deferral of all tax payments for individuals and businesses living in the earthquake area. A substantial part of these deferred payments may never be recovered, due to the large-scale loss of tax records. Second, a debt rescheduling and new subsidised credit programme via the state banks has been introduced to support particularly hard-hit businesses and individuals (see below). Nevertheless, the World Bank estimates that 50 per cent of self- and SME employment in the region will be lost permanently.

Burden on the financial sector

Insurance coverage among small enterprises and in the housing sector is very limited. Payments of claims are estimated to have amounted to $750 million.

The bulk (95 per cent) of these losses have been covered by international reinsurers, entailing an upward adjustment in reinsurance premia though probably not affecting the availability of coverage (in part reflecting over-capacity in the international reinsurance industry). Given the dependence on foreign reinsurers, claims processing has been subject to some months of delay, resulting in liquidity constraints for insured businesses facing major repair and replacement costs. It does not appear that banks were willing to provide bridge financing.

In the banking sector, the emergence of bad loans due to uninsured earthquake losses constitutes a concern. The direct exposure (cash loans outstanding) of banks in the region has been estimated to be about $733 million, of which $119 million is held by public banks and the remainder by private banks.[72] The World Bank estimates that roughly one-third of such outstanding loans could be directly affected by the earthquake, which could in turn lead to defaults and affect capital adequacy of the system – itself coming under closer scrutiny in the context of banking sector reform.

According to a government decree of 28 August 1999, the outstanding debts to Ziraat, Halk and Emlak banks owed by individuals or firms (in the seven cities of the broader region) who have sustained serious damage from the earthquake can be deferred for three years, with grace period of one year for both principal and interest, the latter being set generally at half the current interest rate. New subsidised loans would also be made available to the same applicants, including working capital loans for up to one year, and investment loans up to five years with a grace period of one year for both principal and interest.[73] However, applications for both reschedulings and new loans under the scheme amounted to merely $56 million and $42 million, respectively, i.e. well below the amount of known damage. Along with the decline of market interest rates to below the subsidised lending rates in early 2000, this means that the implied addition to state banks' duty losses will have been minor, but also that the financial help to stricken enterprises will be limited. This could reflect some problems with the design of the subsidised credit scheme. Only applicants who filed for the scheme within three months after the earthquake were considered. Also, it is not clear that the system of independent verification of damage by provincial commissions was rigorous and transparent enough. Scarce public resources might not have been directed to those most in need, particularly small and micro businesses who have fewer personal connections and access to public banks. Indeed, small businesses in the region complain that they are not able to obtain credit to proceed with restructuring. For these firms, access to credit is at least as big a problem as its cost (Chapter III).

Aggregate economic costs of the disaster

Several assessments of the earthquake's aggregate macroeconomic impact have been made, notably by the World Bank, the State Planning

Organisation, and the Turkish Businessmen's Association (TÜSIAD), shown in Table 35. They are based on different methodologies, which makes comparisons difficult but nonetheless allows for a range of plausible quantification. Also, for the most part the estimates were made in the month following the earthquake, when information was still sparse while the effects of the devastating second shock to the Bolu region on 12 November were not factored in. Figure 19 suggests that additional costs of perhaps 50 per cent might be implied by the Bolu shock. Subject to these caveats, the results of these studies suggest the following possible magnitudes of macroeconomic impact:

- Wealth and income losses range from $5 to $14 billion. Destruction of physical capital accounts for the greater part, $3 to over $10 billion, of which housing and enterprise sectors each account for roughly 40 to

Table 35. **Macroeconomic costs of the earthquake**

US$ billion

	TÜSIAD[1]	SPO[2]	World Bank[3]
Direct costs	**10**	**6.6 to 10.6**	**3.1 to 6.5**
Housing	4	3.5 to 5	1.1 to 3
Enterprises	4.5	2.5 to 4.5	1.1 to 2.6
Infrastructure	1.5	0.5 to 1	0.9
Indirect costs	**2.8**	**2 to 2.5**	**1.8 to 2.6**
Value-added loss	2	2 to 2.5	1.2 to 2
Emergency relief expenditures	0.8	. .	0.6
Total damage costs (rounded)	**13**	**9 to 13**	**5 to 9**
Secondary effects			
Current account losses	2	. .	3
Fiscal costs	2	5.9	3.6 to 4.6
Job losses (per cent of labour force in the region)	. .	. .	20 to 50%

1. TÜSIAD first estimated the value of the loss of national wealth by surveys of its members and in co-operation with SPO. It then estimated the associated loss of national income by assuming that economic activity in the region came to a halt for two to three months (with about $50 million lost each day), due not only to loss of physical capacity, but also employee absenteeism, lack of water and energy, supply shortages and transportation difficulties, which depressed overall output regionally as well as nationally.
2. SPO estimated wealth losses on the basis of information given to the government from various sources (including a physical count of destroyed properties) and preliminary estimations based on certain assumptions.
3. The World Bank used an enumerative technique to estimate physical damages (on-site inspections by Bank staff). The GNP impacts are estimated by: a) assuming that the percentage of value added lost due to disruptions to industry and services in the four most severely affected regions is 50, 30, 15, and 8 per cent in 1999 Q3 to 2000 Q2, respectively; b) further assuming that one-third of the disruptions in the first two quarters are offset by increased economic activity in other areas; c) multiplying the net disruption by the weight of the region (7.2 per cent) in national value added.

Source: TÜSIAD (Turkish Industrialisation and Businessmen's Association), "Economic Impact of the Turkish Earthquake", 1 September 1999; SPO (State Planning Organisation), "The Impact of the Turkish Earthquake on the Turkish Economy (A Brief Assessment)", 23 September 1999; World Bank (1999b); and OECD staff estimates.

50 per cent, and infrastructure the remainder. The greatest uncertainty in these estimates (*i.e.*, the widest ranges) appears to lie in the extent of damage to the enterprise sector (particularly to small and micro businesses). The associated income losses range from ½ to 3 per cent of GDP, affecting mainly 1999 and including not only the loss of output due to supply and demand disruptions, but also the cost of emergency relief – a "dead-weight cost" which does not replace damaged structures but diverts resources from other uses all the same.

– Job losses could range from 20 to as much as 50 per cent of the pre-earthquake labour force in the affected region, due to both damage to business premises (demand side) and loss of life and health and out-migration (supply side). Most of these job losses are concentrated in self-employed and small business jobs, of which in turn a large proportion is expected to be semi-permanent.

– Growth in 1999 may have been up to 1 percentage point lower than the SPO baseline (Figure 20), reflecting disruptions to both supply (loss of physical capital and labour force) and demand (loss of inventories, temporarily depressed consumption and investment activity, interrupted input-output linkages across firms) – albeit offset to some extent by the mobilisation of spare capacity in the rest of the country. Initially, these impacts were expected to result in a 2 to 2½ per cent point drop in final GDP. However, the official estimates for 1999 indicate a drop of 5 per cent, suggesting that either the estimates of the earthquake impacts were too optimistic, or that the recession deepened by more than had been initially anticipated (*i.e.*, worsening the baseline). In 2000, by contrast, growth may be up to 1½ points above baseline due to the demand effects of the reconstruction effort which gets underway in that year.

– Inflationary effects will be small or negligible, as substantial excess capacity in the wider economy, together with imports, should diffuse any excess demand pressure arising from the reconstruction. Thus, the government does not consider that the reconstruction poses any risks to the disinflation programme. Even so, price pressure in housing and pockets of the construction materials industry cannot be excluded, as existing spare capacity may not well match the areas of excess demand.

Social costs of the disaster: shelter, social infrastructure and rebuilding needs

Mitigating the displacement of the population by temporary shelter

With around 330 000 housing units destroyed or damaged by the earthquake, about 600 000 people were forced to find emergency shelter. They had three options: *i)* shelter with friends or relatives, *ii)* move to an undamaged second

Figure 20.   **Earthquake impacts on major macroeconomic variables**

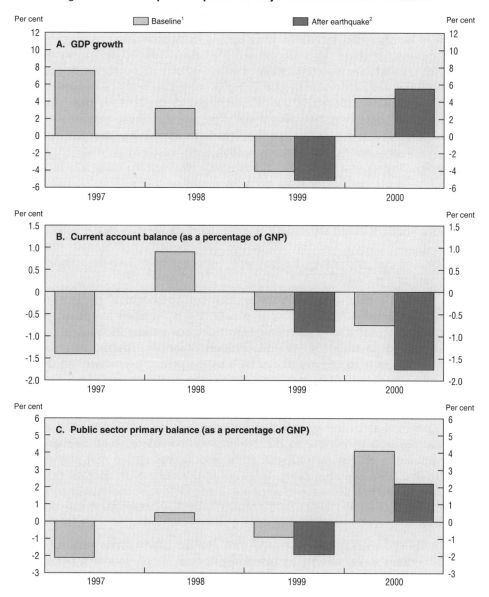

1.   "Baseline" calculated as "After earthquake" less estimated earthquake impacts. GDP growth and current account
     impacts taken from World Bank Marmara earthquake assesment report, while public sector primary balance
     impact is taken from SPO official estimates.
2.   "After earthquake" denotes realisations and official targets for the years 1999 and 2000 respectively.
Source: World Bank, IMF and SPO.

home or rent accommodation, and *iii*) tent shelter in organised camps (more likely for people whose homes were demolished), or in the neighbourhood of the damaged but usually still-standing house.[74] The latter option could also involve the use of vacant public buildings. Only people in category *iii*) were considered to be "homeless": of these, by 1 December 1999, about 200 000 people were registered in 121 tent communities, while another 80 000 to perhaps 200 000 were estimated (by various sources) to be living in individual tents or in public buildings. By implication, at least 200 000 people opted for shelter with friends or alternative second-home or rented accommodation; many of these moved out of the region. Those who chose not to live in a tent town received a "rent allowance" of about $175 per month, on condition that their house was mid- to heavily damaged. However, the cash value of assistance received in camps was far higher – including free health care, food, cooking, clothing, counselling, skills training, schooling, and pocket money – which provided a strong incentive to go there rather than accept the rent allowance, especially for those from the lower economic strata. It could be argued that the large gap between the value of the benefit-in-kind option and the alternative cash benefit, in essence, restricted peoples' choices, including the decision to out-migrate, while making them dependent on the state.[75]

With the cold and damp winter weather approaching, the government decided early on that tents had to be substituted by sturdier temporary accommodations. The search for a solution generated much internal debate. In the end, it was decided to build 30 772 prefabricated homes by public means, while another 10 696 were to be funded and built by the private sector. With an average household size of four, these prefabs were able to house around 165 000 people, so that the units had to be rationed. The cost of a 2-unit prefab (each 30 m^2 unit fully equipped) was $3 300,[76] rising to around $5 000 inclusive of infrastructure costs. Construction of the units was completed by end-November 1999, and by end-year the shift of people to the prefabs was complete. Tent dwellers were given the choice of moving into such a house or accepting the rent allowance in order to find their own arrangements, either in the same or in another city. As of April 2000, around 65 000 people were still living in 54 tent communities, while a total of 300 000 to 400 000 people (100 000 families) were receiving the rent allowance.

Besides assistance associated with shelter, government sought to help people in other ways, notably by extending special social insurance benefits for earthquake victims, insured and uninsured alike. An "earthquake amendment" to the new pension law has reduced the period of mandatory contributions in order for insured members and their dependants to be eligible for death and disability benefit, to just one year (with Treasury covering the shortfall in minimum contributions from the normal four years). This affects mainly monthly payments to dependants of deceased breadwinners as well as disability payments to insured members.[77] The law also provided for the following lump sum payments to be paid regardless of length of service or wage earned: $1 500 for each lost direct relative, and $1 000 for each second degree relative. Financial help was further given in the form of a deferral of all taxes until 2000. Finally, the government has provided extra community services, such as orphanages, child-care facilities, elderly accommodations, and training centres.

Longer-term housing replacement obligations

The latest estimates of the Ministry of Public Works (MPW) indicate that nearly 97 thousand houses were completely destroyed and over 231 thousand damaged, of which 107 thousand moderately and 124 thousand lightly (Table 36). According to the provisions of the (former) Disaster Law, the government is responsible for replacement of destroyed stock and rehabilitation of lightly to moderately damaged stock, though only owner-occupied primary residences are eligible for this guarantee. The World Bank estimates that 55 to 75 per cent of the affected units might satisfy the government criteria.[78] The public cost of replacing a destroyed house is approximately $20 000 (not including land acquisition costs), covering a modest (80 m^2) apartment construction of standard design and location. The average cost of repairing a moderately damaged house is estimated to be $8 000, and a lightly damaged one, $3 000. The MPW is planning to build some 40 thousand new units, with construction due to have started in July 2000 and to be completed by end-year.[79] The preparatory work has involved the rapid

Table 36. **Housing reconstruction cost**[1]
As of 17 August 2000

	Number of units	Cost per unit (US$)	Total damage (US$ million)	Units eligible		Total cost ($ million)	
				Lower bound	Upper bound	Lower bound	Upper bound
Collapsed	96 808	20 000	1 936	53 244	72 606	1 065	1 452
Medium	107 331	8 000	859	59 032	80 498	472	644
Light	124 033	3 000	372	68 218	93 025	204	279
Total	328 172	9 650	3 167	180 495	241 629	1 741	2 375

1. This table replicates the method utilised by the World Bank (applied to the most recent damage assessment reports), which assumes that 55 per cent of the damaged housing is eligible for restitution under government criteria in the lower bound estimate, while 75 per cent is eligible in the upper bound estimate. The latter represents the actual proportion of primary homeowners and assumes that none of them takes the cash benefit in lieu of direct housing benefits.
Source: World Bank (1999b); Turkish authorities; OECD.

mobilisation of engineers and other experts from all around the country to complete the work of damage assessment, determination of holders of property rights, geological and geotechnical surveys to ensure the proper siting of permanent housing settlements, project preparation, and infrastructure construction and repair. The process of tendering the construction contracts has been broadened to allow for bids by foreign construction firms, as well as speeded up, compared with past practices. But despite the scale and pace of reconstruction, there will remain a further 10 to 30 thousand units potentially eligible for full restitution and many more still in need of repair. Ultimately, the government may face $1.7 to $2.4 billion in housing reconstruction costs (Table 36).[80]

In lieu of direct provision, the government is also offering a system of cash benefits towards building or repairing one's own home, which could help to hold down fiscal costs and further speed up the work of reconstruction and rehabilitation. Those who lost their house and are willing to leave the region or to build their own home in the region are given a 20-year no-interest loan of about $10 500. Around 18 thousand people are estimated to have taken this set of options. Owners of damaged homes receive a loan of around $1 000 toward repair of a lightly damaged house and $3 500 for a mid-damaged house, with eligibility for the latter subject to certification by an engineering company. About 88 thousand households have received the former, and 50 thousand the latter benefit. While allowing for more freedom of choice and flexibility – hence more rational redevelopment patterns – the cash benefits are (once again) only at best around half as generous as the corresponding direct government provision. The absolute gap is high in the case of a new home, where the take-up rate may remain low.

Repairing damage to social infrastructure

As regards social infrastructure, damage to schools was extensive: 43 school buildings were demolished and 377 endured severe damage. Until these are rehabilitated, around 25 000 schoolchildren will need to be transported to different school facilities, which requires extra payments for transport, uniforms, books, schoolteachers, and food. The quality of education is also likely to suffer, as classroom size in the schools receiving the overflow will double during the interim period, aggravating capacity bottlenecks already present in this sector (Chapter III). On the other hand, quick mobilisation of extra resources meant that little school time was lost after the earthquake. In the health area, 28 health centres and 10 hospitals were severely damaged, depriving the area of health infrastructure just when it was needed the most. This required deploying temporary prefab health care units and replacing damaged medical equipment, in addition to rehabilitating damaged capacity.

Impact on the Budget

The above earthquake costs will be borne to a large extent by the government budget, namely:

- extra consumption/transfer spending for the relief effort and extra social security spending due to extraordinary death and disability benefits, as well as credit subsidies and tax deferrals/losses for affected businesses and individuals;

- new investment spending for the construction of interim prefabricated homes and the progressive reconstruction and repair of permanent housing and associated infrastructure;

- repairs to damaged transport and communications infrastructure, schools and hospitals.

Table 37 provides the government estimates of these various direct fiscal costs, which are seen to total about 1 per cent of GNP in 1999 and 2 per cent in 2000, $5.9 billion in all. It is seen that expenditures for replacement housing (inclusive of prefabs), at $1.4 billion, accounts for less than one quarter of the total, although as noted, there is an upside risk to the final cost of the government housing guarantee.

Official foreign funding will meet much of the budgetary costs. Total commitments to date stand at $3.8 billion (Table 38): $2.6 billion is in the form of project finance, to be disbursed mainly in 2000 and beyond as the reconstruction proceeds, while $1.1 billion is in the form of budget support, $107 million being already disbursed in 1999. A large part of the project money ($1.0 billion) is being administered through the World Bank-financed Project Implementation Unit (PIU).[81] After official foreign funding, there remains a financing gap of $2.1 billion. To bridge this gap, on 26 November 1999 the government announced an "earthquake package" of one-off tax measures (see Box 3, Chapter II). The total expected revenues from this package are $189 million in 1999 and $1.5 billion in 2000, sufficient to offset a large part of the gap.

By nature the above costs are temporary, so that they do not really impinge on questions of fiscal sustainability; but they come at a critical time for the public accounts. They have to be assimilated against the background of a severe underlying deterioration in 1999, and the subsequent adoption of a very tight stabilisation programme. The overall fiscal effort, needed to offset both baseline budget deterioration and earthquake costs while achieving programme targets, amounts to some 7½ percentage points of GDP in 2000 alone – a speed of adjustment almost unheard of in the OECD context. The stabilisation strategy is buttressed by an impressive number of structural reforms, and the disaster has made these even more difficult yet also more urgent, in part because of the need for re-evaluating the priorities in the use of national resources.

Table 37. **Fiscal impact of the earthquake**

	1999		2000	
	US$ million	Per cent of GNP	US$ million	Per cent of GNP
I. Consolidated budget	1 402	0.8	1 571	0.7
Revenue loss	739	0.4	314	0.1
Expenditure	663	0.4	1 257	0.6
Current	133	0.1	445	0.2
Transfers	306	0.2	463	0.2
Investment	225	0.1	349	0.2
II. Housing	122	0.1	1 242	0.6
Prefabricated houses	122	0.1		
Permanent houses			509	0.2
Payment in cash			283	0.1
Aid for medium-damaged houses			450	0.2
III. Duty losses of public banks[1]			531	0.2
Ziraat			328	0.2
Halk			94	0.0
Emlak			109	0.1
IV. Local governments[2]	81	0.0	65	0.0
V. Funds	169	0.1	371	0.2
Social aid and solidarity fund[3]	169	0.1	261	0.1
Mass housing fund			110	0.0
VI. SOEs[4]			452	0.2
Total public sector	**1 774**	**1.0**	**4 248**	**1.9**

1. The most recent estimates of fiscal costs of the earthquake credit subsidy scheme are considerably lower than the initial estimates shown in the present table.
2. Includes expenditure for sewerage, water, mapwork and development plan, water and sewerage for temporary settlements, and equipment (latter three categories in 1999 only).
3. Includes outlays for death aid, aid for disabled people, emergency aid, shelter aid, restore and shelter aid, and business aid.
4. Refers to the damage recovery costs and includes all SOEs in the region. Moreover, production and sales losses at SOEs are estimated at $632 million.
Source: Turkish authorities.

Overall, the economic and financial repercussions of the disaster have been managed in such a way as to preserve and even enhance confidence in the programme. It was initially feared that indirect budgetary impacts might arise as a result of a higher risk premium on government debt due to the worsened budgetary position and hence a higher debt service burden.[82] Around $1 billion of private capital flowed out of the country in the week after the earthquake. However, capital flows quickly stabilised with the passage of a social security reform bill on 25 August 1999, accompanied by the government's announcement that it would

Table 38. **External financing for Marmara earthquake**
US$ million

Donor	Programme loans	Project loans		Grants	Total
		Managed by PU (World Bank)	Managed by the implementing agency		
IMF	500				500
World Bank					993.8
Import and budget finance	252.5				252.5
MEER project finance		505			505
Reallocation		62.5	173.8		236.3
International Finance Corporation			50		50
European Investment Bank[1]		455	152		607
Council of Europe Development Bank[1]			303		303
Italy[2]			18		18
Spain[2]			60		60
Belgium[2]			4		4
Islamic Development Bank					300
Import trade finance	150				150
Project finance			150		150
Gulf co-operation Council			400		400
Black Sea Trade and Development Bank			10		10
Japan					450
Commodity loan	200				200
Project finance (SMEs)			250		250
South Korea[2]			30		30
EU[1]				35	35
Germany				12	12
Total	**1 102.5**	**1 022.5**	**1 600.8**	**47**	**3 772.8**

1. Assumes $1 = 1.01 euro (as of 24 February, 2000).
2. Tied.
Source: Turkish authorities.

pursue other structural reforms without delay and that it would not finance earth-quake costs by new domestic borrowing. This was followed in short order by a series of important legislative initiatives that served as prior actions for agreement with the IMF. The government's refusal to allow the tragedy to delay reforms or to soften budget targets impressed financial markets and contributed strongly to the turnaround of sentiment which culminated in the sharp fall in interest rates at the turn of the year.

Regulatory issues: towards more effective governance

Uncontrolled urban development

The problems of poor construction and siting described at the beginning of the chapter need to be understood in the context of the extremely rapid process of urbanisation which Turkey has been undergoing, in which the population has been moving *en masse* from the countryside to the cities (Figure 21). The process of urbanisation itself has been part of a momentum to industrialisation which has relied extensively on the informal economy for its underlying dynamic and in doing so may have encouraged a trade-off between economic expansion and orderly development. In practice, despite a "legally governed" real-estate core catering to the needs of the formal business sector and the traditional urban population, the bulk of land development in Turkey seems to have occurred through two informal mechanisms:

- occupation and expropriation of government land by new city-dwellers; and

- *de facto* development of agricultural lands (outside official settlement plans) around cities.

Regular amnesties created moral hazard and thus expanding illegal settlement of the urban peripheries. The proportion of Turkey's urban population living in such settlements is currently close to 40 per cent and since the late 1970s its growth has been explosive (Figure 22).

In effect, Turkey has coped with urban growth through migration by tolerating the illegal construction of housing, often on publicly-owned land,[83] thereby encouraging the construction sector to supply housing at lower cost by eliminating the need to purchase and improve land. Almost by definition, such *"gecekondu"* (overnight houses) settlements have been built without respect for planning rules and in contravention of the building codes. They were not exclusively for the poor, as is often the case in some developing countries; even middle class people have had to compromise on the quality of construction, infrastructure and public services. High inflation also played a role, since it meant that real estate was the only viable long term savings vehicle. This fuelled excess demand for housing and urban land speculation which made the better urban sites too expensive for low and moderate income groups to purchase. The regularisation of illegal settlements was initiated by their residents, who used the process to secure investment in infrastructure and public services as municipalities incorporated their district, and who acquired certification of conformity for their buildings through amnesty even if these still did not meet the standards of the codes. All involved, local and national officials, builders, and property owners, found it convenient to ignore legal measures for town planning and construction.[84] The benefits of this process have been the gradual extension of municipal jurisdiction over illegal settlements,

Figure 21.   **Population in rural and urban areas**[1]
Per cent

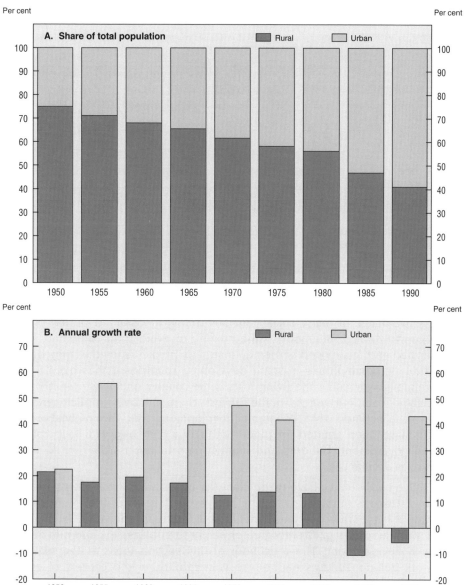

1.   Population census.
Source: State Institute of Statistics.

Figure 22. **Growth of informal settlements**
Number of inhabitants

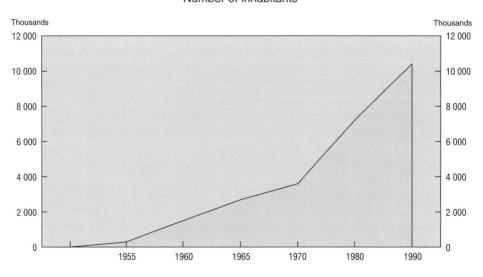

Source: Turkish authorities.

and the avoidance of major social tensions during a sustained period of rapid urban growth through migration, while helping to avoid totally informal, illegal, unequipped and unserviced settlements around Turkish cities that may be seen in favela-type communities in some developing countries. It has been a major factor minimising housing and living costs in the country, and consequently fostering industry's competitiveness. In the process, there has been implicit agreement among all concerned that economic development was the highest priority. Licences have been granted for plots that carry a high risk, with tacit collusion between government, builders and homeowners to bypass the (weak) zoning/ construction ordinances.[85]

The earthquakes have made clear the unsustainability of this framework. In view of Turkey's inherent seismicity and the high costs of the earthquakes, a reckoning of longer run costs and benefits would undoubtedly argue in favour of a model which accords significantly greater weight to public safety and rule of law in economic development. The remainder of this section looks at the regulatory framework behind Turkey's earthquake vulnerability, in the context of existing legislation and its enforcement, which involves accountability and performance at all levels of government. The succeeding section then presents a discussion of the policies and institutions needed to govern the development of a property market in which individuals gradually assume responsibility for finance and insurance.

The need for regulatory reform

Urban planning and land use management, construction quality, and disaster management are all subject to legislation and regulation. Four major laws govern the underlying structure of public responsibilities, legal liability and professional standards: the "Disaster Law" in respect of disaster response; the "Planning Law" in the area of construction and land use control; the "Tender Law" in public construction project contracting, and the "Municipality Law" in urban planning implementation (see Annex IV). The current legal framework has not succeeded in preventing unsafe development, however. The relevant laws and regulations have suffered from both inadequate implementation and non-compliance due to the perverse public and private incentives that they often imply. The lack of clarity concerning responsibilities and principles of co-ordination has also hampered effective co -operation within and across levels of government, as well as between civil society and government. Also, as evidenced above, there is a prevailing culture of an official tolerance of illegal or informal activities in the construction and land use areas. Achieving better safety standards and ensuring that the principles of orderly urban development are more closely followed will entail both an overhaul of legislation, to ensure modern best practice, and better law enforcement. The need for reform is now generally recognised, and a review of regulatory and supervisory practices is under way.

Regulatory reform in the disaster planning and response area

The Disaster Law establishes arrangements for post-disaster management which are highly centralised but poorly co-ordinated both within and across levels of government. In the event of a major natural disaster, fifteen central government ministries – each having its own disaster management unit and plan authorised by the Ministry of Public Works (MPW) – establish a crisis centre in the Prime Minister's office, which mobilises resources to the affected area.[86] The MPW is in charge of overall emergency planning, assistance to victims, temporary shelter and reconstruction (Annex IV). Since disasters, by definition, are of such a magnitude as to overwhelm local and even regional resources, there is a strong argument in favour of such national responsibility. However, due to the concentration of all disaster planning competence and authority within the MPW, most cities in high-risk earthquake zones of Turkey do not have an earthquake response master plan, and there have been no awareness campaigns to inform citizens of risks and appropriate actions to take in an emergency. International best practice indicates the importance of municipalities and provinces being able to develop their own capabilities in disaster management, the lessons of recent global disasters highlighting the contribution of civil society in an emergency, the value of local knowledge, and the benefits of international co-operation.

The Marmara earthquake made clear the inadequacies in the procedures for disaster planning and response, and reforms to address these followed quickly. On 22 November 1999, the government issued a decree creating a new agency, the Emergency Management Agency of Turkey (EMAT), to be housed in the Prime Ministry and charged with comprehensive emergency management. This involves, first, co-ordinating and rationalising hitherto dispersed emergency response functions and responsibilities. To this end, it will be equipped with modern communications, database, and earthquake monitoring facilities, benefit from a comprehensive training and exercise programme (search and rescue activities, fire-fighting, etc.), and engage the public via information and awareness campaigns. Secondly, it will be in charge of developing a national earthquake mitigation plan in co-operation and co-ordination with five pilot municipalities, the results of which will later be applied to other cities in high seismic risk areas.

A related defect of the Disaster Law concerns its rather sparse reference to pre-disaster mitigation, with a resulting lack of coherence between development and emergency planning. This problem is partially addressed with the creation of EMAT. Most seriously, however, the law has dulled risk awareness in the population, while creating a huge contingent fiscal liability, through its broad guarantee of replacement housing. In the immediate aftermath of the Marmara earthquake, decrees were issued to roll back the guarantee and so limit the government's financial exposure. On 1 September 1999, two groups of building owners were excluded from the guarantee: those whose buildings were constructed on others' land without a construction permit, and those who (or their spouses) owned another undamaged building. In December 1999, a decree was issued to remove the guarantee altogether for urban areas in the event of future disasters, being replaced by a new compulsory national earthquake insurance scheme (discussed further below). The decrees on the introduction of compulsory national insurance and of EMAT together form the core of a future revised Disaster Law.

Regulatory reform in the construction and land use area

The Planning Law has suffered from a number of defects which play a key role in undermining the principles of risk mitigation and development control – even though these principles figure among the law's main objectives (Annex IV). As in the case of the Disaster Law, it gives the various central ministries authority for planning and land development, but without a clear delineation of responsibilities and virtually no sanctions for failure to carry these out. In conjunction with a weak institutional backdrop for effective local authority implementation of planning law (discussed below), there is a severe failure to co-ordinate and almost no incentive to implement the law. The attendant regulations and practices have, as a consequence, failed to impose technical and professional standards in the building and planning sector, to keep building codes up to date and prevent collusion between builders and inspectors, or to govern appropriate land use. Most notably:

- There has been little or no criminal and tort liability, and no supervisory agency responsible for *professional standards and liability* for structural engineers, architects, contractors, building inspectors and city planners. Professional training for those in the construction sector, building contractors, sub-contractors, foremen and apprentices, has been left unsupervised.

- *Building codes* have only been periodically updated, but at a pace that has not kept up with international earthquake technology. The majority of the structures subjected to the earthquake were built under the old codes (established in 1975). But even for those built since 1996 (when the codes were revised), the main problem has remained the implementation, monitoring, and control of these codes at the local level. Furthermore, whereas legal standards have been issued for seismic design of principal structural systems, there is no comprehensive, unified building code which would serve as a clear reference for both building engineers and regulatory authorities.

- *Perverse incentives* have arisen insofar as inspecting engineers are traditionally chosen and paid by building contractors or owners. This practice stems from insufficient technical manpower at the municipal level. Low pay and lack of performance management, in addition to the lack of legal sanctions, have further increased the susceptibility of municipal inspectors to illegal payments. The process of tendering government contracts has been so loose as to allow similar abuses in the domain of public construction projects.

- *Zoning ordinances* are unclear and usually flaunted. Urban, regional, and national plans often intersect due to the absence of an established hierarchy among plans, a clear delineation of authority, or a clear mechanism for resolving conflicts. For example, an area designated for parks or greenery in the plans of the local authority can be forced to host the building of a commercial structure due to the intervention of the MPW (or other ministries, such as Tourism or Trade). Added to this is the problem of the informal *gecekondu* settlements on the outskirts of cities, discussed above.

The Planning Law is now under re-evaluation and some of the related regulations have already been changed. An important innovation has been the setting up (by 10 July 2000) of "construction controlling firms" in cities and towns. These firms, composed of groups of engineers having majority ownership, are to take over design-review and construction-site responsibilities from the municipal building departments. A process for the certification of such supervisory firms is being established. The introduction of professional standards and liability for these firms is expected to enhance the rigour of plan-review and inspection procedures significantly. The construction standards to be applied will parallel those of the EU, and those of the Turkish Standards Institute on the use of materials (for example, ready cement must be used in lieu of "own-mixed" cement, elastic instead of rigid steel must be used in frame-work, and steel must be used in the base of industrial buildings, schools and hospitals). The MPW estimates that application of the standards will add 4 to 8 per cent to the cost of new buildings. There will also for the first time be specific municipal and professional responsibilities and penalties for failure to carry out those responsibilities.

It is essential that these steps to improve safeguards and incentives in the building sector are fully enforced, *i.e.* that the practices of the past do not simply reassert themselves within the new framework. In this sense, it will be necessary to fully enforce the new sanctions on the inspecting professions; have full judicial back up of legal liability; put more resources into the training of construction and design engineers; move forward with government procurement and municipal reforms (below), and monitor results. However, beyond this, more work is needed in order to establish a really coherent legal framework for satisfactory land and urban development. Four factors seem essential:

– More rigorous standards must be established.[87] But also, it will be essential that plan standards for closed and open areas, social and recreational facilities, etc. be improved. These will need to take into account planning goals which promote certain environmental, economic, and social outcomes. Direct citizen involvement in development plans, as exists in most other OECD countries, is an important precondition, and will depend to a large extent on progress in municipal reforms (below).

– The problem of lack of co-ordination and of clear delineation of responsibilities of the bodies responsible for different aspects of planning need to be resolved by a careful redrafting of the Planning Law. In parallel, a hierarchy of plans needs to be established nation-wide, including feedback mechanisms to handle spill-over effects.

– Better information about land ownership and a clearer distribution mechanism for land are needed for proper zoning and more orderly land and housing markets. Information about land quality is also needed for better risk assessment in the public and private sectors. Therefore, in addition to a planned World Bank project to improve the land registration and cadastre system in the Marmara region, a national geological survey along with wider public access to detailed geophysical information is advisable. The latter need could be met by establishing a nation-wide computerised Geographical Information System (GIS).

– The problem of the *gecekondu* needs to be resolved. This will certainly require eschewing the repeated use of amnesties. As the problem is strategically related to the economic development process, however, solutions will further need to be part of a global approach to bringing the informal economy within the ambit of state regulations. But even if the inflow into such settlements can be arrested, dealing with the large inherited stock of vulnerable structures is likely to require budgetary resources and effective management.

Reform of government procurement rules

The *Tender Law* has not succeeded in preventing abuses in public procurement. The large amount of money awarded for public construction projects – with little competition or control – has greatly exacerbated unethical practices in the construction sector, not to mention being a considerable waste of taxpayers' money. A major loophole in the law was that state economic enterprises were exempt, being subject to their own (unclear) tender procedures. Another problem was the inefficient structure of the bidding process. Once a tender was announced, only ten days were allowed to enter bids; bidding was based on unrealistic price estimates of the tendering authority; feasibility studies were not required; multiple "commissions" obfuscated procedures; "deferred" tenders (build as money becomes available) were used extensively (Annex IV). These methods favoured insiders, and led to the awarding of contracts where no budgetary appropriations or realistic cost estimates existed. This led in turn to massive misuse of resources, cost overruns, inefficient projects running for years, and indeed unfinished projects. These problems were compounded by the failure to assign responsibility for construction control. The final result was that public buildings such as schools and hospitals had many of the building defects of private houses, and suffered from major devastation in the earthquake.

Since the earthquake, the government has completed a draft new Tender Law, in accordance with EU and WTO norms. The main objectives of the proposed changes are *i*) to implement tenders in a more transparent and competitive way by covering the whole of the public sector, including state enterprises, under a single law; *ii*) to increase the speed and efficiency of project implementation by more realistic tender procedures and pricing mechanisms including: a single "tender commission" and streamlined bureaucratic procedures, a requirement for minimum percentage budget appropriation to open a tender, a 52-day period to enter bids after tender is open, the requirement for feasibility studies, competitive bidding based on the delivery cost of the project, and the abolition of "deferred" tenders; and *iii*) to allocate responsibility for control over the construction process. These reforms would appear to address all of the above serious defects in the old law. Moreover, public construction projects will be subject to the new surveillance mechanism that has been put into place for construction projects in general.

Local authority reform

The local level has, in principle, substantial autonomy over land-use decisions, but within an overall framework of rules and procedures set at higher levels. However, local government capabilities have proved insufficient to respond flexibly to local needs. It may be argued that one of the governance problems affecting disaster outcomes is that functional responsibilities have been devolved to the local level without extending the necessary decision-making powers or accountability. Despite the trend toward more decentralisation embodied in the Municipality Law and its various adaptations and updates, the central government retains considerable powers of control (Annex IV). Another problem is a confusion in the lines of authority due to inconsistencies across the different laws. For example, under the Municipality Law, municipalities are responsible for implementing development control and are under the administrative responsibility of the Ministry of Interior; however the latter does not have the appropriate capabilities to monitor functions related to land use or building safety, which by the provisions of the Planning Law reside with the MPW. Local capabilities also suffer from a lack of internal structural reforms: patronage counts in hiring, while low wages and insufficient incentives for performance reduce efficiency and productivity.

It follows that any empowerment of the municipalities through greater devolution of decision-making would have to be accompanied by greater accountability and citizen involvement to provide the necessary checks and balances. Indeed, when responsibility for development planning was devolved to the municipalities after 1984, it was done without the preconditions laid down in most OECD countries, namely, direct general-public control of development plans and the establishment of mechanisms to provide members of the public with the relevant technical information in the course of exercising this control. In light of these problems, the OECD has previously identified among the principal needs of local government in Turkey as follows: *i)* a more decentralised and less interventionist policy in the planning area with a more responsive attitude to divergent local circumstances; *ii)* greater efficiency, via the development of human and financial resource management aimed at transparency, accountability and control; *iii)* co-operation and joint ventures to deal with the large-scale needs of major cities; and *iv)* the participation of local citizens in government and the development of an urban consciousness.[88]

The government's 5-year Development Plan – the main instrument for co-ordinating government policies including the local level – echoes similar concerns as it emphasises the need to address the absence of decision-making powers in the decentralisation process, the insufficient resources allocated to local administrations, and the lack of consultative mechanisms at the local level (citizen-participation). The process of integration with Europe has given further momentum to the need to adopt new ideas concerning local administrations, including the idea of citizens' rights to participate in the self-government process as a democratic right.[89] With this understanding and parallel to the objectives of the Development Plan, a local authority reform law was drawn up by the government and submitted to Parliament in June 2000. The latter, however, has not yet acted upon it and it would appear crucial that such legislation be passed. Indeed, in its absence, there is a risk that reforms to the Planning Law could fail to be fully effective.

Strategic issues in urban planning and reconstruction

The current reconstruction will have a weighty influence on the future direction for urban development in the affected region, since many of its cities and towns are being virtually built anew. However, this process will profit very little from the above reforms, which will take some time to fully bear fruit, so that important strategic issues may need be addressed within the constraint of the present institutional framework. With respect to the current reconstruction of areas suffering large-scale destruction, including Izmit, Adapazari and Düzce, the responsibility of the government to replace housing gives the central government the initiative, but the decision-making about what is built, where and when would need to involve local levels for a strong component of informed consumer choice to be built into the reconstruction programme. Engaging local government and civil society in land use planning and facilitating measures to reduce risk and improve preparedness at the local level is, however, a complex challenge.

Optimising the reconstruction process

In the aftermath of the 1999 earthquakes, the immediate challenges have been to ensure coherent development/reconstruction of the affected areas and towns, some of which have had their economic viability put in question, while trying to ensure that the defects which magnified the losses in the recent earthquakes are not so catastrophic when the next earthquake hits. Developing a coherent strategy in this respect requires the reconciliation of two potentially conflicting considerations: the desire to move people into new, permanent houses as quickly as possible, thereby reducing the emotional as well as financial cost of interim solutions, versus the opportunity provided by the reconstruction process to introduce improvements in infrastructure, civic facilities, etc., while implementing new measures of code enforcement, insurance, etc. for rebuilt property and districts. Some cities will need to develop a whole new economic base (e.g. Yalova, which lost its entire tourist industry) and there needs to be a strategy to cope with this shift.

The emphasis so far has been on moving people into new, permanent housing and reducing government support for temporary housing as quickly as possible. Some observers have criticised expenditure on temporary housing as wasteful and costly. Indeed, there are reasonable concerns about fostering a dependency mentality, and about people trying to claim benefits on dubious grounds. But in the absence of better maps of the affected sites, of intensive consultations with local populations, and of an assessment of economic and environmental deficiencies in the cities that have been destroyed, the rush to move people into permanent housing may be restricting the options available. In particular, the opportunity to include broad measures of public participation into the strategic planning may be lost. The objective of reconstruction on sustainable lines would be compromised if decisions are made prematurely, on the basis of inadequate information and consultation. For example, because the government's plan to replace houses is limited to owner-occupied housing, landlords will get only one building rebuilt. In the immediate future, therefore, there will be a shortage of rental housing, and the rebuilding strategy does not appear to indicate where rental housing might be built. A shortage of rental housing might compromise mobility at a time when population movement must be expected (with consequences for employers who need to attract workers with certain skills); a failure to plan for rental housing may lead over time to the *de facto* separation of owner-occupied housing from rental properties with a resulting "ghetto-isation" of the latter and a lack of choice for the population.

More generally, the current approach to reconstruction is highly centralised and interventionist. This may be justified by the urgency of the situation. But consideration should be given to the introduction of market forces with the redevelopment programme. This could be based on tradeable vouchers for land auction and partnerships with the private sector for commercial development. It is important for the new situation to be used to progress towards one where central and local interests, state and private, are balanced. The experience of the city of Izmir is instructive in this context (Box 10). Interacting with municipal planners and scientific experts from other countries facing earthquake risks, it has developed a plan of action which brings together different organisations in society and integrates the critical elements required for sale urban development: tools for risk assessment, the principles of selective "retrofitting" (*i.e.* improving to be more earthquake resistant) of existing urban structures, and emergency planning and training procedures. The important lesson here is that the city was able, with international support, to obtain a high degree of co-ordination with other levels of government and civil society, despite the highly centralised legal structure of disaster management in Turkey.

Preparing for the next earthquake

Given the earthquake movement along the North-Anatolian fault, Istanbul is perhaps the city-region now most at risk. As noted above, seismologists expect a severe earthquake in the southern Istanbul region, bordering the Sea of

Box 10.   The Izmir plan of action

The city of Izmir in western Turkey has developed an action plan for managing seismic risk. The main obstacle to co-ordination of such a plan was the highly centralised legal structure of disaster management in Turkey. In light of this constraint, the international "RADIUS" project (Risk Assessment Tools for Diagnosis of Urban Areas against Seismic Disaster) acted as a catalyst in bringing together governmental and municipal organs, the professional chambers, NGOs, etc.* Four working groups were formed in order to deal with the following subjects:

The *assessment of earthquake risks* group (representatives from the chambers of geologists, geophysicists, civil engineers and related departments of the universities):

- the assessment of geological and tectonic structure of Izmir Metropolitan Area, including the study of active faults, landslides, and liquefaction;
- the assessment of past earthquakes in the vicinity of Izmir, the determination of their destructiveness, and the filing of seismic instrumentation records;
- in view of past earthquake experience, the determination of possible geological hazards and the conditions of buildings situated in these areas; evaluation of seismic factors and other disastrous events triggered by earthquakes such as fires, destruction of dams, etc.

The *assessment of buildings and infrastructure* group (representatives of the chambers of civil engineers, architects, related departments in universities, governmental agencies such as Ministry of Public Works, Waterworks, Railways, Turk Telekom, Electricity, municipality subway and construction departments):

- the evaluation of the building stock within city boundaries, classifying them according to their age, construction material, height, etc.;
- the classification of buildings with regard to architectural configuration, foundation type, structural features and existing soil conditions;
- the evaluation of buildings destructed in past earthquakes;
- the evaluation of the infrastructure, including data on location, condition, construction date and materials of structures such as bridges, motorways, subway, airports, seaports, railways, dams, clean water and sewage systems, electrical energy transmission lines and transformers, PTT centres, fire stations, industrial complexes.

The *assessment of social and economic situation* group (representatives of chambers of architects, commerce, industrialists, medical doctors, NGOs, related departments of universities, and the media):

- the evaluation of city community with regard to cultural background, education, age, economic level, living conditions, immigration, etc.;
- determination of the locations of the trade centres, hypermarkets, transportation systems, recreational areas and open spaces, hospitals and clinics, schools, universities, police and army stations, which people frequent.

Box 10.   **The Izmir plan of action** (*cont.*)

The *relief activities and rehabilitation of the buildings* group (representatives of the chambers of civil engineers, architects, city planners, commerce in particular builders and developers, medical doctors and city's health board, civil defence board, NGOs such as mountain rescue teams, amateur wireless network organisation, Agenda 21, fire brigade, army, police force, related university departments):

- the determination of guidelines for urban planning and new development areas which shall be least affected by natural disasters;
- the determination of efficient quality control systems in the construction sector and proposals for new building regulations, etc.;
- a guide to show communities how to behave during and after and earthquake;
- preparation of a guide and documentary films concerning the renovation or retrofitting of hazardous buildings after a major earthquake.

---

* See *www.geohaz.org/project/radius/radiusintro.htm.*

Marmara at some time in the next quarter-century, with the strong possibility of such an occurrence within a decade. In Istanbul, there are known areas of high risk (where liquefaction of soil would occur). A question arises as to whether the people living in these areas should be resettled, or their housing retrofitted. Low-cost improvements may yield significant benefits in terms of resistance to destruction, and could be phased in while preserving existing districts. In the meantime, emergency planning needs to take account of the possibility that some parts of the city will suffer far greater destruction than others. Finally, because the city continues to grow (at a rate estimated at 300 000 newcomers per year), and in the absence of a coherent, enforceable strategy to plan for this growth, illegal settlements and sub-standard construction will continue to be the norm, thus increasing the magnitude of the problem facing those with the responsibility of emergency preparedness.

The elements required to meet any future earthquake emergency are numerous. However, good communications will be a priority. The experience of Kobe should encourage the creation of more areas of open space within the city, where people can assemble, as well as redundant infrastructure, networks and pathways for public services (*i.e.*, excess capacity and multiple pathways), together with massive campaigns of public information and training. Since centralised public services can be easily crippled in time of a disaster, priority will need to be given to retrofitting schools and hospitals, the build-quality of which is generally poor. These could be used as focal points during emergencies.

Most importantly, while options for the future can still be explored in the reconstruction process, there is an urgent need for guidance about metropolitan regional development and appropriate policy instruments. A metropolitan regional review, perhaps in the context of a forum bringing in expert knowledge from OECD Member countries could complement efforts in Turkey to analyse regional conditions. Such a forum could provide an opportunity for the lessons of success and failure in recovery from disaster to be fashioned into best-practice procedures, and could help shape the agenda for the newly-formed national emergency management agency as well as the elaboration of city earthquake master plans.

Enlarging the scope for market-driven economic development

Involving the private sector: the mortgage market

The administrative deficiencies noted above have operated against the background of a perverse set of incentives for the private sector, which have acted to make both the population and the business sector short-sighted with respect to risks. A government guarantee to replace housing after an earthquake has been behind the lack of pressure for better mapping and risk analysis, and an under-developed insurance market. A system of private incentives to risk minimisation has thus failed to develop. At the same time, chronic inflation and associated high real interest rates have prevented the development of a mortgage market. Standard urban planning, micro-zoning according to geophysical information, building code development and enforcement will increase the cost of housing, creating a demand for both a mortgage and insurance market. Indeed, a longer-term consequence of the earthquakes will need to be the development of the two, so far minimally-developed markets for earthquake-resilient and infrastructure-equipped suburban habitable land and that for pricing the natural risk vulnerabilities of individual assets.

The creation of housing-credit and insurance markets should be assisted by a low inflationary environment, which would allow for a longer-term financial planning horizon and help Turkey to attract long-term foreign capital. Moreover, the need to create the conditions for more sustainable urban development comes at a time when the opportunity to make profits from buying government paper are diminishing, promoting a need for alternative domestic savings instruments. However, for mortgage and insurance markets to emerge, legal/institutional impediments to their development will have to be reviewed, giving an impetus to financial market reform. A new action plan, including the securitising of mortgage credits, would need to be developed in order to help form a sound system. Important reforms to the financial system are already taking place that should facilitate financial market diversification (Chapter III).

Reform of the banking sector as it adapts to a low-inflation regime could unleash the development of a mortgage market, which may be instrumental in providing financing for new housing construction. Such a market is already developing, albeit only in the upper segment of the property market. High inflation has thus far prevented the creation of TL-denominated instruments beyond one year, effectively ensuring that the housing industry operates on a pay-as-you-build principle. However, there are some US dollar-denominated transactions in the middle-upper market, the main market vehicle for property investment being Real Estate Investment Companies. These are regulated by the Capital Markets Board since 1995 and are tax-favoured (to allow them to compete with the informal economy which dominates the building industry). These companies seem set to expand, not least because earthquake risks have directed market interest quite clearly towards property compliant with building and zoning codes, which such companies can guarantee. Indeed, the role played by mortgage companies in insisting on building standards and insurance will be a growing stimulus to more orderly development of the housing market as far as new building is concerned.

Managing risks: developing the private sector insurance market

While a natural corollary of a growing mortgage market would be the development of a private insurance market, this would be slow to impact on the current housing stock in Turkey, which is currently severely underinsured. Property owners are usually reluctant to incur the up-front costs of risk mitigation measures because they either misperceive risks, are myopic and/or face severe budget constraints. And judged by its past record and present financial capacity (capital adequacy), the technical abilities of the local insurance industry are limited for handling the earthquake risks. Moreover, when it comes to insuring catastrophic risks, market failures are well-known even in highly developed insurance markets, so that the government has a role to play, as indeed is the case in other OECD economies where the concurrent provision of public and private earthquake insurance is considered a necessity.[90]

Forming the core of a future revised Disaster Law (see above), a government-sponsored "Turkish Catastrophic Insurance Pool (TCIP)" is now being put in place, which will be subject to a coverage limit of $25 000 per house, and will permit additional private insurance coverage (Box 11). The new scheme is to be operational by 28 September 2000.[91] It will require the services of insurance companies as information and collection agents, and could help stimulate development of the sector in the longer run. However, for this to be really effective, the challenge is to reconcile low-cost insurance with the need to generate economic signals which allow individuals to respond to risks. Public provision alters incentives and creates a moral hazard. To enhance the role of insurance in encouraging property owners to take steps to reduce losses from natural hazards such as earthquakes, private

Box 11.   Compulsory earthquake insurance

The prospects of the local insurance industry expanding its coverage, if earthquake insurance were made compulsory, are limited, due to its low capital base (partly reflecting high inflation-protected returns from low risk activities) and the reluctance of leading international reinsurers to provide more capacity to the industry in its present state. In addition, a pure private sector approach is unlikely to succeed, as some insurers will attempt to underwrite only those risks that are overpriced, leading to adverse selection and instability for those who get the wrong part of the portfolio. Well-founded concerns over Turkish building standards are an aggravating factor.

Under these circumstances, it was perceived that a joint public/private sector solution was necessary to reduce the risk borne by the government and the property owners. On 27 December 1999, the Turkish Government approved a Decree-Law on the introduction of compulsory earthquake insurance. This measure represents an important and clear break with the past, when under the *Disaster Law* the government was liable for rebuilding housing destroyed by natural disasters almost free of charge. When the Decree goes into effect on 28 September 2000, those who fail to get insurance will no longer be able to benefit from government aid in the event of a natural disaster.

The Decree paves the way for the creation of the Turkish Catastrophic Insurance Pool (TCIP) that will be the stand-alone provider of earthquake property insurance in the country for up to $25 000.* Coverage in excess of that amount will be provided by private insurers. While initially, in the first several years of its operations, the TCIP will be supported by a contingent line of credit from the World Bank, its major sources of capital support will come from the collected premiums (a flat annual fee of roughly $50 per household), reinsurance and excess of loss treaties and, possibly, issuance of catastrophe bonds. It is envisaged that in ten years, the TCIP will have enough capital to protect Turkish homeowners against catastrophic events larger than that occurred on 17 August 1999, which would effectively relieve the Turkish Government from its large contingent liability due to frequent natural disasters. The risk that the government will be unable to resist political pressure to turn TCIP into an indiscriminate liquidity conduit to victims of a major future earthquake, regardless of their terms of coverage, is limited by the financial design of the programme.

In addition to its core earthquake insurance functions, it is expected that the TCIP would also greatly contribute to the better enforcement of building codes through a commercial arrangement with independent engineering firms that would be retained to certify the construction quality of new residential dwellings to be insured under the plan. However, since there will be a single undifferentiated premium, this will need to come via pressure from the reinsurers rather than a built-in incentive structure. Indeed, care will need to be exercised to ensure that the insurance premium is not treated as a tax and ultimately assimilated into the central government budget. To this end, it is envisaged that after two years' operation, TCIP will introduce either a reduced premium or greater coverage if the insured adopts recommended mitigation practices.

---

*   To reduce moral hazard and encourage top-up cover from the private sector, claims payments will be subject to "average", a method by which loss claims are scaled down in inverse proportion to the value of the property. Thus, only houses worth $25 000 would be able to get the full maximum coverage.
Source: World Bank (1999c).

incentives are needed that internalise risks. This may be the only real solution to enforcement failures noted above, since incentives to favour development over safety will change only slowly and uncoordinated regulatory responsibilities between local and national levels are not yet rationalised. Uncontrolled building on dangerous land may well continue, since it will take great political courage to call out the bulldozers against squatters who have erected buildings. The effectiveness of the proposed new supervisory companies, with professional standards and liability, is uncertain. The greatest boost to home safety in Turkey might thus well lie in private risk-based enforcement to standards in land use and construction. For this to be the case, private insurance should ideally assign risk-related premia to the risk exposures of different types and locations of buildings. The lack of premium differentiation is a drawback here, which should be corrected as cartographic and insurance sector deficiencies are remedied.

An active insurance industry would be instrumental in ensuring the enforcement of building codes, relieving the burden on government in this respect. Indeed, it is because reinsurers do not utilise information on risk to price their products so as to create an incentive to invest in cost-effective mitigation measures that the responsibility of the public sector for enforcing building codes is so high. There is also limited interest by engineers and builders in designing safer structures if it means incurring costs that will hurt them competitively. Interviews with structural engineers concerned with the performance of earthquake-resistant structures indicate that they have no incentive to build structures that exceed existing codes because they have to justify these expenses to their clients and would lose out to other engineers who did not include these features in the design. This would change with the development of insurance and mortgage markets.

Summing up: implications for future disaster readiness

The human and material toll of the two earthquakes have been severe. International assistance, however, has reduced the financial burden to manageable proportions, and the economy is rebuilding and recovering. The disaster has not diverted policy attention from the need for sound macroeconomic policies and the structural reform process has been strengthened by it. On the other hand, many displaced persons remain in temporary shelters, many of the governance factors responsible for the more than 18 thousand deaths and 50 thousand injuries remain in place, and there are important questions with respect to Turkey's preparedness in the event of a probable future major earthquake. The 1999 earthquakes have revealed a relative slowness of response and a human vulnerability to shocks greatly in excess of that observed in other OECD member countries subject to earthquakes.

The World Bank has identified three critical elements that are needed for a comprehensive disaster management strategy: risk identification, risk-reduction, and risk-transfer.[92] This chapter has shown arrangements in Turkey to be deficient on all three levels.

- The process of *risk identification* has been inadequate. The delineation of hazard zones indicating both soil quality and exposure to risk (earthquake zone maps) is fairly rudimentary and geological surveys are out of date and incomplete. Awareness campaigns to inform citizens of risks and appropriate actions to take in an emergency have been absent.

- *Risk reduction* and mitigation have been impeded by a systemic failure to enforce building codes and implement appropriate land use and planning policies, even in relation to known risks. The laws governing development contain loopholes, while local level implementation and monitoring has been inadequate. Planning/construction standards do not correspond to potential hazard exposure, land use and building certification have been compromised, with a lack of a rigorous system of training, licensing and liability in the engineering, building and planning professions.

- Many of the deficiencies stem from the fundamental fact that personal incentive structures have been perverse. The obligation of the government under disaster law to rebuild damaged residences, and the lack of a mortgage market, operate as disincentives to the development of a market for *risk pricing and transfer*. Individual insurance is virtually absent, and even small businesses are under-insured. The failure to properly price and internalise risk has thus amplified the systematic failure to mitigate risks through appropriate behaviour.

Measures are now being put in place to correct many of the above deficiencies (Table 39). With respect to the planning legislation, these include the out-sourcing of design-review and construction-site responsibilities from the municipal building departments, and the introduction of a process for the certification to ensure construction standards parallel to those of the EU. There will be specific municipal and professional responsibilities and attached penalties. There are proposals for state tender reform and for local municipality reform to strengthen governance in the construction and development area. The severe disincentives to proper risk management that are embodied in the disaster legislation are likewise being addressed. The government has introduced a new mandatory national insurance scheme, while abolishing its former guarantees in the housing area. National risk will be transferred to world-wide risk-sharing pools. However, for the moment, the differentiation of risks will remain rather rudimentary and individual incentives to take precautions against earthquake will be inadequate. In this sense, a mortgage market, which would serve to encourage a property insurance market, would be needed. It has been prevented from developing *inter alia* by endemic high inflation, so that the transition to a low inflation

Table 39. **The post-earthquake agenda**

Phase/activity	Turkish action plans	Recommendations for further action
Emergency relief Locate people to shelters, provide social services and food until permanent houses are built	By end-1999 121 tent towns converted into 41 500 prefabricated houses for the winter. Emergency cash to those who find own housing.	Better temporary accommodation (*e.g.* vacant building) for people still living in 54 tent towns.
Preconditions for reconstruction Complete land surveys of geological conditions Complete new land planning based on geological surveys Establish ownership rights for housing guarantee	Completed spring 2000. Needed for land valuation, housing construction, and resumption of commercial activities. Ankara largely in charge, but local mayors want to plan for local needs.	Encourage national/local co-operation in urban planning. Assemble international team of urban planning advisors. Local mayors have ideas, but no expertise in urban planning. Need also to plan for adequate rental housing and needs of business.
Transition during reconstruction Housing construction and installation of basic infrastructure in new areas	Housing construction highly interventionist. State is building 40 000 homes, with supporting infrastructure, entirely designed and allocated from Ankara. Target date for completion end-2000.	Introduction of market forces in redevelopment, for example, giving tradeable vouchers for land auctions, and partnering with private sector for commercial redevelopment. Use the reconstruction to improve cities and their economic base.
Compensation for lost or damaged houses	Mix of interventionist (housing swaps) and bottom-up approaches (cash payments for housing repair or relocation). About 125 000 households affected by the latter.	Compensation should permit as much choice as possible. Cash is better than houses. Tradeable vouchers are a possibility. Incentives better than standardised approaches.
Post-reconstruction and normalisation Move to market-driven economic development	Regulatory reforms to banking sector. Mandatory insurance scheme for buildings. Removal of housing replacement guarantee.	Risk-based insurance for new buildings. Government should provide risk information on land use to sellers/buyers/financiers.
More efficient government land planning and better building standards	Outsourcing of municipal inspections function to private engineering companies with professional standards and legal liability; upgrading of building codes to EU standards; specification of municipal and professional responsibilities and penalties; reform of public contract tendering rules.	Responsibilities in planning law must be clarified with corresponding sanctions. Urban planning standards should be more rigorous with informed citizen input and more methodical distribution of land. Local authority reform to improve implementation of planning. More training of engineers.
Better disaster response management	National emergency management agency set up, consolidating hitherto dispersed emergency planning and response functions.	Follow up on plans to educate the public and to engage the local authorities. Need to retrofit schools, hospitals, and possibly houses, in the short to medium run.

Source: OECD.

regime, now set in train, should be beneficial for individual earthquake awareness. However, it could only impact on the current housing stock with a very long lag.

Whatever measures are taken to ensure better governance and to promote private insurance provision, disaster preparedness, especially in the threatened region of Istanbul, needs to rely on improving the earthquake resistance of the existing housing stock ("retrofitting"). Retrofitting will be enormously expensive, and could only be achieved very gradually, but it would seem inevitable that the government will have to undertake more spending beyond the reconstruction phase in order to avoid yet greater budgetary and human costs in the future. This might involve tax breaks to complement the new national insurance scheme, but the full cost for rehabilitation of low-income housing may have to be borne by the state, especially those in illegal settlements that are not covered by insurance. And in the event of a major earthquake before the new insurance fund has matured, the state will also have to bear a large portion of the insured claims. At the same time, schools, hospitals, and other public buildings in the zones at risk urgently need to be reinforced and earthquake-proofed, so as to become useable as shelters for the most vulnerable members of society. The demands on the budget will thus remain heavy – coming on top of those identified to meet the needs of human capital development, requiring redoubled structural reforms to eliminate wasteful spending, prioritising of expenditures and continuing efforts to strengthen tax administration.

The general policy implications of the recent earthquakes are that their human and material effects are a function of the governance and incentive structures that are in operation, and policy responses to future threats need to take this into account. In this sense, the structural reform responses to Turkey's earthquake vulnerability are part of the same process of modernisation and enhanced transparency which is required for economic modernisation. The progress already underway within the government in enhancing transparency and accountability in the public sector and creating a rules-based market-oriented framework for private-sector initiative should make for an environment which allows a more orderly, earthquake-resistant pattern of urban development than has been apparent in the past two decades.

Notes

1. However, the latter was also assisted by an inflow of about $2 billion attributed to the residual errors and omissions in the balance of payments.

2. See Selasie (1999) for a wider discussion. The same ratio for the average of the OECD countries amounts to about 71 per cent.

3. Following an agreement between the Treasury and the Central Bank, direct Treasury access to Central Bank advances was curtailed from the second half of 1997.

4. Having declined by 38 per cent in 1998, repo operations of banks with their clients rose by 17 per cent in 1999, measured in dollar terms.

5. The path is slightly front-loaded, the rate of depreciation decelerating gradually in the course of the year, and is to be extended on a rolling basis at the end of each calendar quarter.

6. See Mishkin (1999), p. 10.

7. See Kiguel and Liviatan (1992) and Mussa *et al.* (2000) for detailed discussions of the results of such programmes.

8. Public sector civil servants amount to 2 million, including notably, teachers, but also administrative employees, including health and social security employees.

9. By June the take home pay of the civil servants had benefited from an additional one-off 1 per cent increase arising from the abolition of the compulsory contributions to the obligatory savings scheme introduced in 1988. The effects of such a measure on the wages and salaries of employees in the private sector was offset by the introduction of an equivalent compulsory contribution to the unemployment insurance scheme created in connection with the 1999 social security legislation. Under the new system, civil servants are not required to pay a similar contribution.

10. However, to the extent that the demand boom spilled over into the current account, more pressure on domestic prices was avoided.

11. One important underlying motive for the conclusion of the agreement, which has been phased in gradually from January 2000, was the need to achieve the widest possible public consensus around a major social security reform approved in the summer of 1999.

12. The number of workers affected by such negotiations ranges between 220 and 260 thousand, of which more than half in private manufacturing (metal, textile and garment). The remaining part comprises the public workers outside the Public Sector Employers' Associations (mainly general workers employed in the municipalities, including Ankara and Istanbul).

13. As a contribution to this process, parliament has approved a law to switch from backward-looking to forward-looking indexation in the determination of the minimum premium base on social security contributions for 2000-01.

14. The tourism sector appears set to produce results at least as strong as 1998, following a poor 1999.

15. See Ghosh (1999).

16. There is also a special export-credit programme that has been put into place.

17. Chapter II shows that the tax-to-GDP ratio is set to rise by about 1½ percentage points in 2001 (and by about 2 percentage points in comparison with the previous plan for 2001). Real GDP growth is expected to decline by 2 percentage points between 2000 and 2001 (see Table 1). Assuming a tax elasticity with respect to GDP of around 1 and "potential" GDP growth of about 3½ per cent, the "structural" tax ratio rises by about 5 percentage points of GDP between 2000 and 2001, according to OECD calculations.

18. The projected current account deficit is around $9 billion in each of 2000 and 2001, while the estimated 2000 and target 2001 foreign borrowing of the government are each around $8.5 billion.

19. See Folkerst-Landau *et al.* (1995).

20. Many of these Asian countries were committed to the pursuance of an exchange rate target strategy during the 1990s. See Mishkin (1999), for a wider discussion.

21. Under the framework of econometric analysis, Ozatay (1997) and Ozmen and Kogar (1998) investigated the sustainability of debt stock and budget deficit respectively. The conclusions drew the attention to the unsustainability of fiscal balances under current economic conditions and necessity of policy regime changes.

22. Ozatay (1997), Ozmen and Kogar (1998), Atiyas *et al.* (1999), and Ozgun (2000).

23. The short-term advance has not been used as a financing method anymore since the protocol signed between the Central Bank and the Treasury in 1997. Treasury occasionally uses it for liquidity reasons and repays the amount totally within a month.

24. The tax was at first controversial because it was totally unexpected, was levied on interest accruing before introduction of the tax, and applied only to government paper. However, markets adjusted quickly.

25. For the first half of the year, a 15 per cent wage hike was awarded. An additional 4.1 per cent was given in June, reflecting 2.1 per cent inflation compensation and 2 per cent welfare bonus; and a 10 per cent increase was realised for the second half of 2000.

26. Since the appropriations were already determined in the central government consolidated budget as "transfers to SEEs" which is mainly composed of wages and salaries of SEEs' employees, there will be no extra appropriations for energy sector SEEs as transfers from the central government budget. The burden of SEEs will be directly reflected in the consolidated public sector deficit through their accounts.

27. For further discussion see Kogar (1998).

28. The living-standard tax was applied between 1983 and 1999 and removed with the 1998 tax reform. This tax will be levied on the self-employed ensuring a minimum amount of tax collection, with expected additional revenue of between 0.2 and 0.4 per cent of GNP in 2001.

29. The merged banks will be exempt from tax liabilities for three years, while institutions and persons who will buy the banks at a loss will have the right to subtract the losses of those banks from their profits for a five-year period.

30. However, off-balance sheet financial liabilities such as price purchase guarantees provided under BOT energy contracts (see Chapter III) appear to be large but difficult to evaluate precisely in the absence of better monitoring of such off-balance sheet debt.

31. There are also socio-cultural factors at work (see last year's Survey), which impedes the supply of and demand for married women's labour. As education levels rise, so also should women's participation, in line with international patterns (for example, Spain's female participation rate rose dramatically in the 1970s and 1980s)..

32. The end-2000 target is to reduce the premium on grains over world prices from 45 per cent at the start of the year to 35 per cent by end year.

33. The budgets of three core agricultural SEEs, TMO (wheat), TEKEL (tobacco), and TSFAS (sugar) have been included as performance criteria under the stand-by agreement. In 2000, the legal framework for privatising the processing facilities of TEKEL will be established. In 2001, privatisation of tea factories of Caykur and sugar plants of TSFAS will be initiated. Some firms will have to be liquidated, such as TZDAS, the state firm responsible for input supply already in liquidation proceedings.

34. The World Bank is planning to provide technical and financial assistance in these areas, in addition to helping to manage the pilot programme. A vital aspect of the training will be to teach farmers to grow alternative crops.

35. One major reason for denying approvals was that the Danistay saw that the price guarantees offered under the BOT contracts implied large contingent liabilities for the government. This problem is discussed further below.

36. The subsequent law also gave the government authority to extend the right to international arbitration retroactively on a case by case basis.

37. See World Bank (2000b).

38. At the end of 1999, TEAS was selling electricity to TEDAS for about 3.8 cents per kWh including transmission, but was paying private generators around 6 to 9 cents per kWh. As current BOT projects come to fruition, TEAS' losses may grow to a cumulative $9 billion by 2010. See World Bank (2000b).

39. In the longer run, retail sales activities will be separated from the distribution services, and retailers will be able to directly purchase electricity from the generators or from the Trading Company (including the transmission and distribution fees into the tariffs). In addition, "Eligible Consumers" will be free to choose their suppliers by way of "Bilateral Agreements".

40. In 2001 there is to be a sale of 5 per cent of the shares to the company's workers and local investors, with a further 14 per cent of the shares to be sold through an international public offering. Another 10 per cent is to be set aside for the post office.

41. This could be challenged in the courts, however, the first investor claiming that the "rules of the game" have changed.

42. Turkish Airlines 51 per cent strategic sale was expected to be announced in Q4 (rather than Q3) 2000; PETKIM petrochemical company was postponed to 2001 due to restructuring needs of the company (as obsolete Yormca complex will be sold off by the end of 2000); ERDEMIR, a major iron and steel company, has also shifted to 2001 due to a possible merger and acquisition with ISDEMIR, another portfolio company in the sector. Moreover, the lock-up period of Tüpras offering ended in mid-October, not

leaving enough time to launch an immediate deal in Q4 2000, in addition to adverse market conditions. Another tranche of Tüpras and POAS offerings could be expected in first and second half 2001, respectively, depending on the existence of favourable domestic and international market conditions.

43. Privatisations are considered as mergers and acquisitions under the Competition Law. A communiqué issued in 1998 confirmed that competition rules are to be considered in privatisations, by means of "receiving the opinion of the Competition Board as to the post-privatisation course of the dominant positions or concessions held by the public institutions in relevant markets prior to the commencement of bidding transactions, and subjecting the acquisition transaction via privatisation to the consent of the Competition Board after bidding" (Communiqué No. 1998/4).

44. See von Rijckeghem (1997).

45. Demirgüc-Kunt and Huizinga (1999) show that inflation pushes up interest margins for a broad sample of high inflation countries and interpret this as higher inflation implying higher real risk for bank owners, who in turn require higher real returns. Selassie (1999) shows that even after adjusting such margins for the effect of inflation itself (which reduces the real level of a given margin), Turkey stands out as having higher interest margins than any other country in his sample.

46. See Moalla-Fetini (1999).

47. See World Bank (1999*b*).

48. See Rajan and Zingales (2000), who argue that growth is faster where capital market finance is present.

49. By June 2000 the maximum open foreign exchange position was reduced from 30 to 20 per cent of capital, and the minimum capital adequacy ratio was adapted to BIS standards. At the same time, the liquidity ratio which is applied to the exceeded amount of the foreign exchange position of banks was increased from 8 per cent to 100 per cent of the total amount.

50. The level of deposits under the coverage of the Savings Deposit Insurance Fund declines from unlimited to a maximum of TL 100 billion per account until the end of 2000, and to TL 50 billion thereafter.

51. Passage of the related legislation was originally intended for August 2000, but has been delayed.

52. An earlier "decree with the force of law" (KHK) to privatise Vakif was annulled by the Constitutional Court in October 2000.

53. In 1999, the minimum pensionable wage was 4 million TL per day, close to the minimum wage. The September 1999 social security law changed the system, establishing the minimum pensionable wage at 5 million TL per day and indexing it to the CPI (in effect, delinking it from the minimum wage), however on a forward rather than a backward looking basis, in line with incomes policy.

54. These are projections of the World Bank (World Bank, 2000*b*). The government's own projection shows a smaller near-term improvements and a smaller long-term deterioration. The differences stem from differences in GNP projections, mortality rate (World Bank assumes a decline), and assumptions about the age at which people start contributing into the system.

55. Indeed, calculations show that the up-front improvement in system balances is primarily due to increased contributions, as the phase-in of the new minimum retirement age is rather slow.

56. The average wage is about five times the minimum wage, approximately the level of the ceiling in the likely event that the Council of Ministers exercises its discretion to raise the latter further to five times the minimum pensionable wage. The ILO recommends a 60 per cent replacement of previous earnings as an adequate retirement. Thus, the ILO condition would be met for the "average" worker.

57. The government had initially prepared a very ambitious reform proposal but was compelled to modify it in the face of stiff opposition from the labour unions.

58. It covers the members of SSK (private employees' pension scheme), the employees of some organisations which are not covered by SSK such as banks, insurance companies, chambers of trade, and exchange and foreign workers from countries with which bilateral social security arrangements were made.

59. However, there is a contentious discussion going on about what to do with the stock of accumulated savings contributions – give it back to workers or fold it into the unemployment insurance fund.

60. See Blondal and Pearson (1994).

61. In its Letter of Development Policy (March 2000), the government has requested such assistance from the World Bank.

62. This decline in spending reflected the 1994 crisis. According to Turkish data, public spending declined from 4.4 per cent of GNP in 1993 to 2.8 by 1995. However, with the 1997 reform to raise years of compulsory schooling to eight, public education spending (Turkish data) rose from 3 per cent of GNP in 1996 to 3.4 and 3.9 per cent in 1997 and 1998, respectively, before falling back to 3.6 per cent in 1999.

63. See Ahn and Hemmings (2000).

64. OECD (1995).

65. A strong R&D capability has been shown to be a primary determinant of the absorptive capacity for the transfer of technology via multinational firms, whose domestic presence seems to expand considerably. It could be added that a strongly competitive market environment is another factor enhancing the transfer of technology from abroad, because it forces foreign firms to increase the value added in their local operations, with consequent spill-over effects in the local economy.

66. At the same time, the focus of education policy should not be exclusively on science, to avoid the risk that science absorbs many of the highly skilled people that are needed for the economy more broadly.

67. See Wiss, Janney, Elstner Associates, Inc. (1999).

68. A Parliamentary Earthquake Investigation Commission report commented that the 110 people of the Civil Defence Institution had "virtually become lost amongst the 13 600 damaged buildings" after the Marmara quake and that insufficiency of personnel had resulted in a low success rate for rescuing persons from collapsed buildings.

69. There were critical failures in the national infrastructure: i) the main fibre optic cable governing telephone connections into the earthquake region was cut where it crossed the fault line just east of Ismit; ii) two main substations on the electric power grid were damaged, causing a widespread power blackout across Turkey; and iii) an overpass on the motorway between Ismit and Ankara collapsed. Compounding these failures was widespread cellular phone use by outsiders trying to get information from the region, which caused the telephone system to break down completely, and by people driving to the region, which clogged the roads. See World Bank (1999b).

70. The response to the second (November) earthquake was much better co-ordinated, as reflected in part in the far lower ratio of deaths to houses destroyed (.03 versus .26 in August). This was because of lessons learned from the mistakes made in first earthquake, but also because the geographical and seismic magnitude of the shock was not so large as to overwhelm the rescue capacities of the region and nation.

71. Many foreign companies have affiliates nearby in the region, including Goodyear, Pirelli, Honda, Hyundai, Toyota, Renault, FIAT, Ford, Bridgestone, Mannesmann, Lafarge and Bayer.

72. In addition, there are some large-scale enterprises which are established in Istanbul and use loans from Istanbul branches to make investments both in and out of the earthquake region. Including such indirect exposures, the World Bank initially estimated total banking exposure at about double the given estimate.

73. The new loan programme differs from regular subsidised lending operations (Ziraat to the agricultural sector, Halk to small businessmen and artisans, and Emlak for housing) mainly in terms of ease and breadth of access (*e.g.*, large firms as well as SMEs could apply for Halk Bank credits).

74. In many cases the houses were habitable, but the residents were afraid to enter them for fear they would collapse. This reflected the very low level of credibility among the population of official damage assessments (see "Temporary Shelter Report" in World Bank, 1999*c*).

75. Surveys indicate that the tent camp population was relatively poor and poorly educated. Nearly half had owned their houses and 61 per cent had lived in an apartment building; 38 per cent were under treatment for illness, and 64 per cent had experienced psychosocial problems since the earthquake, rising to 79 per cent for children. They tended to develop focused strategies for assuring that they were eligible for as many benefit options as possible, but felt great uncertainty. They exhibited classical symptoms of dependency and victimisation. A significant number were unwilling to move to prefabs because they did not want to lose the fringe benefits associated with camp living. By contrast, those living next to friends and relatives were more likely to have financial resources and emotional support, and more likely to have a plan that the cash from the rental subsidy would support (*ibid.*).

76. This was below market value of $4 200, as the Ministry of Public Works (the sole purchaser) was in a position to set prices and standards for these units.

77. Reflecting the pattern for Turkey as a whole, about three-quarters of the affected population is either a member of a social security fund or the dependent of one.

78. According to the MPW, 70 per cent of the population having lost their shelters are homeowners. Of these, around 75 per cent will have legal beneficiary. This would tend to support the lower band estimate of the World Bank.

79. Original plans were for construction to start in March. However, the MPW later imposed a moratorium on new construction until July in order to allow more time for new inspections and control systems to be put into place (see below). Also, another 6 500 units are being built directly by the World Bank, but approval of the sites (by the MPW) has been subject to some delay. The World Bank is also repairing some 55 000 units.

80. These estimates do not include the cost of relocating entire cities, which could substantially raise the upper bound. For example, the town of Adapazari (capital of Sakarya province) has been planning to relocate all housing 20 km outside the city, due to poor soil quality there (which liquifies easily in earthquakes).

81. The PIU was set up in the Prime Minister's office in the context of an earlier loan project and has now been strengthened to co-ordinate all paperwork, tenders, and disbursements of aid in a transparent way. Appointments of the staff of the PIU must be approved by the Bank, and Bank procurement rules must be followed. Official disbursements via the PIU are moreover largely conditional upon Bank-specified policy reforms in the disaster preparedness area. These include the setting up of: *i*) a national co-ordinating disaster management agency while enhancing the capabilities of the local authorities in coping with a future disaster, and *ii*) a national mandatory earthquake insurance plan; with iii) appropriate modification of the Disaster Law, Urban Planning Law, and State Tender Law (see below).

82. See World Bank (1999*b*).

83. Public land ownership is quite high in Turkey (55 per cent of the territory). This reflects the legacy of Ottoman times when the government owned essentially all the land, together with the subsequent failure to distribute it in a methodical way, but rather by default through *ex post* regularisation of squatting.

84. Often, mayoral candidates promised such amnesties in return for the sizeable number of votes the residents of these squatter communities could deliver.

85. Anecdotal evidence suggests that in some cases building quality and legal observance have deteriorated in the formal sector as well (*e.g.*, builders would add a number of stories to high rise buildings beyond those stipulated in the construction permits, and then secured *ex post* certification from inspectors). This could reflect both competitive pressure from the informal sector and the general attitude of regulatory laxity with which it is associated.

86. For smaller-size crises with more localised effects, the Ministry of Public Works is put in charge of crisis management, with local authorities administering its directives and "Provincial Committees" (purely administrative organs of the central government at the regional level) mobilising resources to the region.

87. The World Bank will be helping Turkey to set up a process for the development, review, and promulgation of a comprehensive unified building code, while clarifying the legal status of the codes, reference standards and public commentary.

88. See OECD (1996).

89. See State Planning Organisation (2000).

90. The New Zealand and California Earthquake Authorities, for example, have found ways to price residential earthquake insurance products, transferring large portions of the risk via reinsurance.

91. However, it did not become fully operational until the end of November 2000.

92. See World Bank (1999*a*).

Bibliography

Ahn, S. and P. Hemmings (2000),
"Policy Influences on Economic Growth in OECD Countries: an Evaluation of the Evidence", OECD, *Economics Department Working Papers*, No. 246.

Atiyas, I. and S. Sayin (1997),
Political Accountability, Managerial Accountability and Budget System: Towards a Proposal for Restructuring, in Turkish, TESEV Publications No. 4.

Atiyas, I. and S. Sayin (1998),
"Budgetary Institutions in Turkey", presented at Mediterranean Development Forum, Morocco, 3-6 September.

Atiyas, I., Y. Gunduz, F. Emil, C. Erdem and B. Ozgun (1999),
"Fiscal Adjustment in Turkey: the Role of Quasi-Fiscal Activities and Institutional Reform", T.C. Hazine Mustesarligi, *Arastirma Inceleme Dizisi* 22.

Blöndal, S. and M. Pearson (1994),
"Unemployment and Other Non-employment Benefits", *Oxford Review of Economic Policy*, Vol. 11, No. 1.

Çilli, H. and C. Kaplan (1998),
"Analysing the Impact of Disinflation on the Banking System: a Conceptual Note", in *Macroeconomic Analysis of Turkey: Essays on Current Issues* (ed. M. Üçer), Central Bank Research Department Publications, pp. 220-241, December.

Demirgüç-Kunt, A. and H. Huizinga (1999),
"Determinants of Commercial Bank Interest Margins and Profitability: Some International Evidence", *The World Bank Economic Review*, Vol. 13, No. 2 (May), pp. 379-408.

Fischer, S. (1982),
"Seignorage and the Case for a National Money", *Journal of Political Economy*, Vol. 90, No. 2.

Fischer, S. (1993),
"The Role of Macroeconomic Factors in Growth", *Journal of Monetary Economics*, Vol. 32, No. 3.

Folkerts-Landau, D., G.J. Schinasi, M. Cassard, V.K. Ng, C.M. Reinhart and M.G. Spencer (1995),
"Effects of Capital Flows on the Domestic Financial Sectors in APEC Developing Countries", in *Capital Flows in the APEC Region* (eds. M.S. Khan and C.M. Reinhart), International Monetary Fund, 31-57, Washington.

Förster, M.F. (assisted by M. Pellissari) (2000),
"Trends and Driving Factors in Income Distribution and Poverty in the OECD Area", OECD, *Labour Market and Social Policy Occasional Papers*, No. 42, August.

Ghosh, A. (1999),
"Turkey's External Current Account", in IMF, Turkey: Selected Issues and Statistical Appendix, December.

Gonenc, R., M. Maher and G. Nicoletti (2000),
"The Implementation and the Effects of Regulatory Reform: Past Experience and Current Issues", OECD, Economics Department Working Papers, No. 251.

Government of Turkey (1999),
"IMF Stand-By Agreement: Letter of Intent dated 9 December 1999", www.tcmb.gov.fr or www.treasury.gov.tr.

International Monetary Fund (IMF) (2000),
Report on the Observance of Standards and Code: Fiscal Transparency, Washington.

Jarvis, C. and A. Selassie (1999),
"The 1999 Social Security Reform", in IMF, Turkey: Selected Issues and Statistical Appendix, December.

Kiguel, M.A. and N. Liviatan (1992),
"The Business Cycle Associated with Exchange Rate-Based Stabilizations", The World Bank Economic Review, Vol. 6, No. 2.

Kogar, C. (1998),
"Operational Budget Balance: Methodological Issues and Application to Turkey", in Macroeconomic Analysis of Turkey: Essays on Current Issues, (ed. M. Üçer), Central Bank Research Department Publications, pp. 171-211, December.

Mishkin, F.S. (1999),
"International Experiences with Different Monetary Policy Regimes", NBER Working Paper, No. 7044, March.

Moalla-Fetini, R. (1999),
"Inflation as a Fiscal Problem", in IMF, Turkey: Selected Issues and Statistical Appendix, December.

Mussa, M., P. Masson, A. Swoboda, E. Jadresic, P. Mauro and A. Berg (2000),
"Exchange Rate Regimes in an Increasingly Integrated World Economy", IMF Occasional Paper, No. 193.

OECD (1995),
National Science and Technology Policy Review: Turkey, Paris.

OECD (1996),
Managing Across Levels of Government, Paris.

OECD (1997),
Energy Policy Review: Turkey, Paris.

OECD (1998),
Fostering Entrepreneurship, Paris.

OECD (1999),
OECD Economic Surveys: Turkey, Paris.

OECD (2000),
Agricultural Policies in OECD Countries: Monitoring and Evaluation 2000, Paris.

Ozmen E. and C. Kogar, (1998),
"Sustainability of Budget Deficits in Turkey with a Structural Shift", METU Studies in Development, 25(1), pp. 107-128.

Oxley, H., T.T. Dang and P. Antolin (2000),
    "Poverty Dynamics in Six OECD Countries", OECD *Economic Studies* 30, 2000/1.

Ozatay, F. (1997),
    "Sustainability of Fiscal Deficits, Monetary Policy and Inflation Stabilisation: the Case of
    Turkey", *Journal of Policy Modelling*, 19(6), pp. 661-681.

Ozgun, B. (2000),
    "An Empirical Approach to Fiscal Deficits and Inflation: Evidence From Turkey",
    T.C. Hazine Mustesarligi, *Arastirma Inceleme Dizisi* 25.

Parker, R., A. Kramer and M. Munsinghe (eds. 1995),
    *Informal Settlements, Environmental Degradation, and Disaster Vulnerability: The Turkey Case
    Study*, The International Decade for Natural Disaster Reduction (IDNDR) and the World
    Bank, Washington.

Rajan, R. and L. Zingales (2000),
    "The Great Reversals: The Politics of Financial Development in the 20th Century",
    OECD, *Economics Department Working Papers*, No. 265.

Saygili K. (2000),
    "Funds System in Turkey" mimeo, SPO.

Selassie, A. (1999),
    "Implications of Disinflation for Banks' Profitability in Turkey", in IMF, *Turkey: Selected
    Issues and Statistical Appendix*, December.

Selçuk, F. and E. Yeldan (1999),
    "On the Macroeconomic Impact of the August 1999 Earthquake in Turkey: A First
    Assessment", Department of Economics, Bilkent University, Bilkent-Ankara, Turkey,
    September.

State Planning Organisation (SPO) (2000a),
    "Restructuring of Public Finance Management and Fiscal Transparency", Report,
    Special *ad hoc* Committee, SPO, March (in Turkish).

SPO (2000b),
    Global Forum on Local Governance and Social Services for All: Turkish Case for Local Administrations,
    Stockholm, May.

Van Rijckeghem, C. (1977),
    "The Political Economy of Inflation: Are Turkish Banks Potential Losers from Stabiliza-
    tion? ", Istanbul Stock Exchange Review, Vol. 3, pp. 1-16.

Wiss, Janney, Elstner Associates, Inc. (1999),
    WJE Earthquake Engineering Update, September.

World Bank (1999a),
    Managing Disaster Risk in Mexico: Market Incentives for Mitigation Investment, Washington, June.

World Bank (1999b),
    Turkey: Marmara Earthquake Assessment, Turkey Country Office, September.

World Bank (1999c),
    *Project Appraisal Document of a Proposed Loan in the Amount of US$505 million to the Republic of
    Turkey for a Marmara Earthquake Emergency Reconstruction Project*, Washington, November.

World Bank (2000a),
    Turkey: Economic Reforms, Living Standards and Social Welfare Study, Washington, January.

World Bank (2000b),
    Turkey: Country Economic Memorandum, Structural Reforms for Sustainable Growth, Washington,
    September.

Annex I

Links between growth and inflation: evidence for Turkey

Empirical support for the view that inflation is harmful to growth remained weak until the 1970s, but built up considerably thereafter as many emerging countries started to experience episodes of high and persistent inflation. This shift in consensus is apparent from Table A1, which provides a recapitulation of the existing empirical literature. Moreover, the available studies suggest that there may be important non-linear effects of inflation on output growth, the link being stronger in cases of high inflation (see amongst others, Bruno and Easterly, 1998; Barro, 1995; Fischer, 1995). Recent work by Sarel (1996) finds the break to occur around an inflation rate of 8 per cent, implying that output growth might accelerate considerably in Turkey should the country meet the target of permanently moving to within a one-digit inflation rate.

Drawing from recent OECD work that explores the links between policy settings, institutions and growth (OECD, 2000), this annex takes a closer empirical look at the relation between inflation and aggregate output growth in Turkey. The estimated equation is derived from a conventional production function with constant returns to scale, which assumes that output is a function of the inputs of physical capital, employment, and the efficiency with which they act together. Within this setting, the steady-state level of output per capita is a function of the propensity to accumulate physical capital, the rate of growth of population, the growth rate of technological efficiency and the rate of capital depreciation.

The empirical approach adopted considers an *inflation-augmented* version of the standard neo-classical growth specification. This is subsequently extended so as to account for the *variability of inflation* as the related higher degree of uncertainty may also have important negative real consequences. Finally, a specific test is carried out to investigate the *direction of causality between growth and inflation*. It is possible, in fact, that the direct link between growth and inflation masks the impact of a set of external shocks that ultimately exacerbate inflationary pressures while also causing slower output growth. Following Fischer (1998), the latter issue is addressed by augmenting the basic model to account for the change of the terms of trade, an important source of supply shocks for Turkey. The analysis uses quarterly data and, in order to control for short-term processes, it introduces different error-correction terms for the various explanatory variables. More specifically, the following specification is estimated:

$$\Delta \ln y_t = a_0 - \phi \ln y_{t-1} + a_1 \ln s^k_{t-1} - a_2 n_{t-1} - \sum_{j=3} a_j \ln \Pi^j_{t-1}$$
$$- \sum_{h=1}^{4} b_{1,h} \Delta \ln y^k_{t-h} + \sum_{h=1}^{4} b_{1,h} \Delta \ln s^k_{t-h} - \sum_{h=1}^{4} b_{2,h} \Delta n_{t-h} - \sum_{h=1}^{4} b_{j,h} \Delta \ln \Pi^j_{t-h} + \varepsilon_t \tag{1}$$

Table A1. **Empirical studies on the real effects of inflation**

Studies		Dependent variable	Nominal variable	Number of countries	Time period	Data frequency	Correlation
Phillips	(1958)	U	ω	1 (UK)	1880-1950	Annual	Negative
McCandless and Weber	(1995)	Yg	μ	110	1960-90	30-year averages	Positive for OECD, zero otherwise
		Yg	π	110	1960-90		Zero
Bullard and Keating	(1995)	Yg	π	58	1960-90	Annual	Positive at very low π, zero otherwise
Geweke	(1986)	Yg	μ	1 (US)	1870-1978	Annual	Zero
Boschen and Mills	(1995)	Yg	μ	1 (US)	1951-90	Quarterly	Zero
Kormendi and Meguire	(1985)	Yg	μ	47	1950-77	28 year average	Zero
		Yg	π	47			Negative
De Gregorio and Edwards	(1992)	Yg	π	12	1950-85	6-year average	Negative
Cardoso	(1992)	w	π	7	1977-89	12-year average	Negative
Barro	(1995)	Yg	π	117	1960-90	10-year average	Negative
		Ig	π				Negative
Bruno and Easterly	(1995)	Yg	π	127	1961-92	Annual	Negative
Ghosh and Phillips	(1998)	Yg	π	145	1960-96	Annual	Negative
Fischer, Sahay and Végh	(1999)	Yg	π	130	1960-97	Annual	Negative
		Cg	π				Negative
		Ig	π				Negative
		e	π				Negative
		CA	π				Negative
Braumann	(2000)	Yg	π	17	1961-97	Annual	Negative
		Ig	π				Negative
		Gg	π				Negative
		w	π				Negative

Note: ω = nominal wage growth   N = employment
μ = money growth   U = unemployment
π = inflation   C = consumption
Y = real GDP   e = real exchange rate
I = real investment   CA = current account
w = real wage
g = when present, the subscript indicates that the reference variable is expressed in growth rate terms

Source: Braumann (2000) and OECD.

where y denotes output per capita, ϕ is the convergence coefficient, s^k is the propensity to accumulate physical capital, n is population growth, Π^i is a vector of several inflation variables affecting per capita output growth, the b – regressors identify error correction terms and ε is the usual error term.[1]

The variables included in the basic regression equation are as follows:

- *Dependent variable* (Δlog y_{-1}). Growth of real per capita output, defined using the measures of aggregate real GDP and the working age population (*i.e.* population aged 15-64).

- *Convergence variable* (log y_{-1}). Lagged real per capita GDP of the working age population.

- *Physical capital accumulation* (log s^k_{-1}). Lagged ratio of real fixed capital formation to real GDP, a proxy for the propensity to accumulate physical capital.

- *Population growth* (Δlog n_{-1}). Lagged growth in the working-age population.[2]

Table A2. **The role of inflation for growth**

	Inflation	Inflation uncertainty	Causality
Dependent variable: Δlog y_{-1}			
Estimation period: 1977:2-1999:4 Explanatory variables:			
Constant	2.988	2.944	3.482
	(3.42)	(3.31)	(4.08)
log y_{-1}	–0.192	–0.189	–0.224
	(–3.36)	(–3.47)	(–4.01)
log s^k_{-1}	0.105	0.102	0.119
	(3.78)	(3.47)	(4.41)
π_{-1}	–0.025	–0.024	–0.026
	(3.04)	(3.00)	(–3.30)
$sd\pi_{-1}$	. .	0.003	. .
		(0.30)	
tot_{-1}	. .	. .	–0.034
			(–2.91)
Δy_{-1}	–0.146	–0.147	–0.131
	(–1.94)	(–1.95)	(–1.83)
Δs^k_{-1}	0.154	0.150	0.166
	(3.45)	(3.26)	(3.88)
$\Delta\pi_{-1}$	–0.029	–0.029	–0.030
	(–4.84)	(4.81)	(–5.33)
R^2	0.690	0.691	0.719
SE of regression	0.022	0.022	0.021
Sum of squared residuals	0.040	0.040	0.036
DW	1.752	1.749	1.713
F-statistics	26.428	22.883	26.258

Note: t-statistics are in brackets.
Source: OECD.

Three measures of inflation were included in the extended growth equation, defined as follows:

- Inflation (π_{-1}). The rate of growth of the private consumption deflator lagged one period.
- Indicator of inflation uncertainty ($sd\pi_{-1}$). The moving standard deviation of the rate of growth of the private consumption deflator, calculated over four quarters.
- Indicator of the robustness of the causal relationship between inflation and growth (tot_{-1}). The lagged change in the terms of trade, calculated using the ratio between the export and import deflators (goods and services).

Table A2 presents the set of estimation results obtained using the OLS technique for a time series specification that covers the period between 1977-Q2 and 1999-Q4, with a total of 90 observations. The coefficient on inflation suggests that a 10 per cent increase in inflation leads to a ¼ percentage point decline in the growth rate of per-capita GDP, while the period of time required to achieve half the transition ranges between three and four quarters. As such, the results are broadly consistent with the findings of the recent literature that has focused on countries with a range of inflation rates similar to those of Turkey.[3]

Aside from the standard tests, the dynamic equation is expanded to account for the role played by inflation uncertainty. However, the new estimate shows that there is little evidence of any impact of inflation variability on the output relationship. This result appears to corroborate the general view that, notwithstanding the severe costs of inflation, Turkish agents display a high capacity to adapt quickly. Finally, the last column of Table A2 expands the initial specification with a variable capturing the importance of a possible external terms-of trade shock. The coefficient on the terms of trade is negative and significant while its insertion does not appear to alter the role played by the rate of inflation. Overall, the result suggests that the causation runs significantly, but not exclusively, from inflation to growth.

Notes

1. Only significant b short-term regressors were retained in the preferred specifications.
2. Though characterised by the proper sign, the population coefficient was not significant and was dropped from the summary table presented below.
3. See Barro (1995) and Fischer (1993), for example.

References

Bassanini, A., S. Scarpetta and P. Hemmings (2001),
"Economic Growth: the role of policies and institutions, Panel data evidence from OECD countries", OECD, *Economics Department Working Papers* (forthcoming).

Barro, R.J. (1995),
"Inflation and Economic Growth", *Bank of England Quarterly Bulletin*, pp. 166-176, May.

Boschen, J. and O. Mills (1995),
"Test of Long-Run Neutrality Using Permanent Monetary and Real Shocks", *Journal of Monetary Economics*, 35, pp. 25-44.

Braumann, B. (2000),
"Real Effects of High Inflation", IMF *Working Paper*, WP/00/85, May.

Bruno, M. and W. Easterly (1998),
"Inflation Crises and Long-Run Growth", *Journal of Monetary Economics*, No. 41, pp. 3-26.

Bullard, J. and W. Keating (1995),
"The Long-Run Relationship Between Inflation and Output in Postwar Economies", *Journal of Monetary Economics*, 47, pp. 97-133.

Cardoso, E. (1992),
"Inflation and Poverty", NBER *Working Paper*, No. 4006.

De Gregario, J. and S. Edwards (1992),
"The Effects of Inflation on Economic Growth", *European Economic Review*, 36, pp. 417-425.

Fischer, S. (1993),
"The role of Macroeconomic Factors in Growth", *Journal of Monetary Economics*, No. 32, pp. 485-512.

Fischer, S., R. Sahay and C. Végh (1999),
"Modern Hyper- and High Inflations", IMF, mimeo.

Geweke, J. (1986),
"The Superneutrality of Money in the United States: An Interpretation of the Evidence", *Econometrica*, 54, pp. 1-21.

Ghosh, A. and S. Philips (1998),
"Warning: Inflation May Be Harmful To Your Growth", IMF *Staff Papers*, Vol. 45, No. 4, December.

Kormendi, R. and P. Meguire (1985),
"Macroeconomic Determinants of Growth", *Journal of Monetary Economics*, 16, pp. 141-163.

McCandless, G. and W. Weber (1995),
"Some Monetary Facts", Federal Reserve of Minneapolis Quarterly Review, Summer, pp. 2-10.

Phillips, A. (1958),
"The Relationship between Unemployment and the Rate of Change of Money Wages in the United Kingdom", *Economica*, 100, pp. 283-299.

Sarel, M. (1996),
"Nonlinear effects of inflation on economic growth", *Staff Papers*, International Monetary Fund, Vol. 43 (March), pp. 199-215.

Annex II

EU Accession Partnership: economic priorities

In December 1999, the European Council in Helsinki welcomed Turkey as a candidate country to join the Union on the basis of the same criteria as applied to the other candidate countries. It was decided that an "Accession Partnership" be drawn up, containing priorities for Turkey's membership preparations. These are identified in the Commission's 2000 Regular Report on Turkey's progress toward membership. The Partnership – adopted by the Council on 4 December 2000 – is the key feature of an enhanced pre-accession strategy to stimulate and support political and economic reforms in Turkey,[1] and to target assistance so as to provide support for overcoming particular problems in view of accession. The EU funds allocated to Turkey will amount to about €180 million per year in grants.[2] Before end-2000 Turkey should adopt a National Programme for the Adoption of the Acquis, *i.e.* to integrate the community "acquis" (accumulated body of law and regulations) into national legislation, and to implement it.

The priorities of the Partnership imply the substantial commitments in both the political and the economic policy area, which have to be fulfilled in order to be able to start negotiations. The economic commitments (the subject of this annex) are due to start in 2001 and to be eventually completed over the medium term with a full adaptation of community law in these areas:

- Ensure the implementation of the current *disinflation and structural reform programme* agreed with the IMF and World Bank, in particular to ensure the control of public expenditures; swift implementation of the financial sector reform aiming at guaranteeing transparency and surveillance; proceed with agricultural reforms; and continue with privatisation of state owned entities taking into account the social component.

- Prepare a pre-accession *fiscal surveillance procedure* consisting of an annual notification of fiscal positions, in line with EU procedures, and presentation of a Pre-accession Economic Programme (PEP).

- On the Internal Market:

  • continue alignment of intellectual property legislation and strengthen fight against piracy;

  • accelerate alignment of European standards, certification and conformity assessment marking, and reinforce the corresponding structures with equipment and training;

  • speed up work related to specific sectors (foodstuffs, cosmetics, pharmaceuticals, textiles) and the framework legislation transposing New and Global Approach principles, create compatible administrative infrastructure, and remove technical barriers to trade;

- adapt legislation designating the responsibility of state aid control to provide basis for transparency and monitoring;
- align public procurement system with community acquis, to ensure greater transparency and accountability.

– On *taxation*, align excise duties and VAT with respect to rates, scope of exemptions, taxable scope and structure; ensure that new tax measures comply with principles of Code of Conduct for Business Taxation.

– In *agriculture*, develop a functioning land register, animal identification and plant passport systems, and improve administrative structures to monitor markets and implement environmental and rural development measures.

– In *fisheries*, establish administrative structures for monitoring of resource exploitation, resource management policy, inspection and control measures, and improvement of fishing fleet register.

– In *transport*, align legislation on maritime safety standards and implement and enforce, adopt action plan to improve performance of Turkish flag register, strengthen maritime administration.

– In the area of *statistics*, develop further demographic, social, regional, business, external trade and agricultural statistics, and bring the business register up to EU standards.

– On *employment and social affairs*, tackle problem of child labour, ensure trade union rights are respected and abolish restrictive provisions on trade union activities, and support social partners' capacity building efforts to develop and implement the acquis.

– In *energy*, establish independent regulatory authority for gas and electricity sectors and grant it the authority and means to carry out its tasks effectively, adopt EU gas and electricity directives and open up markets.

– In *telecommunications*, align with EU acquis in areas of licensing, interconnection and universal service, further liberalise, strengthen capacity building of independent regulator to implement regulations.

– On *regional policy*, introduce regional policy criteria for planning process, develop policy for economic and social cohesion with a view to diminishing disparities, and establish structures for monitoring and evaluation.

– On *culture and audio-visual policy*, align audio-visual legislation and strengthen TV/radio regulatory authority.

– On *environment*, transpose and implement Environmental Impact Assessment directive; as adapt acquis develop institutional, administrative and monitoring capacity to ensure environmental protection, with special focus on nature protection, water quality, and waste management.

– In *customs*, ensure enforcement of new Customs Code; align legislation in particular on free trade zones, dual use goods technologies, precursors and counterfeited and pirated goods.

– In the areas of *administrative and judicial capacity, justice and home affairs*:

- accelerate modernisation and improve capacity of public administration to adopt, implement and manage acquis via training and co-ordination between ministries;
- effective border control to prevent illegal immigration and trafficking in drugs and humans, and enforcement of veterinary and phytosanitary controls;
- strengthen financial control functions, improve efficiency of customs and modernise tax administration and anti-fraud capacity; upgrade food control administration;

- improve operation of the judicial system and promote training in Community law and its application and in JHA affairs; adopt legal, administrative and budgetary framework for programme management;
- enhance the fight against corruption, organised crime, drug trafficking and strengthen capacities to deal with money laundering, as adopt acquis in these areas.

Notes

1. The main principles guiding these reforms and priorities are in the Copenhagen criteria for membership which state: *i)* that the candidate state has achieved stability of institutions guaranteeing democracy, the rule of law, human rights and respect for and protection of minorities; *ii)* the existence of a functioning market economy, as well as the capacity to cope with competitive pressure and market forces within the Union; and *iii)* the ability to take on the obligations for membership, including adherence to the aims of political, economic and monetary union.

2. This includes €127 million per year out of MEDA funds and about €50 million per year for three years based on the European Strategy for Turkey, adopted by the Luxembourg Council in December 1997.

Annex III

Inflation-related revenues of the banking system

Both the government, via the central bank, and the commercial banks have benefited from high inflation over the past two decades. Inflation diminishes the real value of banking-sector liabilities, insofar as Turkish-lira denominated demand deposits are interest-free (or nearly so), as are reserves held at the central bank. The commercial banks invest these deposits in high-yielding bonds, while the central bank passes on its "seignorage" gains to the government by explicitly or implicitly funding the central government deficit, to that extent avoiding the need for the latter to issue high-yielding paper. This annex provides estimates of the (hidden) gains from inflation accruing to the government and the banks.

Central Bank seignorage

The narrowest technical definition of seignorage is the profit from coining money: the difference between the intrinsic and face values of coins. A wider definition would incorporate the profits of the central bank arising from the issue of all base money, calculated as the difference between what the bank pays on its liabilities (cash and reserves) and what it receives on assets (government overdrafts and treasury bills, etc.). In economic terms the definition of seignorage is the negative of the *real rate of interest on cash and reserves* (divided by GNP). On the basis that the central bank pays no interest on its liabilities and inflation (π) increases at the same rate as the monetary base ($\Delta m/m = \pi$), this would be equivalent to a tax rate of $(\Delta m/m)(m/y) = \Delta m/y$. By issuing monetary assets at a rate equal to (identical with) the inflation rate, the central bank is "taxing" money holders (the commercial banks, who pass the loss on to their depositors) at that rate.[1] In practice, in an open economy like Turkey which is subject to unforeseen terms-of-trade shocks, there is no year-to-year correspondence between inflation and money creation. The operational definition of the tax on money balances is thus $-(i - \pi)(m/y)$, where i is the effective rate of interest paid on cash and reserves. Where no interest is paid on required reserves, as in Turkey, the tax rate simplifies to $\pi(m/y)$.

Like other tax bases, this one is affected by the tax itself: the amount of "seignorage" revenue depends on the willingness by the banks and public to hold money balances, which will decline as inflation rises. Because of this erosion of the base, inflation needs to be constantly ratcheted up in order to preserve the same amount of seignorage. In developing countries, this almost invariably degenerates into hyper-inflation. By contrast, formerly high-inflation and seignorage-dependent OECD economies such as Italy, Iceland, Portugal and Greece have disinflated and moved towards more orthodox tax methods. Turkey is unique among OECD economies in being able to maintain high levels of seignorage for so long. Table A3 shows that as inflation rose during the 1980s and early 1990s central bank reserve money (cash in circulation and bank reserves), as a proportion of GDP, fell from 9 per cent in 1986 to less than 7 per cent in the mid 1990s – a normal, but rather slow, decline in real

Table A3. **Banking system balance sheets**

As a percentage of GDP; end of period

	1986	1990	1995	1998	1999	2000[1]
I. Central Bank						
Assets						
Foreign assets	5.2	6.2	11.4	13.2	17.9	13.5
Claims on central government	18.6	8.1	7.7	0.9	..	..
Claims on commercial banks	1.4	1.1	0.4	4.0	4.1	2.9
Other claims	0.1	0.2	0.0	0.0	0.0	0.0
Liabilities						
Reserve money	9.0	7.3	6.5	6.7	8.9	6.8[2]
of which: Cash in circulation	2.5	2.9	2.4	2.0	2.4	1.8
Foreign liabilities	13.7	6.5	9.9	8.0	8.3	6.1
Central government deposits	2.0	1.3	1.3	1.6	2.5	1.6
Capital accounts	0.3	0.3	0.2	0.8	1.7	0.8
Other liabilities (net)	−0.6	0.3	1.2	0.6	0.1	0.7
II. Commercial banks						
Assets						
Reserves	6.7	4.3	4.1	4.7	5.9	4.3
Foreign assets	4.0	3.7	7.6	7.0	10.4	7.1
Commercial loans (claims on private sector)	18.6	15.7	17.8	22.4	22.2	18.6
Domestic securities (claims on government)	5.2	5.1	5.3	15.9	27.4	17.7
Other claims	0.0	0.1	0.1	0.2	0.6	1.1
Liabilities						
Demand deposits	7.3	4.8	2.5	2.7	3.1	2.1
Time and saving deposits	13.1	10.5	12.4	17.5	23.1	15.6
Foreign currency deposits	..	5.4	14.8	16.6	23.4	18.6
Central government deposits	5.4	5.2	1.9	2.9	4.4	3.5
Foreign borrowing	2.3	2.8	4.1	8.8	12.6	9.4
Capital accounts	5.4	5.2	1.9	2.9	4.4	3.5
Other liabilities (net)	1.4	−2.1	−4.7	−5.2	−7.9	−5.9

1. June 2000 figures.
2. Reached 9.6 per cent in September, used in Figure A1.
Source: IMF, *International Financial Statistics.*

base money demand in response to high inflation. As a result, central bank seignorage, defined as the real rate of return from money creation, $\pi(m/y)$, fell slowly from a peak of 5 per cent in 1988 to 3½ per cent in 1993 (Figure A1). Experience since 1994 seems to contradict the normal experience of high-inflation countries, base money stabilising relative to GDP and even rising after 1998 with the decline in inflation. Seignorage rose once more towards 4¾ per cent of GDP by 2000.

The reasons for this rise are partly regulatory and institutional: i) bank customers were required to open demand deposits in order to benefit from the interest-bearing instruments of repos and mutual funds; ii) reserve requirements apply both to Turkish lira and foreign currency deposits; and iii) extra-government agencies (see Chapter II), which are counted in the private sector, have been required to hold their cash balances as demand deposits in the pool of official deposits. The seignorage estimates are thus biased upwards since the mid-1990s, being partly a function of growing off-balance sheet and off-budget transactions,

Figure A1. **Inflation revenues of the Central Bank**

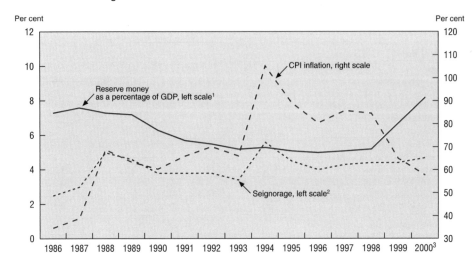

1. Reserve money measured as year average stock.
2. Defined as CPI inflation times ratio of reserve money to GDP.
3. OECD estimates based on year-to-September data.
Source: OECD.

and should not be taken as a refutation of the fact that seignorage revenues are difficult to sustain with a high but stable inflation rate. Nevertheless, the magnitude of "inflation tax" on money balances, of between 4 to 5 per cent of GDP and 15-20 per cent of total tax revenues appears to correspond well with the experiences of Italy in the 1970s and Iceland, Portugal and Greece in the mid-1980s.

Table A3 also reveals that seignorage revenues accruing to the central government via the erosion of government debt vis-à-vis the central bank was the primary instrument by which the government debt-to-GDP ratio was stabilised up to 1998. A consolidation of the central bank and government accounts gives rise to a formulation for debt dynamics wherein the level of inflation needed to stabilise the debt-to-GDP ratio is a negative function of the primary balance, at given interest rate, or alternatively, a positive function of the gap between real interest rates and growth for a given level of the primary balance.[2] Debt dynamics are expressed by the following equation:

$$dk = -p + (r - g)k - (\pi + g)/v$$

where k denotes government debt to GDP ratio, p the primary balance, $r - g$ the gap between the real interest rate and the real growth rate, π the rate of inflation, and v the velocity of base money. Setting $dk = 0$ gives:

$$\pi = -vp + v(r - g)$$

as the formula for stability in the debt-to-GDP ratio. A stable velocity of base money implies a stable rate of inflation, while a lower primary balance or higher real interest rate relative to growth, imply that a higher rate of inflation is needed to stabilise the debt ratio. In 1999, when $(r - g)$ surged to 50 per cent in response to the emerging market crisis, the debt ratio exploded from 44 to 58 per cent in the absence of a hike in inflation, given tight monetary policy in that year.

Commercial banks

Insofar as the public is willing to hold low-interest TL-denominated demand deposits, commercial banks likewise profited from the "inflation tax". (In the case of the state banks, accounting for almost half of bank liabilities according to Table 27, these profits accrued to government.) Such demand deposits typically have earned 5 per cent interest annually, against twenty times as much for time deposits. However, to obtain profits from demand deposits over and above those from time deposits, costs associated with the collection and maintenance of demand deposits need to be taken into account (*e.g.*, higher reserve requirements, free ATM services, servicing of more frequent turnover in the accounts). Given bank competition and the existence of close substitutes for TL-denominated demand deposits, notably foreign currency deposits and repos, it would be expected that costs closely track revenues. Thus, the net real return on demand deposits relative to time deposits, $-(i_d - i_t)$, has been estimated at 15 per cent.[3]

Applying this rate of return to the ratio of demand deposits to GDP, *i.e.* $-(i_d - i_t)$ (d/y), gives an estimate of bank seignorage of some ½ per cent of GDP during the 1990s. This has fallen from around 1 per cent in the mid-1980s, given that real demand deposit holdings have declined from around 7 to 3 per cent of GDP (Figure A2). While more significant than the decline in real base money demand, broader real money demand has also not responded

Figure A2. **Inflation revenues of commercial banks**

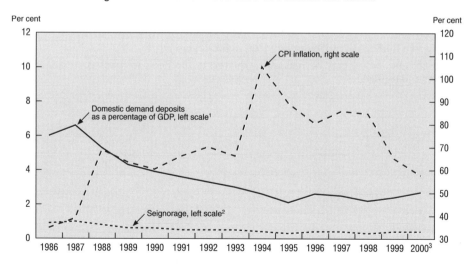

1. Domestic demand deposits measured as year average stock.
2. Defined as 0.15 times ratio of domestic demand deposits to GDP.
3. OECD estimates based on year-to-September data.
Source: OECD.

dramatically to the persistence of high inflation.[4] Inflation-related earnings were boosted by the earning of "float" income, *i.e.*, resources temporarily available to banks before they are credited to bank customers, which may also be expected to be high in the presence of high inflation.

The shift to low inflation

The extent of inflation revenues gives some indication of the reduction in profitability to be expected from the stabilisation in prices. However, the commercial banking sector is a heavy net debtor in foreign currency terms and will gain from the real appreciation of the exchange rate. The table suggests that – in the absence of reverse currency substitution – such gains could amount to around 2 per cent of GDP with a 10 per cent real appreciation in 2000 (as projected by the OECD), more than offsetting the losses associated with declining inflation. The state banks would benefit much less from this effect than would private banks, as the former hold a much smaller proportion of their liabilities in foreign currencies (Table 26 above). The opposite would hold true for the Central Bank, where a large proportion of assets are held in foreign currency.

Notes

1. See Fischer (1982) (referenced in bibliography).
2. See Moalla-Fetini (1999) (referenced in bibliography).
3. See Van Rijckeghem (1999) (referenced in bibliography).
4. Again, one reason may be regulatory, related to the need for bank customers to hold demand deposits.

Annex IV

Legislation and regulation with respect to development and natural disaster readiness in Turkey[1]

General framework laws

The *Act on Measures and Assistance Regarding Natural Disasters Affecting General Public Life* (No. 7269) (hereinafter the *Disaster Law*), enacted in 1959 and amended in 1968, determines procedures for natural disaster management. The law specifies the protective and preventive measures, as well as regulating the activities to be undertaken before, during and after natural disasters; it defines guidelines for terms and conditions of assistance to be provided to affected people and determines procedures for natural disaster management. The Ministry of Public Works and Settlements (specifically, its General Directorate of Disaster Affairs, or GDDA) is placed in charge of most aspects of disaster management and response. These include: *i*) providing emergency aid and securing co-ordination among the relevant institutions during and after a disaster; *ii*) implementing the measures to provide temporary shelter immediately after the disaster and undertaking the reconstruction and rehabilitation activities of damaged housing, work places and infrastructure facilities; *iii*) taking measures to realise and co-ordinate planning, project preparation, implementation, management and control activities in disaster areas as well as in disaster-prone areas; and *iv*) establishing regional centres for the production and storage of prefabricated structural elements aiming at the accommodation of people and co-ordination of emergency assistance in cases of disasters. The law has provided for the establishment of the "Disasters Fund" which is relatively free of the customary constraints associated with expenditures from the national budget processes, so as to provide quick support for agencies involved in disaster relief.[2] An important feature of the law is its broad guarantee of replacement of damaged owner-occupied primary residences at nominal cost.

The *Planning Law* (No. 3194), variously known as *Development Law* or *Construction Law*, with associated statutes, determines rules for urban planning and land use, with the objective of providing guidelines for the construction of the buildings. In the law, it is stated that "regional planning" relates to the socio-economic structure of the region, emphasis being given to the sectoral development targets and infrastructural needs as prepared by the State Planning Organisation. "Urban planning" includes all aspects of city planning and is the responsibility of the municipalities. Urban planning comprises the details on construction, construction permission, and conditions on the determination of measures, construction techniques and design principles, etc. The Ministry of Public Works and Settlements (Public Works) has the authority to intervene in the "urban plans" if necessary, but the law leaves the responsibility for implementation and construction inspection to the municipalities. Thelatter being under the control of the Ministry of Interior Affairs, their legal responsibility is minimised. For example, in the case of a disaster arising from the insufficient control of construction, there is no legal sanction for municipalities. Municipalities are directly involved in each stage of the construction: from project inspection to construction permission via the related departments. However, a major criticism arises from the insufficient number of capable technical personnel to carry out the process (see below).

According to the *Planning Law*, during construction the control is carried out by engineers and "controllers" who have no legal power to increase the effectiveness of their control while the career qualifications of the controller are not mentioned in the law. Moreover, the owner and/or constructor of the building has no responsibility in terms of building weaknesses and faces no legal commitment or liability. These factors tend to undermine the objectives explicitly written into the law to evaluate the risk factors determining potential disaster areas and to take the necessary precautions to minimise loss of life and property. Specifically, the law requires (but has not achieved): i) the development of a seismological and strong ground motion network for the country; ii) the establishment of a national information centre for processing of all kinds of earthquake data, such as the preparation of earthquake catalogues and earthquake hazard maps of Turkey; iii) the determination of measures, construction techniques and design principles for the structures to be built in the earthquake zones; and iv) the development of methods of repair and structural strengthening of buildings damaged by earthquakes or prone to be affected by disasters, including training and monitoring activities.

The *State Tender Law* (No. 2886), or *Tender Law*, sets the conditions for public contracting and implementation of public construction projects, with the exception of the State Economic Enterprises, which are excluded from the provisions of the law. The law allows for the following tender procedures which have given rise to a number of abuses and inefficiencies: i) it is possible to accept bids and conclude a tender without asking for a feasibility study of the project; ii) so-called "deferred tenders" are made possible by the formation of a "deferred commission" which can open a tender for a project for which there is yet no appropriation from the budget; iii) there are other commissions besides the tender commission which leads to the possibility of misuse and delays in the tender process; iv) the pricing of the project is done through unit price estimation by the "public entity" which opens a tender, as the basis for bids; this leads to improper pricing of the project as its costs rise over the years; v) the announcement date of the tender is 10 days, which does not give time to prepare an efficient project; vi) the "warrant amount" for participating in the tender (a nominal sum which is then reimbursed if the bid is rejected) is too low to prevent frivolous offers; vii) there is no responsibility of the contractor for construction quality control.

Laws governing local authority implementation

The main legislation that gives powers and responsibilities to municipalities, including the responsibility for development control, is the *Municipalities Act of* 1930 (No. 1580), or the *Law on Municipalities*, supplemented by many other Acts and constitutional provisions. According to this law, the major services for which municipalities are responsible are: urban planning and implementation, mapping, regulation of construction and the issuance of construction permits; land development and the opening up of new settlement areas; urban renewal; organisation and management of public infrastructure; construction and maintenance of parks and other green areas; provision of fire-prevention and fire-fighting services; establishment and management of recreational, sports, cultural facilities, health and social welfare facilities; municipal policing; environmental regulation; protection and conservation of historical and natural areas; vocational training; planning and construction of social housing, social assistance and meeting other social needs.

Over the years, there has been a significant re-evaluation and expansion in the scope of municipal activities to meet the changing needs of urban life. In 1984, a different type of municipal administration, namely metropolitan municipalities, defined as "cities which comprise more than one district within their own boundaries", was introduced by the *Act on Metropolitan Municipalities* (No. 3030). It was first set up in Istanbul, Ankara, and Izmir, and currently there are 15 such entities. Their responsibilities include: to draw up city master plans; to approve the application plans drawn up by district municipalities and to supervise the implementation of them; to implement and co-ordinate city-scale joint ventures; to co-ordinate and control the activities and conflicts among municipalities within its boundaries; and to implement large-scale public utilities, infrastructure, parks and other projects. The laws further define a dispute settlement procedure in the case of conflicts in the execution of these duties between the mayor and municipal executive committee, in which case the municipal council has the final say on the issue.

According to the various relevant *revenue laws*,[3] municipal administrations obtain their income from three main sources: *i*) local direct tax revenues and property tax on the real estate base; and *ii*) tax sharing, with 9.25 per cent of the tax collected by the central government going to the municipalities, mainly in accordance with their populations; and *iii*) a variety of non-tax revenues. The Bank of Provinces, established in 1933, furthermore helps local authorities both financially and technically, especially the smaller ones with limited capabilities, notably by making town plans or constructing infrastructure projects on their behalf or by providing short, medium and long-term loans and surety for their commercial borrowing. The Bank is a semi-autonomous body tied to the Ministry of Public Works.

According to Article 127 of the Constitution, the central administration has administrative trusteeship over the local governments, in order to ensure the functioning of local services in conformity with the general public interest and integral unity of administration, as well as to increase the effectiveness of local authority activities. The supervision mainly takes the form of approval, postponement, cancellation, and permission for some decisions (in addition to the suspension and dissolution of the local elected persons and organs pending a process of judicial review). The administrative trusteeship of the local authorities is generally exercised by the Ministry of Interior, and of regions by provincial and district governors. The MOI has recently (1994) delegated some of its supervisory powers to provincial governors to reduce the excessive concentration at the centre. In some cases, the authority to supervise local decisions is given to the Council of Ministers, other individual ministries, or the Council of State. The Audit Court is also empowered with trusteeship competence on local authorities with respect to expenditure control.

The above legal structure has basically prevented local authorities from working more efficiently and effectively, while at the same undermining the overall administrative structure. These problems can be classed into the following six categories:

– *Inappropriate distribution of functions between central government and local authorities*. Although the constitution prescribes that local duties are, in principle, to be carried out by the local authorities, this has not yet been realised. Many local duties are still being performed by provincial and regional units controlled from the centre. The local authority share of public expenditure in Turkey is around 13-14 per cent, which is far lower than that of the rest of the OECD.

– *Insufficient financial resources*. Local authorities have not had sufficient incomes in relation to their duties and responsibilities, despite the fact that the Constitution prescribes otherwise. Moreover, the capability of creating new income sources is very limited; they can levy taxes and other financial obligations only within the limits set forth by legislation.

– *Insufficient organisation and personnel*. Local authorities lack the capability to found organisations and employ personnel which their functions require. Strict limits on these activities are set by the central administration and legislation (for example, the right of review by central government over all local hirings).

- *Unnecessary practice of trusteeship*. Much of the practice of trusteeship by central adminis- trations over the local authorities is unnecessary and impairs the efficient functioning of the latter.
- *Lack of transparency and participation*. Transparency and participation have not developed in the domain of local government, due to the fact that semi-public professional organ- isations and civil associations are not represented in the commissions, while taxation and other financial obligations cannot be put directly to the voters by the local author- ities. Consequently, public (citizen) control has been inadequate.
- *Over-dependence on central government*. Local authorities have been over-dependent on the centre, owing to financial dependence and too much trusteeship. This undermines local authorities in developing their own identity and inhibits local democracy.

Notes

1. Most of the information for this annex has been provided by the Turkish authorities, both central and municipal.
2. A second fund, the "Earthquake Fund", was later established using earmarked excise tax revenues to provide further financial support to the activities of the GDDA, and the "Civil Defence Fund" was also established.
3. Notably, the Act on Municipal Incomes (No. 2464), the Act on Property Tax (No. 1319), and the Act on Revenue Sharing (No. 2380).

Annex V

Calendar of main economic events

1999

June

Following the April election results, a new three-party coalition government headed by Mr. Ecevit receives a vote of confidence from Parliament.

The Banking Law goes into effect, providing for establishment of an independent bank regulatory and supervisory agency.

Parliament adopts the 1999 budget.

July

The government sets second-half civil-servant wage rises at 20 per cent.

The government announces an economic relief package which contains tax breaks for companies in financial distress, eases lending regulations, provides extra resources for Eximbank and postpones the tax declaration of interest earnings for a period of three years.

August

Standard and Poors sets single B rating on Turkey and confirms outlook as stable.

Parliament passes a set of constitutional amendments which provide a constitutional basis for privatisation and allow for international arbitration for dispute settlements involving foreign investors.

7.4 magnitude earthquake devastates Turkey's north-western provinces of Kocaeli, Sakarya and Yalova, located in the Marmara region.

Parliament adopts social security reform bill, raising retirement age to 58-60 for new workers and extending insurance premium payments.

Withholding tax on repos and deposits is raised to 12 and 13 per cent, respectively.

September

The Government releases a package of relief measures for earthquake victims, including provision of mass housing projects, debt relief and social security assistance.

Turkey joins G-20 group.

October

IMF approves US$501 million in emergency earthquake assistance for Turkey.

2000 budget submitted to Parliament. Civil servant wage rises are set at 25 per cent for whole of 2000 (15 per cent in first half plus 10 per cent in second).

Parliament passes a new customs law aimed at harmonising Turkey's relevant legislation with that of the EU and ensuring compliance with its international agreements.

November

7.2 magnitude earthquake devastates the north-west province of Bolu.

World Bank approves US$757.5 million in earthquake loans to Turkey.

Organisation for Security and co-operation in Europe (OSCE) summit held in Istanbul.

European Parliament confirms €600 million earthquake assistance loan to Turkey through European Investment Bank.

The Government introduces earthquake taxes including retroactive taxes on Treasury bonds and bills and one-off taxes on corporations, individual income, real estates, motor vehicles and monthly taxes on cellular phone bills; withholding tax on repo and bank deposits raised by 2 percentage points.

December

Central Bank announces new monetary and exchange rate policies for 2000-02, which keep lira depreciation against an exchange rate basket at the inflation target.

EU accepts Turkey as official candidate for membership.

S&P affirms Turkey's B foreign currency rating, changes outlook to positive.

VAT rates on luxurious goods raised by two percentage points from 23 to 25 per cent, and on general VAT from 15 to 17 per cent. VAT on basic food materials remains unchanged at 8 per cent.

Amendments to banking law become effective, with a view to bringing the banking system up to EU standards.

The Government hands over five small and medium-sized banks (Yurtbank, Egebank, Sumerbank, Esbank, Yasarbank) to the Deposit Insurance Fund, bringing the total to eight, and shuts down an investment bank (Birlesik Yatirim) as part of a banking rehabilitation operation.

IMF approves Turkey's letter of intent for a three-year $4 billion stand-by arrangement to back Turkey's disinflation programme, aimed at reducing inflation to 5 per cent by 2002.

World Bank pledges $3 billion over three years in support of Turkey's structural reforms.

2000 budget adopted by targeting a primary surplus of 5.4 per cent of GNP.

2000

January

Auction interest rate declines sharply (to 37.9 per cent compounded) in the first government bond auction of the year.

Turkey issues a bond with 30 years maturity in US market, in the amount of $1.5 billion.

Legal amendments for telecommunication sector passed, allowing more competition and privatisation.

Legal amendments made in order to apply international arbitration clause retroactively.

February

International rating agency JCR upgrades Turkey from BB to BB+.

New interest rate mechanism is set for state-owned Ziraat and Halk Banks, in order to eliminate duty losses arising from credit subsidies.

Real estate rent hikes limited to 25 per cent in 2000, and to 10 per cent in 2001, by amending the related law.

March

Implementation of the agricultural sector reform started in the pilot zone.

Banking Regulatory and Supervisory Board appointed.

Tender made for the privatisation of a 51 per cent stake of POAS, Petroleum Distribution Company, with winning bid at $1.3 billion.

Central Bank announces the value of the exchange rate basket for 2001Q1.

April

GSM licence sold to an international consortium for $2.5 billion; second license remains unsold.

Public offering of 31.5 per cent of the shares of Tüpras, Petroleum Refinery Company, with $1.2 billion obtained.

S&P revises Turkey's long term foreign currency rating from B to B+. Fitch-IBCA also upgrades it from B+ to BB–.

Competition Board approves privatisation of 20 per cent of Turk Telekom by block sale.

Government puts off Akkuyu nuclear plant tender.

May

25 budgetary and 2 non-budgetary funds eliminated between February and May.

Primary dealership for government bonds and bills introduced.

World Bank approves $759.6 million Economic Reform Loan to support public expenditure management, social security, agriculture and infrastructure.

June

Unemployment insurance goes into effect.

Support price of cereals declared in line with targeted inflation, this decision being regarded as an indicator of the commitment of the authorities to the economic programme.

VAT rate on liquid petroleum gas used in motor vehicles is raised from 17 to 40 per cent, while the annual technical inspection fee for LPG-run motor vehicles is increased by 2000 per cent.

Economic and Social Council reconvenes in order to build consensus among social partners for the disinflation programme, without the participation of DISK and TZOB.

Level of deposits under the coverage of Saving Deposit Insurance Fund declines from unlimited to a maximum TL 100 billion per account until the end of 2000, and to TL 50 billion thereafter.

Parliament approves bill giving government the right to enact "decrees with the force of law" (KHK).

July

Following the second stand-by review, a second supplementary letter of intent is approved by IMF Board of Executive Directors and the third tranche amounting to SDR 221.7 million released.

Treasury auction sees lowest yield for 20 years with 28.27 per cent.

Cabinet puts nuclear plant on indefinite hold.

September

Bank Regulation and Supervision Agency begins its operations.

Turk Telekom block sale tender is cancelled due to potential investor concerns about management rights, leading to a delay in meeting privatisation targets.

Measures are taken to curb domestic demand, notably: Resource Utilisation Support Fund rates applied to interest payments on consumer credits increased from 3 to 8 per cent; VAT imposed on automobiles with an engine capacity over 1600 cc increased from 25 to 40 per cent.

IMF postpones next tranche of standby loan to December.

October

Constitutional Court cancels the law empowering the government to issue decrees having the force of law; also cancels decree on the privatisation of Vakifbank.

2001 budget is submitted to Parliament with the ambitious target of 3.5 per cent of GNP budget deficit and 7.5 per cent primary surplus. Civil servants' wage rises set at 10 per cent for the first half of 2001.

Motor vehicle tax rate is increased for luxury cars and fee on consumers loans (Resource Allocation Fund rate) is increased from 3 to 8 per cent.

Banking Regulation and Supervision Agency (BRSA) announces that two mid-sized banks, Etibank and Kapital Bank, are transferred to Savings Deposits Insurance Fund.

Deposit Insurance Fund asks for $6.1 billion from the Treasury to inject into the eight banks under its administration since end-1999.

Criminal investigation is started for Ege Bank.

November

The third/fourth stand-by review is completed by IMF mission, whereupon the government announces a significant tightening of the fiscal targets for 2001.

A supplementary tax package is sent to Parliament. It covers the extension of special communication, transaction taxes, basic education contribution levies and share from the regulatory boards' surpluses until the end of 2002 while giving authority to the cabinet to increase special transaction and basic education taxes by up to 10 times; gives authority to the cabinet to raise motor vehicle tax and motor vehicle purchase tax rates by up to 50 times and by up to 20 times more on certain vehicle types; and reimposes the "Living-Standard" tax for self-employed business.

The government forwards foreign capital incentive draft law to Parliament aiming at stimulating foreign capital investments. It gives cabinet authority to determine the foreign capital process, including foreign currency, machinery, equipment, patent, and trademark considerations brought by foreign capital, and to eliminate the preliminary permission process for foreign capital.

Draft decree is prepared for corporate tax law regarding tax exemptions for mergers and acquisitions in the banking sector.

The fee on consumer loans is increased from 8 to 10 per cent, and for other types of credits from 3 to 5 per cent.

Vakifbank's privatisation law goes into effect.

Public banks bill goes into effect allowing commercialisation and privatisation of the three state-banks, Ziraat Bank, Halk Bank, Emlak Bank.

Banking Regulation and Supervision Agency announces the Action Plan concerning the sale of eight bailed-out banks under the management of Savings Deposit Insurance Fund.

The new national compulsory earthquake insurance scheme becomes fully operational.

Banking probes widen, begin to unsettle markets.

BASIC STATISTICS:

INTERNATIONAL COMPARISONS

	Units	Reference period [1]	Australia	Austria
Population				
Total	Thousands	1997	18 532	8 072
Inhabitants per sq. km	Number	1997	2	96
Net average annual increase over previous 10 years	%	1997	1.3	0.6
Employment				
Total civilian employment (TCE)[2]	Thousands	1997	8 430	3 685
of which:				
Agriculture	% of TCE	1997	5.2	6.8
Industry	% of TCE	1997	22.1	30.3
Services	% of TCE	1997	72.7	63.8
Gross domestic product (GDP)				
At current prices and current exchange rates	Bill. US$	1997	392.9	206.2
Per capita	US$	1997	21 202	25 549
At current prices using current PPPs[3]	Bill. US$	1997	406.8	186.3
Per capita	US$	1997	21 949	23 077
Average annual volume growth over previous 5 years	%	1997	4.1	1.9
Gross fixed capital formation (GFCF)	% of GDP	1997	21.5	24.1
of which:				
Machinery and equipment	% of GDP	1997	10.3 (96)	8.8 (96)
Residential construction	% of GDP	1997	4.4 (96)	6.2 (96)
Average annual volume growth over previous 5 years	%	1997	7.3	2.8
Gross saving ratio[4]	% of GDP	1997	18.4	23
General government				
Current expenditure on goods and services	% of GDP	1997	16.7	19.4
Current disbursements[5]	% of GDP	1996	34.8	48
Current receipts	% of GDP	1996	35.4	47.9
Net official development assistance	% of GNP	1996	0.28	0.24
Indicators of living standards				
Private consumption per capita using current PPP's[3]	US$	1997	13 585	12 951
Passenger cars, per 1 000 inhabitants	Number	1995	477	447
Telephones, per 1 000 inhabitants	Number	1995	510	465
Television sets, per 1 000 inhabitants	Number	1994	489	480
Doctors, per 1 000 inhabitants	Number	1996	2.5	2.8
Infant mortality per 1 000 live births	Number	1996	5.8	5.1
Wages and prices (average annual increase over previous 5 years)				
Wages (earnings or rates according to availability)	%	1998	1.5	5.2
Consumer prices	%	1998	2.0	1.8
Foreign trade				
Exports of goods, fob*	Mill. US$	1998	55 882	61 754
As % of GDP	%	1997	15.6	28.4
Average annual increase over previous 5 years	%	1998	5.6	9
Imports of goods, cif*	Mill. US$	1998	60 821	68 014
As % of GDP	%	1997	15.3	31.4
Average annual increase over previous 5 years	%	1998	7.5	7
Total official reserves[6]	Mill. SDR's	1998	10 942	14 628 (97)
As ratio of average monthly imports of goods	Ratio	1998	2.2	2.7 (97)

* At current prices and exchange rates.
1. Unless otherwise stated.
2. According to the definitions used in OECD Labour Force Statistics.
3. PPPs = Purchasing Power Parities.
4. Gross saving = Gross national disposable income minus private and government consumption.

EMPLOYMENT OPPORTUNITIES

Economics Department, OECD

The Economics Department of the OECD offers challenging and rewarding opportunities to economists interested in applied policy analysis in an international environment. The Department's concerns extend across the entire field of economic policy analysis, both macroeconomic and microeconomic. Its main task is to provide, for discussion by committees of senior officials from Member countries, documents and papers dealing with current policy concerns. Within this programme of work, three major responsibilities are:

- to prepare regular surveys of the economies of individual Member countries;
- to issue full twice-yearly reviews of the economic situation and prospects of the OECD countries in the context of world economic trends;
- to analyse specific policy issues in a medium-term context for the OECD as a whole, and to a lesser extent for the non-OECD countries.

The documents prepared for these purposes, together with much of the Department's other economic work, appear in published form in the *OECD Economic Outlook, OECD Economic Surveys, OECD Economic Studies* and the Department's *Working Papers* series.

The Department maintains a world econometric model, INTERLINK, which plays an important role in the preparation of the policy analyses and twice-yearly projections. The availability of extensive cross-country data bases and good computer resources facilitates comparative empirical analysis, much of which is incorporated into the model.

The Department is made up of about 80 professional economists from a variety of backgrounds and Member countries. Most projects are carried out by small teams and last from four to eighteen months. Within the Department, ideas and points of view are widely discussed; there is a lively professional interchange, and all professional staff have the opportunity to contribute actively to the programme of work.

Skills the Economics Department is looking for:

a) Solid competence in using the tools of both microeconomic and macroeconomic theory to answer policy questions. Experience indicates that this normally requires the equivalent of a Ph.D. in economics or substantial relevant professional experience to compensate for a lower degree.

b) Solid knowledge of economic statistics and quantitative methods; this includes how to identify data, estimate structural relationships, apply basic techniques of time series analysis, and test hypotheses. It is essential to be able to interpret results sensibly in an economic policy context.

c) A keen interest in and extensive knowledge of policy issues, economic developments and their political/social contexts.

d) Interest and experience in analysing questions posed by policy-makers and presenting the results to them effectively and judiciously. Thus, work experience in government agencies or policy research institutions is an advantage.

e) The ability to write clearly, effectively, and to the point. The OECD is a bilingual organisation with French and English as the official languages. Candidates must have excellent knowledge of one of these languages, and some knowledge of the other. Knowledge of other languages might also be an advantage for certain posts.

f) For some posts, expertise in a particular area may be important, but a successful candidate is expected to be able to work on a broader range of topics relevant to the work of the Department. Thus, except in rare cases, the Department does not recruit narrow specialists.

g) The Department works on a tight time schedule with strict deadlines. Moreover, much of the work in the Department is carried out in small groups. Thus, the ability to work with other economists from a variety of cultural and professional backgrounds, to supervise junior staff, and to produce work on time is important.

General information

The salary for recruits depends on educational and professional background. Positions carry a basic salary from FF 318 660 or FF 393 192 for Administrators (economists) and from FF 456 924 for Principal Administrators (senior economists). This may be supplemented by expatriation and/or family allowances, depending on nationality, residence and family situation. Initial appointments are for a fixed term of two to three years.

Vacancies are open to candidates from OECD Member countries. The Organisation seeks to maintain an appropriate balance between female and male staff and among nationals from Member countries.

For further information on employment opportunities in the Economics Department, contact:

**Management Support Unit
Economics Department
OECD
2, rue André-Pascal
75775 PARIS CEDEX 16
FRANCE**

E-Mail: eco.contact@oecd.org

Applications citing "ECSUR", together with a detailed *curriculum vitae* in English or French, should be sent to the Head of Personnel at the above address.

Did you Know?
This publication is available in electronic form!

Many OECD publications and data sets are now available in electronic form to suit your needs at affordable prices.

CD-ROMs

For our statistical products we use the powerful software platform Beyond 20/20™ produced by Ivation. This allows you to get maximum value from the data. For more details of this and other publications on CD-ROM visit our online bookshop **www.oecd.org/bookshop** or **www.oecdwash.org.**

STATISTICS VIA THE INTERNET

During 2000 we are launching SourceOECD/statistics. Whilst some statistical datasets may become available on the Internet during the second half of 2000 we anticipate that most will not be available until late 2000 or early 2001. For more information visit **www.oecd.org/sourceoecd** or **www.ivation.com.**

BOOKS AND PERIODICALS IN PDF

Most of our printed books are also produced as PDF files and are available from our online bookshop **www.oecd.org/bookshop.** Customers paying for printed books by credit card online can download the PDF file free of charge for immediate access.

We are also developing two new services, SourceOECD/periodicals and SourceOECD/studies, which will deliver online access to all printed publications over the Internet. These services are being developed in partnership with ingenta. For more information visit **www.oecd.org/sourceoecd or www.ingenta.com.**

OECD DIRECT

To stay informed by e-mail about all new OECD publications as they are published, why not register for OECD Direct?

OECD Direct is a free, opt-in, e-mail alerting service designed to help you stay up to date with our new publications. You've a choice of different themes so you can adapt the service to your fields of interest only. Registration is free of charge and there is no obligation. To register, simply follow the instructions at the top of the online bookshop's home page **www.oecd.org/bookshop**. We don't use your e-mail address for any other purpose and we won't give them to anyone else either – you'll just get what you registered for, e-mails announcing new publications as soon as they are released.

Le saviez-vous ?
Cette publication est disponible en version électronique !

Pour répondre aux besoins de ses clients, l'OCDE a décidé de publier un grand nombre d'études et de données sous forme électronique à des prix très abordables.

CD-ROM

Nos bases de données statistiques fonctionnent avec le logiciel Beyond 20/20™ produit par Ivation. Ce logiciel, convivial et très simple d'utilisation, vous permet d'utiliser au mieux les données.
Pour plus de détails et pour consulter la liste des publications sur CD-ROM, visitez notre librairie en ligne : **www.oecd.org/bookshop.**

STATISTIQUES SUR INTERNET

SourceOECD/statitics sera lancé au cours de l'an 2000. Ce nouveau service commencera à être opérationnel à partir du second semestre de l'an 2000 et nous envisageons de diffuser la totalité de notre catalogue de statistiques pour la fin de l'an 2000/début 2001.
Pour plus d'information : **www.oecd.org/sourceoecd** ou **www.ivation.com.**

LIVRES ET PÉRIODIQUES EN VERSION PDF

La plupart de nos publications sont également disponibles en format PDF. Vous pouvez les trouver dans notre librairie en ligne : **www.oecd.org/bookshop.**
Les clients de notre librairie en ligne, qui font l'acquisition d'un ouvrage imprimé en utilisant une carte de crédit, peuvent télécharger gratuitement la version électronique, pour une lecture immédiate.

Nous développons actuellement deux nouveaux services, SourceOECD/periodicals et SourceOECD/studies, qui vous permettront d'accéder en ligne à toutes nos publications. Ces services, qui sont actuellement en voie de développement en association avec ingenta, ne seront dans un premier temps disponibles que pour les versions en langue anglaise. Une étude est en cours pour élargir ce service aux publications en langue française. Pour plus d'information, visitez les deux sites **www.oecd.org/sourceoecd** ou **www.ingenta.com.**

OECD DIRECT

Pour être informé par e-mail de la parution de nos toutes dernières publications, enregistrez dès maintenant votre nom sur **www.oecd.org/bookshop.**
OECD Direct est notre service « Alerte » gratuit qui permet aux lecteurs qui le souhaitent de recevoir par e-mail des informations sur la sortie de nos nouvelles publications. Une série de thèmes est proposée et chacun pourra choisir en fonction de ses propres centres d'intérêt. L'inscription est gratuite et sans obligation. Pour enregistrer votre nom, il vous suffit de suivre les instructions figurant en haut de la page d'accueil de notre librairie en ligne **www.oecd.org/bookshop.** Soyez assurés que nous n'utiliserons pas votre adresse e-mail à d'autres fins et ne la transmettrons en aucun cas. Vous ne recevrez par e-mail que des informations vous annonçant nos nouvelles publications dès lors qu'elles sont parues.

www.oecd.org/sourceoecd

For more information about all OECD publications
contact your nearest OECD Centre, or visit
www.oecd.org/bookshop

Pour plus d'informations sur les publications de l'OCDE,
contactez votre Centre OCDE le plus proche
ou visitez notre librairie en ligne :
www.oecd.org/bookshop

Where to send your request:
Où passer commande :

In Central and Latin America / En Amérique centrale et en Amérique du Sud

OECD MEXICO CENTRE / CENTRE OCDE DE MEXICO
Edificio INFOTEC
Av. San Fernando No. 37 Col. Toriello Guerra
Tlalpan C.P. 14050, Mexico D.F.
Tel.: +525 281 38 10   Fax: + 525 606 13 07
E-mail: mexico.contact@oecd.org   Internet: www.rtn.net.mx/ocde

In North America / En Amérique du Nord

OECD WASHINGTON CENTER / CENTRE OCDE DE WASHINGTON
2001 L Street N.W., Suite 650
Washington, DC 20036-4922
Tel.: +1 202 785-6323
Toll free / Numéro vert : +1 800 456-6323   Fax: +1 202 785-0350
E-mail: washington.contact@oecd.org   Internet: www.oecdwash.org

In Japan / Au Japon

OECD TOKYO CENTRE / CENTRE OCDE DE TOKYO
Landic Akasaka Bldg.
2-3-4 Akasaka, Minato-ku
Tokyo 107-0052
Tel.: +81 3 3586 2016   Fax: +81 3 3584 7929
E-mail : center@oecdtokyo.org   Internet: www.oecdtokyo.org

In the rest of the world / Dans le reste du monde
DVGmbH
Birkenmaarsstrasse 8
D-53340 Meckenheim
Germany
Tel.: +49 22 25 9 26 166/7/8   Fax: +49 22 25 9 26 169
E-mail: oecd@dvg.dsb.net

OECD Information Centre and Bookshop/
Centre d'information de l'OCDE et Librairie
OECD PARIS CENTRE / CENTRE OCDE DE PARIS
2 rue André-Pascal, 75775 Paris Cedex 16, France
Enquiries / Renseignements : Tel: +33 (0) 1 45 24 81 67
E-mail: sales@oecd.org

ONLINE BOOKSHOP / LIBRAIRIE EN LIGNE : **www.oecd.org/bookshop**
(secure payment with credit card / paiement sécurisé par carte de crédit)